T0358381

MANAGING SUPPLY CHAIN AND LOGISTICS

Competitive Strategy for A Sustainable Future

MANAGING SUPPLY CHAIN AND LOGISTICS

Competitive Strategy for A Sustainable Future

Ling Li

Old Dominion University, USA

World Scientific

NEW JERSEY · LONDON · SINGAPORE · BEIJING · SHANGHAI · HONG KONG · TAIPEI · CHENNAI

Published by

World Scientific Publishing Co. Pte. Ltd.

5 Toh Tuck Link, Singapore 596224

USA office: 27 Warren Street, Suite 401-402, Hackensack, NJ 07601

UK office: 57 Shelton Street, Covent Garden, London WC2H 9HE

Library of Congress Cataloging-in-Publication Data

Li, Ling, 1954–

    Managing supply chain and logistics : competitive strategy for a sustainable future / Ling Li.

    pages cm

    Includes bibliographical references and index.

    ISBN 978-9814602426 (hardcover : alk. paper) -- ISBN 9814602426 (hardcover : alk. paper)

    1. Business logistics. 2. Business logistics--Case studies. I. Title.

    HD38.5.L5247 2014

    658.7--dc23

                         2014026662

British Library Cataloguing-in-Publication Data

A catalogue record for this book is available from the British Library.

In-house Editor: Sandhya Venkatesh

Printed in Singapore

Dedication

Dedicated to the memory of my parents

Preface

This book is written for managers, executives, students, and business professionals who are keen to invest in a sustainable future through effective supply chain management. It can also be used as a textbook for upper-level undergraduates, for MBA students, or for those preparing for their Association of Operations Management (APICS) examinations.

During the last seven decades, the discipline of supply chain management has progressed from dealing with inventory, warehouse, and transportation management issues to dealing with matters of strategic discussions, both in the boardrooms of global enterprises as well as in the offices of mid- and small-sized firms. In the information age, the traditional economic models bounded by regions and countries have evolved into a more globally-oriented economy. This new environment enables global collaboration in creating a supply network for conducting world-wide supply chain operations. To a nation, its supply chain and its material management are the arteries of its economy. They determine the metrics used to evaluate the level of modernization and the economic power of a nation.

The drivers of the modern supply chain management are information technology and container transportation. The former has shortened geographic distances by providing a virtual information highway, and the latter has lowered the cost of transportation which helps to justify the shipment of large volumes of goods from the eastern hemisphere to the western hemisphere (or vice versa). In 1970, the cost of one megahertz of computing power was \$7,600. By the end of the 20th century, it was 17 cents. The cost of storing one megabit of data in 1970 was \$5,256. In more recent times, the cost of storing one megabit is less than 17 cents.[1] Since the 1960s, technology has enabled business to create tools for effective materials management. At the same time, containerization has dramatically stimulated the formation of the global supply chain. Today, 90 percent of the world's trade moves in containers. Each year, about 100 million container cargos, in over 5,000 container ships, crisscross the oceans.

This book focuses on investing in a sustainable future through building a competitive supply chain by applying viable value creation strategies, operational models, decision-making techniques, and information technology, and big data science. The book focuses on supply chain management and the support of new initiatives such as Collaborative Planning, Forecasting, and Replenishment (CPFR); big data science; knowledge management; and business intelligence. In addition, the book promotes cross-functional decisions, and fosters decision- making capability and problem solving skills. By examining cutting-edge supply chain management issues, this text captures the current trends as presented below. It offers:

- **Broad global perspective.** The book features increased treatment of globalization and related operational issues, such as managing demand, transforming demand, transportation, and logistics.
- **Expanded coverage of collaborative supply chain practices.** The book presents an expanded treatment of collaborative planning, forecasting, and replenishment in supply chain.
- **Integrative technology framework.** The book offers an integrated framework for discussing current information, technology applications across the supply chain, and the expanded use of technology within specific operations and logistics operational areas.

---

[1] Federal Reserve Bank of Dallas (1999). "The new paradigm," 1999 Annual Report. Date of access: June 2007.
http://www.dallasfed.org/fed/annual/1999p/ar99.pdf.

- **Balanced approach.** The book takes a balanced approach to illustrating both the successes and failures in supply chain management, by illustrating them with cases and examples.
- **Case-based industry practice analysis.** The book provides real-world cases to demonstrate various supply chain management strategies and tactics.
- **Spreadsheet-based quantitative problem solving methods.** The book provides methods to solve quantitative problems. Actual Excel screens are used to illustrate the use of the methods and to make it easier for readers to replicate the examples and problems, following the illustrated Excel commands.

The book has twelve chapters. Chapter 1 invites you to participate in a journey to explore the broad and deep connectivity of the global supply chain. Chapter 2 provides an analysis of successful supply chain models, as well as some failed examples. Chapters 3 to 9 discuss the components of supply chain management and illustrate an array of decision-making methods used. Chapter 10 highlights the issues related to a sustainable supply chain, and Chapter 11 presents the impact of information technology and big data science on supply chain management. Finally, Chapter 12 introduces supply chain performance metrics and discusses how best to achieve sustainable growth and development.

Many critical issues arise when trying to manage a sustainable supply chain in a competitive world. First, supply chain integration poses a major challenge, because integration requires cohesive decision-making across the supply chain. Second, a supply chain is a dynamic system with its own life cycle, and consequently, supply chain relationships evolve constantly. Third, integrating data, information, and knowledge in a supply chain poses practical problems. Furthermore, tacit knowledge embedded in an enterprise can be difficult to express and communicate. This book offers a feasible approach to managing a volatile business. Readers of this book will be able to use the theory and methods presented herein to solve supply chain management practical problems.

The book profiles industry leaders such as the retail giant Walmart and its everyday low price strategy; the electronic innovator Dell Inc., its direct-sell model and its integration of traditional retailing methods in recent years; and the apparel pioneer ZARA and its reasonably-priced fresh, fashionable, and trendy clothes. Choosing a suitable strategy is critical to building sustainable supply chain. History has recorded that Walmart has evolved from a local retailer to a global enterprise, having chosen the right design of supply chain. Kmart, on the other hand, traveled off the appropriate trajectory and filed bankruptcy protection with the US federal government in 2001.

This book looks to illustrate these and other business' stories as a means of explaining supply chain management. I want to thank you for choosing this book as an enlightened resource on your journey to invest in a sustainable future.

Ling "Lynn" Li, PhD
Professor of Operations and Supply Chain Management
Head, Maritime and Supply Chain Management Program
Fellow, Association of Operations Management (APICS)
E.V. Williams Research Fellow
Old Dominion University
USA

Acknowledgements

It is my pleasure to acknowledge all those who have supported me and have contributed to the success of this manuscript.

I am grateful to my colleagues and my students at Old Dominion University, USA. I thank Alison Schoew for her careful editing and proofreading of this manuscript. Her excellent work has made this book a better presentation. I want to thank my editor at World Scientific Publishing Ms. Sandhya for her persistent support and insightful suggestions.

My father deeply believes that publishing a book is the achievement of a major milestone for any professor. He would be very happy to see that I have completed this project.

Contents

PART 1: STRATEGIC ISSUES AND SUPPLY CHAIN DESIGN

PART 2: PURCHASING, PROCUREMENT, AND SUPPLY
RELATIONSHIPS

PART 3: DEMAND AND SUPPLY INTEGRATION IN SUPPLY CHAIN

PART 4: LOGISITCS NETWORK DESIGN AND TRANSPORTATION

PART 5: EMERGING ISSUES IN SUPPLY CHAIN

PART 6: SUPPLY CHAIN PERFORMANCE AND EVALUATION

List of Tables

List of Figures

Part 1

Strategic Issues and Supply Chain Design

Chapter 1
Supply Chain Management and Strategy

Chapter 2
The Right Design of a Supply Chain

Chapter 1

Supply Chain Management and Strategy

1.1 Understanding the Supply Chain and Supply Chain Management

Supply chain management is a relatively new field of management study in comparison with the traditional business fields such as marketing, finance, and production management. The newness of the field results from the concept of using an integrated management for order fulfilling activities. In the early 1960s, MIT professor Jay Forrester studied the interrelationship between suppliers and customers and uncovered the phenomenon that inventories in a supply pipeline tend to fluctuate more as they are further away from the customer. This phenomenon leads either to unfilled orders or to too much in inventory. In the early 1980s, Harvard professor Michael Porter suggested that companies could be more competitive if they were better able to manage the interrelationship of their inbound logistics, outbound logistics, operations, sales and marketing, and customer services. Porter used the term "value chain" to discuss the process upon which the current supply chain framework is built.

The current version of the *Supply Chain* encompasses all of the activities in fulfilling customer demands and requests, as shown in Fig. 1.1. These activities are related to the flow and transformation of goods from the raw materials stage to the end user, as well as the associated flows for information, service, and funds. There are four stages in a supply chain: the supply network, the internal supply chain (the manufacturing plants), the distribution systems, and the end users. Moving up and down the stages are the four flows: the material flow, the service flow, the information flow, and the funds flow. The interrelationship in a supply chain is connected by business activities.

For example, the procurement links the supply network and manufacturing plant, distribution links the manufacturing plant and the distribution network, and commerce or e-commerce links the distribution network and the end users (see Fig. 1.1).

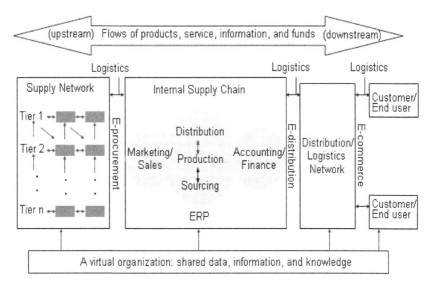

Fig. 1.1 Supply chain in an e-business environment.

Let us consider the case of the purchase of a Dell computer. The supply chain begins with the *need* for a computer. In this example, a customer places an order for a Dell computer through the Internet. Since Dell does not have distribution centers or distributors, this order triggers the production of that computer at Dell's manufacturing center, which is the next stage in the supply chain. Microprocessors used in Dell's computer may come from Advance Micro Devices (AMD); a complementary product like a monitor may come from Sony. Dell receives such parts and components from these suppliers, who belong to the upstream stage of the supply chain. After completing the order according to the customer's specification, Dell then sends the computer directly to the user through UPS, a third party logistics provider. This ***responsive supply chain*** is illustrated in Fig. 1.1. In this order fulfillment process, Dell Computer is the captain of the supply chain; it selects the suppliers, forges partnerships with other members of the supply chain, fulfills orders from customers, and follows up the business transaction with services.

Now, consider a case of purchasing a pack of Perdue Farms chicken breasts at Sam's Club, a warehouse wholesale club. When customers buy trays of chicken breasts at Sam's Club, the demand is satisfied from inventory that is stocked in a Sam's Club distribution center. Production at a Perdue Farms manufacturing facility is based on forecast demand, using historical sales data. Perdue Farms runs a vertical supply chain that begins with the eggs, continues to the grains that feed chicks, and is followed by manufacturing, packaging, and delivery.[1] This is an *efficient supply chain* and is illustrated in Fig. 1.1.

These two different types of supply chain, responsive supply chain and efficient supply chain, will be discussed in detail in section 1.6.2.

Supply Chain Management is a set of synchronized decisions and activities utilized to efficiently integrate suppliers, manufacturers, warehouses, transporters, retailers, and customers so that the right product or service will be distributed at the right quantities, to the right locations, at the right prices, in the right condition, with the right information, and at the right time, in order to minimize system-wide costs while satisfying customer service requirements. The objective of Supply Chain Management (SCM) is to achieve a sustainable competitive advantage.

A company's supply chain in an e-Biz environment can be very complicated. Fig. 1.1 illustrates a simplified supply chain because many companies have hundreds and thousands of suppliers and customers. The supply chain in Fig. 1.1 includes internal supply chain functions, an upstream supply network, and a downstream distribution network. The logistics function facilitates the physical flow of material from the raw material producer to the manufacturer, and then to the distributor, and finally to the end user.

---

[1] Li, L. (2013). Perdue Farms: A Vertically Integrated Supply Chain, ed. Chuck Munson, "*The Supply Chain Management Casebook*," (Pearson Education, Inc. One Lake Street, Upper Saddle River, NJ).

The *internal supply chain* of the focal manufacturing company in the middle of Fig. 1.1 includes sourcing, production, and distribution. **Sourcing**, or the procurement function of a company, is responsible for selecting suppliers, negotiating contracts, formulating the purchasing process, and processing orders. The **Production** function is responsible for transforming raw materials, parts, or components into the product. The **Distribution** function is responsible for managing the flow of material and the finished goods inventory from the manufacturer to the customer. Enterprise Information Systems (ERP) integrate the entire company's information system, process and store data, and link functional areas, business units, and product lines in order to assist managers in making business decisions. As an IT infrastructure, ERP influences the way in which companies manage their daily operations and facilitates the flow of information among all of the supply chain processes of a firm.

The *supply network* on the left-hand side of Fig. 1.1 consists of all the organizations that provide materials or services, either directly or indirectly. For example, a computer manufacturer's supply network includes all of the firms that provide its needed items (ranging from such raw materials as plastics and computer chips, to subassemblies like hard drives and motherboards). A supplier of motherboard, for instance, may have its own set of suppliers (*second-tier suppliers*) that provide inputs and that are also part of the supply chain.

The *distribution network* on the right-hand side of Fig. 1.1 is responsible for the actual movement of materials between locations. Distribution management involves the management of the packaging, storing, and handling of materials at receiving docks, warehouses, and retail outlets. A major part of distribution management is transportation management, which includes the selection and the management of external carriers or internal private fleets of carriers.

Commerce or E-commerce uses advanced technology to assist business transactions in a web-based environment and facilitates the transaction of information flow and fund flow. E-commerce involves business-to-business (B2B) transactions such as Covisint.com (an on-line industrial collaboration platform), business-to-customer transactions such as Amazon.com (B2C), customer-to-business (C2B) transactions such as Priceline.com, and customer-to-customer (C2C) transactions such as eBay auctions. E-commerce is conducted through a variety of electronic media. These electronic media include the Internet of Things (IoT), electronic data interchange (EDI), electronic funds transfer (EFT), radio frequency identification (RFID), bar codes, fax, automated voice mail, CD-ROM catalogs, and a variety of others.

Distribution instructs where to locate the sources of supply and advises how to access them, as well as how to move the materials to the retailers or to the end user via the Internet or a web-based environment.

Procurement is a function that acquires material needed for manufacturing the goods. E-procurement completely revolutionizes a manufacturing or distribution firm's supply chain, creating a seamless flow of order fulfillment information from manufacturer to supplier.

Now that we have characterized the nature of supply chain management, we are ready to make a few relevant points:

1. The objective of supply chain management is to be efficient and cost-effective through collaborative efforts across the entire system.
2. The role of supply chain management is to produce products that conform to customer requirements.
3. The scope of supply chain management encompasses the firm's activities from the strategic level through the tactical and operational levels, since it takes into account the efficient integration of suppliers, manufacturers, wholesalers, logistics providers, retailers, and end users.

1.2 Virtual Integration in the Supply Chain

There are two important technological innovations that have made supply chain virtual integration possible: the advent of advanced **information technology** and **container boxes**. The former shortened the geographic distance by providing a virtual information highway and the latter has lowered the cost of transportation which has helped to justify shipping a large volume of goods from the eastern hemisphere to the western hemisphere. Between the two innovations, information technology and container boxes, information technology plays the more important role in extending the supply chain beyond a firm's business boundary to involve global business and trading partners. Virtual integration is discussed in this section, and containerization will be discussed in the next section.

Virtual integration is using information technology and information to blur the traditional boundaries among the suppliers, manufacturers, distributors, logistics providers, and end users in a supply chain. Today, the virtual cooperation between various firms in a supply chain is apparent through suppliers' and customers' ability to trade over the Internet in real-time in order to create maximum value. Virtual integration offers the advantage of a tightly coordinated supply chain that has traditionally come through vertical integration. In the age of virtual organizations, managers, engineers, professional staff, and technical workers are no longer the lone custodians of the corporate knowledge base. Knowledge is shared across cultural boundaries, time boundaries, and space boundaries in order to create strategic frontiers in global and virtual enterprises.

The seamless virtual integration of the firms within a supply chain requires real-time automation of the inter-organizational business processes that span across trading partners. Today, Enterprise Information Systems are a state of the art technology that enables supply chain partners to integrate and coordinate their supply chain processes. Within an organization, ERP systems create a central data structure which ensures that information can be shared across all of functional levels in real time.

The traditional arm's length transaction from one stage of a supply chain to the next is illustrated in Fig. 1.2(a).[2] In this view, organizations view their suppliers and customers as adversaries who are not to be trusted. This prevents their entry into successful long-term relationships. Performance is often narrowly viewed, and procurement decisions are

---

[2] Source: Magretta, J. (1998). The Power of Virtual Integration: An Interview with Dell Computer's Michael Dell. *Harvard Business Review*, March 1.

often based solely on price. Business relationships are viewed in terms of a zero-sum game in which there is a clear winner and a clear loser.

The integrated supply chain model that Dell Inc. has created is illustrated in Fig. 1.2 (b). This model focuses on the mutual trust and respect of supply chain members, utilizes a just-in-time manufacturing strategy, and eliminates third-party retailers. With this integrated supply chain, Dell only holds five days of inventory, and has a build cycle of two days (on most systems). The integrated supply chain includes joint improvement projects, training seminars, workshops, and meetings between the organizations' top management members. As the degree of communication increases between customers and suppliers, higher levels of informal information sharing can be seen.

(a) Supply chain model: a value chain with arm's length transactions from one layer to the next

Fig. 1.2(a) Supply chain in an e-biz environment.

(b) Dell's direct supply chain model: forge partnership with suppliers and eliminate third-party distribution

Fig. 1.2(b) Supply chain in an e-biz environment.

(c) Virtual integration: works faster by blurring the traditional boundaries and roles in the value chain

Fig. 1.2(c) Supply chain in an e-biz environment.

Still one more step ahead of the integrated supply chain is virtual integration, which blurs the walls of supply chain organizations, as illustrated in Fig. 1.2 (c). The trend of mass-customization forces many companies to focus on their core competences, and thus requires them to outsource a wide range of functions including design, manufacturing, and distribution. This trend drives the need for a virtually integrated supply chain.

1.3 The Container Box

One of the most significant economic developments of transportation in the second half of the 20th century was the introduction of shipping containers by Malcolm McLean. In the mid-1950s, McLean came up with the idea of taking a fully loaded container from a tractor-trailer and placing it onto a ship or a railroad car without breaking bulk. In this way, shipments could be kept together and are protected from damage in handling. Labor costs went way down, cargo turnaround time at the ports decreased significantly, and productive time for container ships increased.

Containerization has dramatically stimulated the formation of a global supply chain. It is estimated that 90 percent of the world's trade today moves in containers. Each year, about 100 million container cargos in over 5,000 container ships crisscross the oceans. Containerization allows for dramatic improvement in port and ship productivity and helps to lower the cost of imported goods. For example, it took 50 days in 1970 for a standard shipment to travel from Hong Kong to New York, but today, in containers, that same trip takes only 17 days. Just as Marc Levinson commented, the shipping container has made the world smaller and the world economy bigger.[3]

After its economic reform in 1979, China gradually became the world manufacturing center and its trade volume with North America, Europe, Asia, and Africa is steadily increasing. As Walmart, the world's largest retailer, shifts its sourcing and purchasing focus to China, the demand for container shipping skyrockets. The Asian countries have responded quickly. The massive construction of container ports in China, Thailand, and Malaysia during the 1990s is an investment in a global supply chain.

---

[3] Levinson, M. (2006) *The Box: How the Shipping Container Made the World Smaller and the World Economy Bigger* (Princeton University Press, USA).

In 2012, the Port of Shanghai (China) and the Port of Singapore ranked number one and two respectively in terms of container handling volume. Rotterdam (The Netherlands) which was the 3rd busiest container port in 1990, and was ranked number eleven on the list of world busiest container ports in 2012. The Port of Los Angeles ranked number 16 in 2012.[4]

1.4 From Material Management to Supply Chain Management

Information technology was the key driving force for moving from material management to supply chain management during the second half of the 20th century. In 1970, the cost of one megahertz of computing power was $7,600. By the end of the 20th century, it was 17 cents. The cost of storing one megabit of data was $5,256 in 1970. It is less than 17 cents now.[5] Ever since the 1960s, technology has enabled businesses to create tools to ease the management of materials. The stages of the business model evolution are illustrated in Fig. 1.3, with Bill of Materials (BOM) processor appearing in the early 60s, Material Requirement Planning (MRP) entering the scene in the 70s, Manufacturing Resource Planning (MRPII) in the 80s, Enterprise Resource Planning (ERP) in the 90s, and supply chain management (SCM) packages coming into use in the early 21st century. The impact of advanced technology on materials and on supply chain management has been phenomenal.

In the early 1960s, a BOM processor was written on a 1400 disk computer. In mid-1960s, the first use of the computer for planning material was introduced and was named Manufacturing Resource Planning (MRP). IBM was the first to introduce MRP software to the market. The significance of MRP is that it identifies what product is required by the customer, compares the requirement to the on-hand inventory level, and calculates what items need to be procured and when.

---

[4] World Shipping Council, "Top 50 World Container Ports", 2013.
[5] Federal Reserve Bank of Dallas, (1999). "The new paradigm," 1999 Annual Report. www.dallasfed.org/fed/annual/1999p/ar99.pdf.

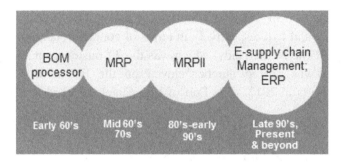

Fig. 1.3 Evolution of e-supply chain.

By itself, MRP does not recognize any capacity limitation. It will schedule order release even if the capacity is not available. This was a problem, so Closed-loop MRP was then introduced to include capacity requirement planning as a part of material requirement planning. Advancements in computer capacity have made the extra mathematical computations needed for capacity planning available and affordable.

In the mid-1980s, Manufacturing Resource Planning (MRPII) evolved out of MRP. MRPII is a method for the effective planning of all of the resources of a manufacturing company. MRPII closed the loop not only with firms' capacity planning and accounting systems but also with their financial management systems. Consequently, all of the resources of a manufacturing company could now be planned and controlled, once the information became more accessible using MRPII.

In the 1980s, the proportion of labor cost decreased and the proportion of material cost increased due to automation in the production process. Reduction in inventory and a shortening in lead time became inevitable, if a business was to survive its competition. Companies searched for new business paradigms that would lead to competitive advantages. Just-In-Time (JIT), Theory of Constraints (TOC), and Total Quality Management (TQM) are examples of several strategies that helped companies to improve their production processes, to reduce costs, and to successfully compete in a variety of business environments.

The late 1980s and early 1990s witnessed the shift of "time to market." Customers demanded to have their products delivered when, where, and how they wanted them. JIT requires cooperation along the entire supply chain with the ultimate goal of maximizing the profit of the supply chain. The beginning of JIT started along the assembly line and was not necessarily controlled by a computer but by a Kanban card. Sending a Kanban card or an empty container upstream along the assembly line was the signal to replenish inventory. A phone call to the supplier with an order was the trigger to deliver the next order. Companies worldwide began to embrace the philosophy of JIT and the supplier partnership as a way to remain competitive.

In the 1990s, increased globalization and the Internet continued to catch on. In order to improve competitiveness, companies began to realize the potential of information technology to dramatically transform their business. Instead of automating old, inefficient processes, companies began to reengineer business processes, using technology as the enabler. This led to the development of ERP systems that gave complete visibility to the organization, integrating systems that previously stood alone. ERP became more acceptable during the mid- and late-1990s. It should be noted, here, that ERP is not just MRPII with a new name. ERP is the next logical level in the sophisticated evolution of computer tools for use in material and supply chain management. ERP systems offer an integrated view of information across the business functions within a company and provide the potential for several different companies to collaborate.

During the late 1990s and the beginning of the 21st century, electronic communications (as opposed to paper transactions) began to allow for a decrease in the amount of lead time required to replenish inventory. Cutting lead time minimizes the risk of uncertainty in demand and decreases the probability of over- or under-stocking inventory. The 1990s marked the wide use of the Internet. This provided a great opportunity for companies to integrate E-commerce into their business models. The primary emphasis during that period was business-to-customer (B2C). Today, the emphasis expands to include business-to-business (B2B). Back-end system integration, especially supply chain management, provides greater visibility and more strategic capability for companies to improve profitability and competitiveness.

A supply chain consists of all of the stages involved, either directly or indirectly, in fulfilling a customer request. A supply chain includes manufacturers, suppliers, transporters, warehouses, retailers, third-party logistics providers, and customers. The objective of supply chain management is to maximize the overall value generated, rather than the profit generated, in a particular stage of a supply chain.

1.5 The Changing Paradigm of Supply Chain Management

Today, there is new tempo and there are new ways of thinking about supply chain management and how it can fit the global economy. Maybe it is that touch of global reality that has motivated business managers to tie the links of a new global supply chain together that has caused the advancement of the paradigm of supply chain management. Table 1.1 illustrates four new paradigms in today's supply chain:

(i) from cost management to revenue management,
(ii) from a functional focus to an order fulfillment process focus,
(iii) from inventory management to information management, and
(iv) from a transactional relationship to a strategic partnership.

Here's an example. American theater owners have known for quite some time that a person who buys a movie ticket might also buy a soft drink and popcorn when he watches the movie. But when businesses, such as Walmart, have tried to think the same way, by moving their focus from the delivery of one product to the delivery of a basket of products, new challenges have emerged: (1) Supply chain operations must move from cost management (How much did a customer spend on this product?) to revenue management (How much did the business make overall?) with a new emphasis on customer relationship management and order winning; (2) Supply chain operations must move from a functional focus (Should we produce the product in-house?) to an order fulfillment process focus (Should we work with partners in the supply chain and outsource?) with an emphasis on the integrated delivery of goods and service; (3) Supply chain operations must move from inventory management (What product should we keep in stock to satisfy demand?) to information management (What products is this customer likely to buy?) with an emphasis on quick response systems and knowledge management; and (4) Supply chain operations are moving from an arm's length transactional relationship (What products/services do businesses need from each other?) to a strategic partnership (What products/services can businesses provide together?) with an emphasis on a win-win strategic collaborative relationship.

Table 1.1 The changing paradigm.

Existing Paradigm	New Paradigm	Indicators
Cost management	Revenue management	Customer Relationship Management (CRM) and order winning
Functional focus	Order fulfillment process	Integrated goods and service delivery flow
Inventory management	Information management	Quick response and knowledge management
Arm's length transactional relationship	Strategic partnership	Win-win strategic collaborative relationship

1.6 Supply Chain Management Models

1.6.1 Competitive priorities and manufacturing strategy

The ability of a supply chain to compete based on cost, quality, time, flexibility, and new products is shaped by the strategic focus of its supply chain members. A firm's position on its competitive priorities is determined by its four long-term structural decisions: facility, capacity, technology, and vertical integration, as well as by its four infrastructural decisions: workforce, quality, production planning and control, and organization. The cumulative impact of infrastructural decisions on a firm's competitiveness is as important as its long-term structural decisions.

Manufacturing strategy focuses on a set of competitive priorities such as cost, quality, time, flexibility, and new product introduction. It classifies production processes into five major types: project, job shop, batch production, assembly line, and continuous flow. "Make-to-order", "engineer-to-order", "build-to-order", "assemble-to-order", and "make-to-stock" are a few of the manufacturing strategies used to address competitive priorities to help businesses compete in the market place.

Make-to-order or **Engineer-to-order** produces products that are made with unique parts and drawings required by customers. Product volume is very small and typically is one-of-a-kind, built in a job-shop environment. The cycle time from order placement to order delivery is usually long because of the unique nature of each customization. MRP planning is extremely important in engineer-to-order.

Build-to-order, on the other hand, produces customized products in low volumes after the manufacturer receives the orders. Build-to-order items are usually ordered in very small volumes and require a high technical competency, a strong product performance design, and effective due date management.

Assemble-to-order is the strategy used to handle numerous end-item configurations and is an option for mass-customization. Assemble-to-order items use standardized parts and components. They require efficient and low-cost production in the fabrication process, and flexibility in the assembly or configuration stage to satisfy individualized demand from customers.

Make-to-stock involves holding products in inventory for immediate delivery, so as to minimize customer delivery time. This fits into the category of the push system, in which demand is forecast and production is scheduled before the demand is even there.

1.6.2 Efficient supply chain and responsive supply chain

One of the causes of supply chain failure is the lack of understanding of the nature of demand. This lack of understanding can lead to a mismatched supply chain design. Fisher (1997) suggested two distinctive approaches, the functional efficient supply chain and the market responsive supply chain, to design a firm's supply chain.

Table 1.2 Efficient supply chain and responsive supply chain.

	Efficient supply chain	Responsive supply chain
Demand	Constant, based on forecasting	Fluctuate, based on customer orders
Order fulfillment lead time	Allowed longer fulfillment lead time	Short lead time or one based on quoted due date
Product life cycle	Long	Short
Product variety	Low	High
Supplier relationship	Long-term	According to product life cycle
Supplier selection	Low cost, consistent quality, and on-time delivery	Flexibility, fast delivery, high-performance design quality
Production	Make-to-stock	Assemble-to-order Make-to-order Build-to-order
Manufacturing Capacity cushion	Low	High
Inventory	Finished goods inventory	Parts, components, subassembly

The purpose of a market responsive supply chain is to react quickly to market demand. This supply chain model best suits the environment in which demand predictability is low, forecasting error is high, the product life cycle is short, new product introductions are frequent, and the product variety is high (Table 1.2). The responsive supply chain design matches competitive priorities that emphasize quick reaction time, development speed, fast delivery times, customization, and volume flexibility. The design features of a responsive supply chain include flexible or intermediate flows, high-capacity cushions, low inventory levels, and a short cycle time.

The purpose of an efficient supply chain is to coordinate the material flow and services to minimize inventories and to maximize the efficiency of the manufacturers and service providers in the chain. This supply chain model best fits the environment in which demands are highly predictable, forecasting error is low, the product life cycle is long, new product introductions are infrequent, the product variety is minimal, production lead time is long, and order fulfillment lead time is short. An efficient supply chain design matches a firm's competitive priority that emphasizes low-cost operations and on-time delivery. The design features of an efficient supply chain include line flows, large volume production, and low-capacity cushions.

1.6.3 Clock-speed of product, process, and organization life cycles

Fine (1999) suggests that each industry evolves at a different rate, depending in some way on its product clock-speed, process clock-speed, and organization clock-speed. For example, the entertainment industry is one of the fast-clock-speed industries. Motion pictures can have a product life measured in hours. The number of movie viewers is greatest during Christmas time; thus, a large number of movies are released during this period. The process for the entertainment industry changes rapidly. New processes for delivering entertainment products and services to our homes and offices evolve daily; smartphones, iPads, TV, PCs, Facebook, YouTube, and CD and DVD players are just a few examples. Organization structure is dynamic as well. The contractual relationships among media giants such as Time Warner, Disney, and Viacom are negotiated, signed, and re-negotiated constantly to accommodate changes in product and process design.

The aircraft industry, on the other hand, is a slow-clock-speed product industry. For example, the Boeing Company measures its products' clock-speed in decades. Almost fifty years after the Boeing 747 was first introduced, the profit generated from selling the Boeing 747 is still flowing in. The Boeing 747, which was produced and sold in 2000, still has the same manufacturing plant as it had when Boeing made the first of these aircraft.

Somewhere in the middle of the clock-time continuum is the automobile industry. This product does not change as fast as that of the entertainment industry, nor does it change as slowly as the aircraft industry. Passenger cars, for example, have a product life of three to five years. As for its process clock-speed, each time that an auto manufacturer makes a new design, it expects much of that investment to be obsolete in four to five years.

Supply chain design should reflect the nature of the product's clock-speed; it is essential to understand what requirements would make it more likely for one to have an effective supply chain or vice versa. Analyzing the clock-speed of the product, along with its manufacturing process and organizational structure, enables us to see with greater clarity and accuracy the future needs of our customers.

1.6.4 Pull and push manufacturing processes

All of the manufacturing processes in a supply chain fall into one of two categories: push or pull. In the push process, production of a product is authorized based on forecasting, which is done in advance of customer orders. In the pull process, on the other hand, the final assembly is triggered by customer orders (Fig. 1.4).

In a pure push manufacturing process, make-to-stock is the primary production approach as shown in the example of the demand for chicken breasts at Sam's Club (in Fig. 1.4). Demand is forecast based on historical sales data. The need of the end users is satisfied from inventory. The production lead time is relatively long and the finished goods inventory is more than that of the pull system. The major technical sophistication that has been applied to the supply chain is Perdue Farms' vertical integration, which focuses on "We do it all for you."

In the pull manufacturing approach, end users trigger the production of computers at Dell's manufacturing factory (as shown in Fig. 1.4). The major production strategy is make-to-order, assemble-to-order, and build-to-order. In a pull scenario, demand uncertainty is higher and cycle time is shorter than it is in the push approach, thus, the finished goods inventory is minimal. Dell is an obvious leader in supply chain management. The major technical sophistication that has been applied to the supply chain is Dell's direct model, which focuses on "Have it your way."

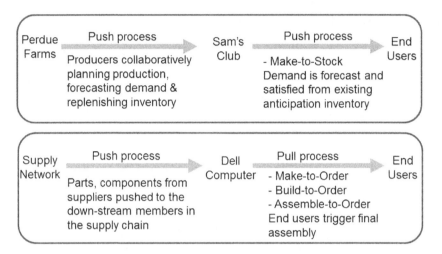

Fig. 1.4 Pull vs. push process.

The decision of whether to use a push or a pull approach is important in the design of a supply chain. Demand uncertainty and variations are treated differently in these two systems. In a push system, safety stock is used to manage demand variability, while in a pull system, flexible capacity is required to meet demand variability. Both inventory and capacity represent financial expenditures. Therefore, developing effective supply chains is crucial to the achievement of a business' cost-effective goals as well as to help it deliver what the customer needs at the right time, in the right place, and in the right quantity.

1.7 Extending the Enterprise: Collaborative Planning, Forecasting, and Replenishment (CPFR)

1.7.1 The basics of CPFR

The essence of recent supply chain development is collaboration across the supply chain. Lack of collaboration in a supply chain leads to inefficient production, redundant inventory stock, and inflated costs. Two examples are given to illustrate the above points:[6]

(1) It often takes a package of cereal more than three months to be delivered from the factory warehouse to a supermarket shelf, due to ineffective distribution strategy.
(2) It takes a car an average of 15 days to travel from the factory to a dealer's showroom, which in real time, usually only requires 4 to 5 days traveling time; this is a significant misuse of valuable time.

Many suppliers and retailers have observed the phenomenon of demand fluctuation in the upstream of the supply chain. Hau Lee describes demand fluctuation for diapers in supply chain.[7] In examining the demand for Pampers disposal diapers, Proctor & Gamble noticed that retail sales of the product were uniform; there was no particular day or month in which the demand was significantly higher or lower than any other. The distributor's orders placed to the factory fluctuated much more than did the retail sales. In addition, P&G's orders to its suppliers fluctuated even more widely. This phenomenon of increasing variability in demand in a supply chain is referred to as the **bullwhip effect**. The bullwhip effect is essentially the artificial distortion of consumer demand figures as they are transmitted back to the suppliers from the retailer.

One way to address the bullwhip effect caused by order batching is to work collaboratively to plan production, to forecast demand, and to replenish inventory. This will lead to smaller order sizes, smoothed production volumes, and more frequent order replenishments. The result is a smoother flow of smaller orders that the distributors and manufacturers are able to handle more efficiently.

In recent years, retailers have initiated collaborative agreements with their supply chain partners to establish ongoing planning, forecasting, and replenishment processes. This initiative is called Collaborative

---

[6] Source: David Simchi-Levi (2002) presentation at Conference on Optimization in Supply Chain Management and E-commerce, Gainesville, Florida.
[7] Lee, H L., Padmanabhan, V., Whang S. (1997). The bullwhip effect in supply chains. *Sloan Management Review*, 38(3), pp. 93-103.

Planning, Forecasting, and Replenishment (CPFR). The Association for Operations Management defines CPFR as follows:

"Collaboration process whereby supply chain trading partners can jointly plan key supply chain activities from production and delivery of raw materials to production and delivery of final products to end customers."[8]

The objective of CPFR is to optimize supply chain outcomes through improved demand forecasts, with the right product being delivered at the right time, at the right quantities, to the right locations, at the right prices, in the right condition, with the right information, with reduced inventories, avoidance of stock-outs, and improved customer service. The value of CPFR lies in the broad exchange of forecast information to improve forecasting accuracy when both the buyer and seller collaborate through joint knowledge of sales, promotions, and relevant supply and demand information.

1.7.2 Major activities of CPFR

Three major activities constitute CPFR: planning, forecasting, and replenishment. There are a few steps involved in each activity.

Planning: Planning starts with a contract that details the responsibilities of the companies that will collaborate with each other in providing the right products for customers. Contract terms are negotiated first. Then, a joint business plan regarding demand management, sales promotion, production quantity, timing, and inventory level can be developed.

Forecasting: First, the customer demand is predicted for all of the participating firms. Any differences in demand forecast among the participating firms is identified and resolved. Finally, a feasible sales forecast for all participating firms is developed. Modifications may be made periodically to reflect the changes in market demand.

---

[8] "The Association for Operations Management" is formerly known as "American Production and Inventory Control Society" (APICS).

Replenishment: First, orders for all participating firms are estimated. Any differences among participating firms are identified and resolved. Finally, an efficient production and delivery schedule is developed. Orders can then be fulfilled.

The idea of collaborative planning, forecasting, and replenishment was initiated at the annual Retail Systems Conference and Exposition in the mid-1990s. Later, the Voluntary Interindustry Commerce Standards (VICS) committee developed a nine-step process model as a guideline for implementing CPFR to facilitate the coordination that is needed in a supply chain. This committee documents best practices for CPFR and creates guidelines for implementing CPFR. The nine steps for effectively implementing CPFR are as follows:

Step 1: Develop a Collaboration Arrangement
Step 2: Create a Joint Business Plan
Step 3: Create a Sales Forecast
Step 4: Identify Exceptions to the Sales Forecast
Step 5: Resolve/Collaborate on the Exception Items
Step 6: Create an Order Forecast
Step 7: Identify the Exceptions to the Order Forecast
Step 8: Resolve/Collaborate on the Exception Items
Step 9: Generate Order

These nine steps have guided companies to successfully implement CPFR. For example, Sears (a US department store) and Michelin (a French tire producer) began discussions on collaboration in 2001. Later that year, they implemented a CPFR initiative which followed the VICS' nine steps. The mutual goal of the two companies was to improve their order fill rate and to reduce inventory at Sears' distribution centers as well as at Michelin's warehouses. After implementing CPFR, Sears distribution-center-to-store order fill rate increased by 10.7 percent. The combined Michelin and Sears inventory levels could be reduced by 25 percent. This practice indicates that collaboration can offer companies the opportunity to transform and radically improve their supply chain performance. Such a transformation can have dramatic benefits and can create competitive advantages.

1.7.3 CPFR in practice

Companies that are able to establish collaborative supply chains will have a significant competitive edge over their competitors. Prominent companies are already leading the way. Companies such as Walmart, Dell Inc., and Proctor & Gamble share point of sales data with all of the other companies in their respective supply chains. The companies in these supply chains also share inventory data with each other. Sharing this kind of information provides a basis for each company to be able to make decisions about its own activities that will yield better efficiencies, as well as more profits, for itself and for the supply chain as a whole.

Collaboration in production, forecasting, and replenishment brings a number of benefits. First, the bullwhip effect is diminished because all of the companies in the supply chain have access to real time sales data and can share sales forecasts. This allows every member in the same supply chain to develop a better production plan, ideal inventory levels, and more realistic delivery schedules. Next, everyone in the supply chain shares the rise and decline in customer demand. Any needed adjustments to previously planned production levels are made accordingly. No retailer loses sales revenue due to lack of inventory or loses profit due to surplus stock. Collaboration is not easy to implement, and it will take time to become more common in business use.

More recently, innovative consumer goods manufacturers and retailers are forging partnerships to advance the implementation of CPFR. For instance, Compaq is working with 850 of its trading partners to conduct purchasing planning over the Internet, and Thomson Electronics is doing CPFR with 50 of its retailers. In addition, more trading partners have launched pilots. Canadian Tire is treading new ground with seven of its suppliers, and New Balance and Timberland are setting the pace in the shoe industry with selected retailers. Further, Schering Plough and Johnson & Johnson are taking the lead with Eckerd Drug, and Mitsubishi Motors is collaborating with its dealers to reduce its customer lead time to two weeks.

The benefits of CPFR include reduced inventory, reduced safety stock, and reduced stock out probability. Nevertheless, it is still a challenging process to integrate a disconnected forecasting and planning process across the entire supply chain. A key issue in improving collaborative efforts revolves around the partners getting their own supply chain processes in order.

1.8 Impact of Globalization in Supply Chain Management

In late November of 2006, I visited a shopping mall in the southern Virginia area. A majority of its merchandise had been manufactured offshore. In the same month in Hanoi, Vietnam, 21 Asian-Pacific Economic Cooperation (APEC) countries were holding the 14th annual APEC Economic Leaders' Meeting. The APEC leaders acknowledged the role of comprehensive Regional Trade Agreements / Free Trade Agreements (RTAs/FTAs) in advancing trade liberalization. They also agreed that RTAs/FTAs would lead to greater trade liberalization and to genuine reductions in trade transaction costs.

Globalization is inevitable. As we look five to ten years down the road, we can be sure about one thing: the continued liberalization of trade. As more and more countries open up to world trade, more and more companies seek the most cost effective way to produce and deliver products. Companies of various sizes realize that they have to be part of the global supply chain in order to remain in business and to stay competitive.

1.8.1 Supply chain management issues in the US

During the past 20 years, the United States has been at the forefront of developing new supply chain management models, reengineering operations processes, and advancing technologies for supply chain management. Walmart, Dell Inc., and HP (as well as many other companies) have already demonstrated their ability in managing the supply chain in the new environment of electronic commerce.

As one of the world's largest consumers, producers, and traders, the US has a number of advantages as it advances its use of supply chain management. First, the population of the US uses the same language, currency, and technology. Additionally, the culture of this large country is much more similar than cultures in neighboring countries from the other parts of the world, even though there are some variations from region to region within the country. Second, it has a well-developed transportation infrastructure. Its sea and airport facilities are adequate to handle the flow of imports and exports. Its intra-country freight rail system is very productive and its highway system is more than sufficient to connect all of the activities within its supply chain. Third, its technology is readily available to all participants in the supply chain. The assumption that there will be ease in telecommunication and convenient access to the Internet is a feature of US supply chains. From the aspect of technology, the US leads both Europe and Japan in the deployment of e-commerce systems.

1.8.2 Supply chain management issues in Europe

In recent years, the European Union has done much to unify the continent, but there are still major differences in local markets, culture, legal regulations, politics, taxation requirements, economic development, wealth, and geography. Markets vary greatly from country to country, especially since the emergence of new democracies in Eastern Europe. Influencing these differences is the wide variety in cultures from region to region. Although some standard issues in the areas of quality, health, environment, and timeliness are beginning to emerge, the level of consumer service values vary widely across Europe. The differences among countries' value systems force manufacturers to focus on customization at the most local level.

Also, the transportation infrastructure varies from country to country across Europe. The geography of a country affects its accessibility, which in turn influences both transportation methods and distribution networks. For example, Italy has chosen to use a more localized distribution network because of its compartmentalized geography. The Netherlands, on the other hand, tends to use a more centralized distribution network because of its relatively accessible geography. These transportation and distribution issues have led some firms to establish regional stockholding distribution centers, which may reduce the need for and the reliance on extensive distribution networks and may reduce dependency on transportation. A considerable disadvantage to using localized transportation systems in Europe is the continent's relatively low usage of rail to transport freight. Poorly maintained infrastructures in some Eastern European countries, as well as differences from country to country in rail gauge size, technical standards, and height/width allowances are the issues that have slowed down the development of supply chain management in Europe.

Finally, the application of current technology also varies from country to country. Unlike the situation in the US, the availability of reliable Internet access and current technologies is not always a given in all of the countries throughout Europe. The variation in Internet access from region to region has had a significant impact on the ability of firms to conduct collaborative planning, forecasting, and replenishment within their supply chains, in order to compete on a global level.

Although the continent and its countries are fighting to overcome some inherent challenges, Europe has made some significant strides forward and has implemented innovations that will help to overcome some of these challenges. Mobile commerce (m-commerce), vehicle tracking and dispatching, radio frequency identification (RFID) tags, silent commerce applications, and collaboration are few examples of recent developments in Europe. Its high level of cell phone usage has led to the development of mobile networks that are integrated into back end operations. Expanding on these wireless application advancements, Europe also uses an increasing number of vehicle tracking and distribution systems. The European Union has initiated a mission to bring the whole of Europe into a single accepted standard, which may include the development of "freight corridors" via road, rail, and water, in order to address distribution both within countries and regions, as well as across the continent as a whole.

1.8.3 Supply chain management issues in Asia

Supply chain management in Asia is considered to be more fragmented and less competitive than SCM in the United States or in Europe, but the gap between these regions is closing. First, the Asian market is made up of many countries which vary in culture, religion, political system, language, legal system, and stage of economic development. Some of the major countries include China, Japan, India, Australia, Indonesia, South Korea, and Thailand. This list of countries presents an obvious diversity, from a variety of aspects. Culturally speaking, most Asian cultures differ greatly from Europe and the United States. As an example, Asian culture values relationships greatly, and they are established over time and past dealings. This precludes the establishment of quick business deals. The focus tends to be on the establishment of respectful relationships over time.

In addition, the transportation infrastructure in many of the developing countries in Asia is less comprehensive, as compared to that in the US and in Europe. Traditionally, rail transportation was the dominant public transportation in countries such as India, China, and Japan. But air transportation has been undergoing fast development in recent years, and highway construction is advancing at a rapid pace. For example, China is aggressively developing its highway system as well as improving the efficiency of its rail freight industry. In 2000, 50,000 kilometers of new highway were added in China. By December 2012, China had a 5,800 mile high-speed railway, which is the world's longest high-speed railway system.[9]

Finally, technology is also a major concern to the development of efficient supply chains in Asia. There is weak access to and limited availability for the use of information technology in many developing Asian countries. The lowering of production costs has been prevalent throughout Asia. However, the opportunity to reduce costs now lies in the development of efficient logistics and distribution systems, which has traditionally been a weak area throughout Asia. The use of information technology can greatly assist in this regard.

Collaboration is an area of opportunity in Asia. Currently, many of its collaborative efforts have been informal. As more formal forms of collaboration develop, especially at the industry level, greater efficiency can be achieved and greater savings will occur. One of the main areas that must be developed in order to enable this increased collaboration is

---

[9] Deng, S. "World's longest high-speed rail line makes debut". Xinhua, Dec. 26, 2012.

information technology. Data integrity must be increased and information must be available upon request. This may require that some companies undergo a certain amount of re-engineering in their supply chains. In the near future, the outsourcing of logistics and supply chain functions will pay great dividends in the Asian market. As manufacturing companies begin to compete for a larger piece of the global market, they will need to compete on a variety of levels – more than just Asia's traditional level of low-cost labor. Quality and cycle time management will be essential. To capitalize on supply chain efficiency, many small manufacturing companies, who lack certain capabilities, will need to turn to third party logistics providers in order to attain a competitive efficiency.

1.8.4 Supply chain management issues in Latin America

Latin American countries can offer US-based firms an opportunity to expand their lists of suppliers and to cut down on costs. The NAFTA agreements give the US access to Mexico's low labor market. However, differences in currency, transportation, infrastructure, political systems, and laws are just some of the hurdles which face US businesses looking to take advantage of the opportunity for growth in Latin America.

Technology is also a major concern to the development of efficient supply chains in Latin America. While computers are common in Mexico and in other Latin American countries, high-tech communications are not as reliable there as they are in the US. There are fewer people are networked via the Internet than there are in the US, which makes it difficult to automate supply chains and to reliably monitor inventory as it passes from one link to another. In the rural area, technology is old or even not available.

Because of Latin America's technology disparities, a company looking to connect with suppliers there will either have to invest in a mixed infrastructure involving electronic data interchange (EDI), Web, phone, and fax systems or will have to link up with third-party logistics providers that offer the needed interfaces. For example, Ryder (a US trucking firm) transports 3,000 different parts from Latin America for an automotive manufacturer that assembles trucks in Indiana. To keep track of inventories, Ryder uses a mixed radio, cell phone, and EDI communications system. Each Sunday, Ryder gets an e-mail with the plant's requirements. Half of the parts makers are either online or have EDI capabilities; the other half requires phone or fax-based transactions. The company had to build a considerable infrastructure in order to facilitate various communication devices.

1.9 Supply Chain Management Issues in the BRIC Countries

In 2003, Jim O'Neill, an economist at Goldman Sachs, a US investment management firm, proposed the concept of the BRIC countries in the report "Dreaming with BRICs: the path to 2050." The acronym "BRIC", which stands for Brazil, Russia, India, and China, represents the emerging markets that may rise to eclipse the economic power of US, Italy, France, Germany, UK, and Japan, the G6 countries. The Goldman Sachs' report projects that in about 40 years, based on GDP growth, income per capita, and currency movements, the BRIC countries' economies, together, could be larger than the combined economies of the G6 countries, in terms of US dollars. Furthermore, of the current G6 countries, only the US and Japan may be among the six largest economies (in terms of US dollars) by 2050.

The BRICs are among the most populous countries in the world. The four countries cover almost 42 percent of the world's population. According to the World Bank, in 2007, the BRICs collectively held over 14 trillion US dollars in GDP (at purchasing power parity). On almost every scale, the four countries would be the largest entity on the global stage. These four economies are among the largest and fastest growing markets and represent unprecedented opportunities for businesses all over the world, whether they are retailers, distributors, logistics service providers, manufacturers, or software developers.

Brazil. When Brazil was included in the "BRIC" group in 2003, it had just narrowly missed bankruptcy. Its long-term growth since the 1970s had averaged less than 2% annually per capita. But in 2003, the world's oil prices began to climb, and that has provided the basis for Brazil's current stellar economic growth. Interestingly, Brazil's ethanol program, deployed during the oil crisis of 1979-82, which had been considered a hopeless project for a couple of decades, suddenly became the bonanza of the country. Rising oil prices made Brazilian sugarcane the world's cheapest and the most economically and ecologically efficient source of newly-fashionable ethanol. The current economic growth rate in Brazil is 5%, and it is likely that Brazil will sustain this growth rate with its improving credit position. Brazil has rich natural resources and occupies an immense area along the eastern coast of South America. With this unique position, the current view of Brazil's role in the global supply chain focuses on it exporting of energy and its container transportation.

Russia. Russia's economy is significantly different from that of the pre-1991 Soviet Union. The Putin government has produced huge economic growth, averaging nearly 10% per annum since 2000, including a growth rate of 8.1% in 2007. With rising oil prices since 2004, Russia's economic growth has been almost entirely driven by high oil prices. The Russia government is set on the task of controlling all economic activities in the energy sector. Russia is primarily natural gas and oil export economy, which makes it important in supporting the steady growth of the global supply chain. On the other hand, its growing economy has created a larger number of middle class consumers that need the global supply chain to provide new products and services.

India. Since 2003, India has been one of the fastest-growing markets, leading to steady increases in per capita incomes, rising consumer demand, and improvements in productivity and efficiency. India's economic growth was 9% in 2007. Inflation in India is a big problem. In the past few years, higher commodity and energy prices have greatly affected the country. India's position is made more difficult by the poverty of much of its population. The Indian government has restricted exports of rice and has subsidized other foods and gasoline. Needless to say, these subsidies and restrictions make the budget deficit worse, and will pose an additional problem when they are lifted, since that could lead to the soaring of consumer prices. Nevertheless, India is reintegrating with the global economic structure.

China. Among the four BRIC countries, China plays the most important role in the global supply chain. China has 1.3 billion people and is the second largest economy in the world (after the United States). As Goldman Sachs projected, it is quite possible that China will exceed the US, in terms of GDP, by 2040.

In 1979, China's leader Deng Xiaoping launched a series of sweeping economic reforms which opened up China's market to the world. This historic transition has fundamentally changed the way that the Chinese economy functions. The economic reform now allows the operations of private firms, joint venture projects with foreign companies, and more local collective businesses. In 1992, the 14th National Congress of the Communist Party of China set up a reform blueprint for a socialist market economy. A new company law which reflected the economic reform was approved in 1993 and was implemented in 1994. Since then, the business enterprise has become an independent legal entity, with separation of ownership and management. This structural change within China's manufacturing sector has laid the foundation for China to become a "world manufacturing center" as well as a key player in the global supply chain.

By the end of the 20th century, North American and European companies sought to further reduce their costs, in order to meet customer demand. As such, the location of low-cost manufacturing centers became vital to the solution. Meanwhile, China's economic reform provided fertile soil for the global supply chain to grow. During the past fifteen years, many US and European firms have moved their manufacturing operations to China, either through outsourcing or through joint ventures.

1.10 Summary

1.10.1 Supply chain management challenges

Supply chain integration is difficult, for two primary reasons: first, the supply chain is an integrated system that requires cohesive decisions to optimize system profit and value. In practice, different facilities in the supply chain may have different, sometimes even conflicting, objectives. Second, the supply chain is a dynamic system which has its own life cycle and which continually evolves. For example, customer demand, as well as supplier capabilities, can change over time. So do supply chain relationships.

Supply chain managers are facing a number of important challenges. For example, supply chain design and strategic collaboration can be quite difficult because of the dynamics and the conflicting objectives employed by different facilities and partners. Inventory control is another tough issue. What is the effect of inventory on a system's performance? Why should a supply chain member hold inventory?

Distribution network configuration involves decisions 1) regarding warehouse locations and capacities; 2) determining production levels for each product at each plant; and 3) setting transportation flows between facilities to minimize total production, inventory, and transportation costs and to satisfy service level requirements.

The sharing of data, information, and knowledge is a challenge in the virtual integration of a supply chain. It must be noted that a large portion of corporate technical knowledge is difficult to articulate and tacitly resides in the minds of knowledge workers. To what extent can emerging information technologies help to explicate complex tacit knowledge so that it can be shared across dispersed or virtual organizational environments?

1.10.2 Road map for supply chain management

This book is about managing the supply chain through collaboration and is divided into six major parts:

- Strategic Issues and Supply Chain Design (Chapters 1 and 2);
- Purchasing, Supply Networks, and Strategic Sourcing (Chapters 3 and 4);
- Demand Transformation in the Supply Chain (Chapters 5, 6, and 7);
- Distribution Networks and Transportation (Chapters 8 and 9);
- Emerging Issues and Big Data Science in Supply Chain Management (Chapters 10 and 11);
- Supply Chain Management Performance and Evaluation (Chapter 12).

The flow of topics throughout the book reflects the theme of how supply chain management can provide a sound basis for market competitiveness and for sustainable growth through collaboration.

Once we are clear about the concept of supply chain management, the discussion is extended. We will learn how to create supply network and how to build strategic partnerships, how to transform our customers' demands into goods, and how to deliver the right products to the right customers at the right time and right place.

Since the driver of the evolution in supply chain management is information technology, the cutting-edge e-solutions that trigger many of the current initiatives in supply chain management are discussed. In the last portion, the book's focus is on evaluating effective supply chain performance, which is interfaced with every supply chain stage.

After the initial wave of e-business, many companies realize that beneath the Internet application are the sourcing structure and the need for physical distribution. Supply chain management is concerned with more than just the movement of materials from raw material producers to manufacturers, and finally to the end users. The goal of supply chain management is to create value for the supply chain members with an emphasis on the end users. The mechanism used to realize value-added activities in a supply chain is collaborative planning, forecasting, and replenishment among the supply chain members.

References

Boalow, J. (2000). "Transformation of Economy Real." *Houston Chronicle*, July 16.

Butler, S. (2000). "The economy downshifts; the Fed tries to do what's never been done before: engineer a soft landing." *U.S News and World Report*, June 19.

Chopra, S. and Meindl, P. (2001). Supply Chain Management: Strategy, Planning, and Operations. (Prentice Hall, Upper Saddle River, NJ).

Deans, P.C. and Karwan, K.R., Eds. (1994). Information Technology and Lead-time Management in International Manufacturing Operations.

Global Information Systems and Technology: Focus on the Organization and Its Functional Areas. (Idea Group Publishing, London).

Domeika, B., and Crawford, F. (2001). "Focusing on success." Dec. http//:www.optimizemag.com/issue/002/custorner4.htm.

Findlay, C. (2002). "Europe's Unique Supply Chain Opportunities, Challenges, and Innovations." *ASCET*, 4, May 16.

Ferrer, J. (2003). "European Supply Chain Management Characteristics and Challenges." *ASCET*, 5, July 26.

Fine, C.H. (1999). Clockspeed. (Perseus Books, Reading, MA).

Fisher, M.L. (1997). "What is the right supply chain for your product?" *Harvard Business Review*, March-April 1997, pp. 105-116.

Forrester, J. (1961). Industrial dynamics. (Pegasus Communications, Waltham, MA).

Goldman Sacks Group Inc., 2003. Global Economics Paper #99, "Dreaming the BRICs: the Path to 2050."

Handfield, R.B. and J. Ernest L. Nichols (2002). Supply Chain Redesign. (Prentice Hall, Upper Saddle River, NJ).

Hutchinson, M. (2008) "Hit the BRICs for a Global-Investing Double Play." Aug. 5. http://www.moneymorning.com.

Krajewski, L.J., Ritzman, L.P. (2002). Operations Management, (Prentice Hall, Upper Saddle River, NJ).

Lee, H. (1997). "Information distortion in a Supply Chain: The Bullwhip Effect," *Management Science*, 43, pp. 4.

Levinston, M. (2006). *The Box: How the Shipping Container Made the World Smaller and the World Economy Bigger* (Princeton University Press, USA).

Magretta, J. (1998). "The power of virtual integration: An interview with Dell computer's Michael Dell." *Harvard Business Review*, March-April.

Ptak, C.A. (2000). ERP: Tools, Techniques, and Application for Integrating Supply Chain (The St. Lucie Press, New York).

Simchi-Levi, D., P. Kaminsky, et al. (2003). Designing and Managing the Supply Chain. 2nd edition (McGraw-Hill, New York).

Steermann, H. (2003). "A practical look at CPFR: the Sears - Michelin experience." *Supply Chain Management Review*, July/August 2003, pp. 46-53.

VICS (2000). CPFR Guidelines. Voluntary Inter-industry Commerce Standards, http://www.cpfr.org.

The New Darwinism (2002). http//:www.optimizemag.com/issue/006/management2.htm.

Chapter 2

The Right Design of a Supply Chain

2.1 Design the Right Supply Chain

Today, supply chain managers are overwhelmed with a range of leading-edge supply chain strategies and new business initiatives. However, not all of these initiatives and strategies are appropriate for every business. Supply chain managers need to understand the constraints of the supply of their products and the uncertainties of the demand from their customers before they try to match these constraints and uncertainties with the right supply chain strategies. A framework for analyzing supply chain practices based on the constraints of various industry environments is proposed in Fig. 2.1.

This figure depicts the integration of an efficient supply chain and a responsive supply chain view (the clock-speed view), with the level of supplier collaboration that we discussed in Chapter 1. In designing their supply chain in an e-Biz environment, companies must integrate the various aspects of competitive priority, the nature of the product, and the complexity of the manufacturing process, in order to be successful. When designing a supply chain, some fundamental principles of the value chain should be exploited in order to be able to respond quickly to the dynamic business environment. As such, supply chain design needs to be fine-tuned constantly to match the evolving industry paradigm.

When new product introductions are frequent and product variety is high, the responsive supply chain option is more attractive, because it reacts quickly to market demand. When the product life cycle is long, the demand is relatively stable, and the demand volume is high, the efficient supply chain is more appropriate. Both the responsive supply chain and the efficient supply chain can be applied to fast, medium, and slow clock-speed products.

A product's clock-speed can be fast, medium, or slow. The product life cycle and its manufacturing process life cycle determine the production volume, the choice of supply chain collaboration level, and the type of supply chain design.

The level of collaboration in a supply chain is closely associated with the product's clock-speed and the production process. The collaboration spectrum on the left-hand side in Fig. 2.1 indicates, at one end, *virtual companies* which outsource most of their business activities through the marketplace and form a virtual business process.

At the other end of the spectrum are *vertical integration* companies which have complete ownership of the business and manage almost everything in-house from the production of raw material to the distribution channel to the final users. As vertical integration gets more involved and complicated, many global corporations have autonomous divisions within their organizations to manage day-to-day operations. Autonomous divisions are responsible for a whole production process, the products produced, or the services provided.

In the middle of the collaborative spectrum is *strategic alliances* and joint venture. At this level, companies synergize resources, knowledge, expertise, location advantage, and capabilities to share responsibilities, benefits, risks, and setbacks. A *strategic alliance* is defined as an agreement between two or more organizations in order to synergize the strengths of involved parties. In today's supply chain market, organizations with complementary strengths forge alliances to gain a competitive edge in order to reduce risks and costs. Thus, strategic alliances are particularly applicable when business uncertainty and complexity are increasing in a global market.

A *joint venture* is a sealed contractual agreement that unites two or more business entities for the purpose of carrying out a particular business undertaking. All parties agree to share in the benefits and the losses of the business. The term "joint venture" is sometimes used interchangeably with "strategic alliance"; however, a strategic alliance may engage competitors.

An *"arm's-length relationship"* is a pure transactional relationship. When the particular transaction is over, the relationship is over. In logistical services, this type of relationship is known as a "you call, we haul" relationship.

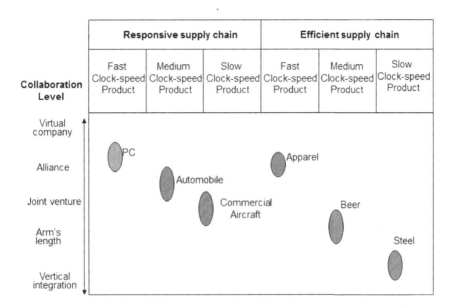

Fig. 2.1 Product life cycle and supply chain design.

2.2 Responsive Supply Chain in the Manufacturing Industry

2.2.1 Responsive supply chain and a fast clock-speed product: The personal computer

The PC industry is a fast clock-speed industry which faces short product life cycles. PC producers adopt the responsive supply chain strategy to reduce the order cycle, the production cycle, and the procurement cycle. Let us consider Dell Computer as an example.

Dell Computer designs, manufactures, and sells a wide range of systems that include desktops, notebooks, workstations, and network servers directly to customers in the global market through the Internet and call centers. Dell also markets software and peripherals as well as service and support programs. Centered on the two key elements of a direct business model and an intense customer focus, Dell strives to eliminate retailers in order to reduce product delivery cycle time and cost (Fig. 2.2a). Customers can order PCs directly from Dell and can have the computers configured to meet their needs. The orders are directly routed to the manufacturing floor and from there the PCs are built, tested, and sent to the customer, all within 5-7 days after the customer placed his or her order.

Fig. 2.2 (a) Dell's direct selling model using strategic alliances and virtual integration.

The traditional PC supply chain has a longer supply chain because it has a distribution network as an additional link in the supply chain (Fig. 2.2b).

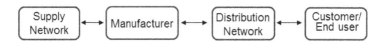

Fig. 2.2 (b) Traditional PC supply chain structure.

In order to reduce its procurement cycle time, Dell shifted from a traditionally-fashioned assembly line to cellular manufacturing techniques and to established strategic alliances with its key suppliers. It forged alliances with reputable suppliers rather than manufacturing its own parts and components. Since new parts and components are introduced so fast that inventory is obsolete in a matter of months or even more quickly, Dell itself holds only a ten-day inventory. Meanwhile, Dell provides its inventory data and production needs to its suppliers at least once a day. Collaboration with suppliers enables Dell to operate with only a few hours of inventory for some parts and a few days of inventory for other parts. Dell's direct model capitalizes the benefits of e-commerce and the Just-in-Time production strategy.

As a responsive supply chain which produces fast clock products, Dell's core competence lies in its virtual supply network, JIT production system, pull model, and flexible assemble-to-order or configure-to-order manufacturing strategy.

2.2.1.1 Dell is cloning a push model

A week before Father's Day, Sunday June 9, 2013, Best Buy advertised Dell computers.[1]

The following questions raise supply chain issues that are pertinent to Dell's decisions:

1. Why has Dell decided to integrate a retailer in its supply chain?
2. At what product life stage will a push model become worth Dell's effort to restructure its supply chain from a pure pull model to a hybrid model of push and pull strategies? Why?
3. Will the traditional PC supply chain model reduce costs for Dell? Or will it increase Dell's market share? How?

---

[1] The information in the figure was based on the advertisement distributed to customers on Sunday June 9, 2013.

2.2.2 Responsive supply chain and medium clock-speed product: The automobile industry

The auto industry is a medium clock-speed industry. New models are introduced every four to six years and the variety of configurations is abundant. Passenger cars are made in an assemble-to-order (also called configure-to-order) fashion. The challenge in this production environment is to manage hundreds of suppliers and to react quickly to market needs (Fig. 2.3). The auto supply chain is led by the supply chain captain, which is an auto maker such as General Motors (GM) or Toyota, with numerous suppliers in the upstream of the supply chain and a number of dealers in the downstream of the supply chain.

Let's take General Motors as an example of a passenger car producer. GM is one of the world's largest industrial corporations and is a full-line vehicle manufacturer. It operates in 397 facilities on six continents and employed more than 212,000 people in 2013. GM has a long list of product lines, including Buick, Cadillac, Chevrolet, GMC, Holden, Opel, Baojun, Isuzu, Vauxhall, and Wuling. GM also has a few major joint ventures in China and Korea including SAIC-GM, SAIC-GM-Wuling, FAW-GM and GM Korea.[2]

These different product lines require GM to manage thousands of parts and components produced by hundreds of suppliers. Thus, GM employs strategic collaboration and joint ventures to manage this medium-clock supply chain. To be more responsive to market needs and to reduce initial research and development costs, GM needs to focus on its core business and product lines. GM forges partnerships with suppliers rather than designing and manufacturing all of its own parts and components. In order to guarantee the steady supply of aluminum that is used in everything from wheel covers to power trains, General Motors signed a 10-year, multi-billion dollar agreement with Alcan Aluminum to buy aluminum at predictable prices.[3] GM also has a joint venture with Alcan Aluminum to co-develop new automotive applications.

---

[2] Date of access: www.gm.com.
[3] "GM, Alcan Sign 10-Year Pact." Date of access: Feb. 11, 2009. www.cbsnews.com.

Strategic alliances and joint ventures ensure GM a smooth flow of material at a minimum cost. General Motors continues to advance vehicle electrification in batteries, electric motors, and power controls. As such, Oracle and Hewlett-Packard are at the top of GM's supplier list. Downstream on GM's supply chain, cars and trucks made by GM are connected with customers around the world through its 21,000 dealers and through rental car companies such as Hertz Global Holdings and Avis Budget Group (Fig. 2.3).

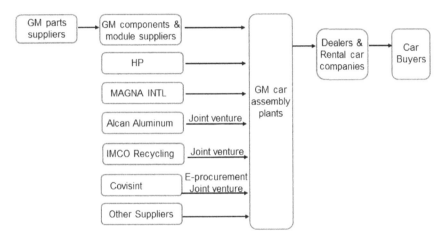

Fig. 2.3 GM's supply chain using joint venture and strategic alliances.

With approximately 18,500 suppliers around the world, managing the relationship between GM and its suppliers is crucial to its success in the global market place. GM has honored its best suppliers each year since 1992. The criteria for the Supplier of the Year Award include the supplier's performance in the areas of delivering innovative technology, superior quality, timely crisis management, and competitive, total-enterprise cost solutions. The award recognizes the significant contributions of GM's suppliers to GM's global performance achievements. The 2012 winner list includes suppliers in Brazil, Canada, China, Denmark, Germany, Japan, India, Italy, Mexico, Norway, Russia,

Spain, Switzerland, Taiwan, UK, and the United States.   Of the 83 recipients in 2012, 46 are repeat winners.[4]

As it is a responsive supply chain which produces medium clock-speed products, GM's core competence lies in its auto-design-and-assemble expertise, its global sourcing, its reliable supply network, and its assemble-to-order manufacturing strategy.

2.2.3 Responsive supply chain and slow clock-speed product: Commercial aircraft

A commercial aircraft is a slow clock-speed product which is highly customized and is traditionally manufactured in a make-to-order production environment. The product technology lasts for 10-20 years, sometimes longer.

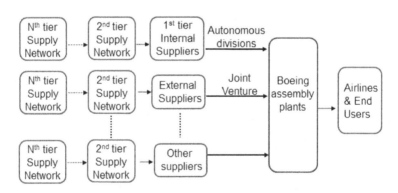

Fig. 2.4 Supply chains for commercial aircraft.

The Boeing Company is the world's largest aircraft manufacturer with revenue totaling $81.7 billion in 2012.   As a global enterprise, Boeing contracts with over 26,000 suppliers and partners around the world. Its supply chain network includes manufacturers, service providers, and technology partners.[5] It has more than 170,000 employees in 70 countries. Boeing relies on both internal and external suppliers for

---

[4] Source: Date of access: May 25, 2013. hppt://www.gm.com.
[5] Source: "Boeing Overview," Date of access: June 8, 2013. www.Boeing.com.

its five to six million parts and components (Fig. 2.4). Boeing's suppliers have their own supply network and the supply chain is very long and complicated. The goal of Boeing's supply chain is to produce the right parts and components, and put them into the right airplane, in the right sequence.

Boeing has had experiences with unreliable suppliers which have resulted in a delay in the arrival of orders. These unreliable suppliers and changed delivery schedules forced Boeing to shut down two of its major assembly lines for a month in 1997, which resulted in a significant loss. Today, Boeing is proactively restructuring its supply chain and its production systems to make sure that such problems never happen again. Phasing out its World War II-era technologies, Boeing is heavily investing in new production systems that include Baan's ERP system, CimLink's factory floor control system, i2 Technologies' forecasting system, Trilogy's product configuration system, and RFID integrated solution systems.

Instead of making one-of-kind, customer-specific airplanes, Boeing is moving toward a small-batch production system which allows it to start building planes even before an order is placed by the customer. The new system reduces cycle time dramatically. Customers will no longer have a 36-month wait from the time they order a plane to the time it is finally delivered. Boeing Commercial Airplanes is now striving to deliver commercial aircraft in eight to twelve months.

2.2.3.1 Boeing 787 moves to batch production and reduces cycle time

When Boeing wanted to reduce the amount of time it took to build its new Boeing 787 Dreamliner, it had to rethink how it built commercial aircraft. In the past, Boeing relied on thousands of suppliers to provide it with the parts and systems for the planes, and then Boeing would assemble everything itself. This method took a long time. In order to be more cost-effective and to reduce its new product development cycle time, Boeing adopted the **modular design method.** In doing so, Boeing came up with a plan in which its suppliers would design and build major sections and modules of the planes, and then the suppliers would ship the sections and modules to Boeing for final assembly and testing. This modular design approach has enabled Boeing to complete the 787's final assembly in just three days (instead of the 30 days that it had spent on performing the final assembly for Boeing 737).

To do that, Boeing had to improve how it collaborated with key suppliers all over the world. Boeing involves about 50 tier-1 strategic partners in its 787 supplier network. These suppliers play a proactive role and serve as "integrators." The tier-1 suppliers produce modules or sections using different parts and subsystems manufactured by tier-2 suppliers or even by raw material suppliers. By outsourcing 70% of the development and production activities in the 787 program, Boeing is able to leverage suppliers' ability to develop different parts, to shorten its production cycle time, and to reduce its financial risk.

On January 16, 2013, one of the Dreamliner passenger jets made an emergency landing in Japan. A battery error had triggered emergency warnings, which was described by a Japanese transport ministry official as "highly serious." Japan Airlines Company Ltd. immediately grounded its 24 Dreamliners and the U.S. Federal Aviation Administration (FAA) asked Boeing to stop flying the Boeing 787 Dreamliner until safety concerns were addressed. After extensive redesign, the new battery was recertified at the end of April 2013. The first modified 787, an Ethiopian Airlines plane, took off on April 27, 2013. Other airlines are not likely to resume operations until June, giving them time to complete tests and training.

The following questions raise supply chain issues that are pertinent to Boeing's decisions:

1. Why did Boeing move from a one-of-a-kind production strategy to batch production?
2. What are the potential benefits that Boeing would gain through developing a strategic supplier network and outsourcing 70% of the 787 production?
3. Could the battery problem be a side effect of outsourcing and cycle time reduction? Discuss the potential risks that Boeing faces. What can Boeing do to reduce these risks?

Boeing forges joint ventures and partnerships with suppliers from their large customers' native countries. Both Japanese and Chinese airlines are Boeing's major customers for commercial aircrafts. Since commercial aircraft is a slow clock-speed product, the supply chain is fairly stable. A number of Japanese companies, such as Mitsubishi Heavy Industries (MHI), Kawasaki Heavy Industries (KHI), and Fuji Heavy Industries (FHI), have supplied Boeing for more than 30 years. More recently, Boeing established "working together" relationships with China. In fact, several Chinese factories produce major assemblies and parts for Boeing airplanes.

As a responsive supply chain which produces slow clock-speed products, Boeing's proficiency lies in its airplane design and configuration expertise, its global supply chain management, and its aircraft assembly.

2.3 Efficient Supply Chain in the Manufacturing Industry

2.3.1 Efficient supply chain and fast clock-speed product: The Apparel industry

The apparel and footwear industries produce large batch, fast clock-speed garments. Thus, the efficient supply chain model that echoes throughout the apparel industry is a critical strategy for its success. The fact that the apparel industry continues to experience relentless deflation is an indication of the complexities of supply chain management. Today, a popular business model applied in the apparel industry is to keep the core business, the design, and the color selection at the company's headquarters or in its home country and to outsource labor-intensive production offshore.

The Limited is a mall-based fashion retailer that offers high-quality, private-label apparel for women. Founded in 1963 in Columbus, Ohio, the Limited was the foundation name for Limited Brands, Inc. The Limited was acquired by Sun Capital Partners, Inc., an investment firm in August 2007[6]. The Limited Brands, Inc. currently has five retail brands: Victoria's Secret, Bath & Body Works, Pink, Henri Bendel, and La Senza.

To transfer from the traditional make-to-stock production strategy to the replenish-to-sale business model, The Limited has developed enhanced relationships with its suppliers. For example, The Limited established a relationship with Li & Fung Co., a fabric and garment supplier in Hong Kong, which in turn works to identify local materials that it can obtain with a short lead-time. Orders for colors and fabrics can be changed much more quickly as a result of this cultivated supplier network. Retailers can go online to change the color, size, and/or style of their garment orders as the items are being made (Fig. 2.5).

Fig. 2.5 (a) ZARA's supply chain model using strategic alliances.

Fig. 2.5 (b) Traditional apparel industry supply chain model.

Two of the vital links in a supply chain are customer order forecasting and demand management. These links serve as preludes to apparel retailers' production planning, capacity management, and order fulfillment. The Limited tries to accurately predict its customers' needs with the delayed differentiation method or "postponement," which is a recent trend in the apparel industry. The Limited asks its manufacturers to reserve a certain amount of production capacity in an effort to delay key decisions regarding size, color, volume, shipping dates, and destinations. Traditionally, the lead-time was six months, but this

---

[6] Source: date of access: May 2013. www.thelimited.com.

strategy allows the product to be shipped almost immediately after it has been completed.

As an efficient supply chain which produces fast clock-speed products, the core competence of the Limited lies in its fashion design, color choice, supplier relationship management, JIT production, logistics management, knowledge of free trade agreements and tariffs, and replenish-to-sale distribution system.

2.3.1.1 ZARA does everything by itself, from procurement to delivery

Established in 1979 with only six stores, today ZARA is a brand name in the fashion business. ZARA's corporate concept is to provide customers with fresh, fashionable, trendy clothes at a reasonable price.

ZARA has reinvented the efficient, fast-clock supply chain in a number of ways. Unlike many fashion producers who outsource their production components to low-cost labor countries or regions, ZARA vertically integrates its supply chain, from design to retailing. Its cycle time for the design and production process is only 30 days, much faster than the traditional production process. In order to get quick response from its suppliers, ZARA purchases no more than 4% of its raw materials from any one of its 260 suppliers. On the other hand, more than 50% of products have been produced by ZARA's own factory or by its holdings factory in Spain. ZARA manages its own distribution system, while most fashion companies outsource theirs to 3rd party logistics providers. Through vertical integration, ZARA maintains high visibility at each phase in its supply pipeline. Therefore, ZARA is able to respond to the fashion that is the best fit for each season and reduce the number of items that do not fit the taste of customers. ZARA is an image of fresh, modern, and new, especially as Kate Middleton has been seen in ZARA's outfits at several glamorous events.

The following questions raise supply chain issues that are pertinent to ZARA's supply chain practices:

1. If vertical integration has enabled ZARA's success, why do so many apparel and footwear companies choose to keep design in their

headquarters and outsource labor-intensive manufacturing portions to low-labor-cost regions or countries?

2. In the apparel and footwear industry, which supply chain activities call for collaboration and what will be the elements of such collaboration?

3. As both a manufacturer and retailer, how does ZARA integrate downstream business (distribution and retailing) and upstream components (sourcing and production)? Discuss the different sets of skills and resources required for each phase in a fashion supply chain.

2.3.2 Efficient supply chain and medium clock-speed product: Anheuser-Busch, Inc.

The beer industry is a medium clock-speed process industry. Due to its volume production and its need for internal vertical integration, an efficient supply chain is a good match. Beer production is planned in batches.

In the prepared food industry, the producer has already incurred more than 85% of the production cost before the demand takes place. This is true of beer, which is a unique blend of malt extract, barley, hops, rice, and water. Consequently, great care must be taken to create and maintain the quality of the finished product. If any of the product spoils or does not meet quality standard, it must be discarded, and a total loss is incurred.

Anheuser-Busch is the world's largest brewer. It has been brewing beer for more than 150 years and blends old-world brewing method with today's new technology. The company was acquired by InBev in 2008 and was renamed as Anheuser-Busch InBev. Currently, Anheuser-Busch has 12 breweries, all located in the US, and has capitalized on its reputation for consistent and quality products. In order to produce the right amount of beer at the right time, Anheuser-Busch controls the majority of its supply chain, including agricultural supply, brewing, packaging, and distribution. Anheuser-Busch owns and operates 13 distribution centers and collaborates with more than 500 independent wholesalers to deliver its products to retailers.[7]

---

[7] Source: Date of access: May 2013. http://anheuser-busch.com.

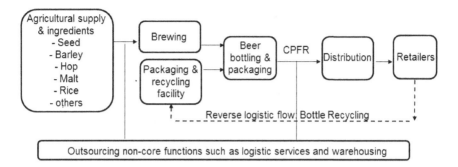

Fig. 2.6 Supply chains for Anheuser-Busch.

Packaging and recycling are important components for any beverage producer. Anheuser-Busch owns packaging and recycling production plants, which provide a source of reliable and quality bottles and cans for its beer operation (Fig. 2.6).

Anheuser-Busch outsources its transportation program to third-party logistics providers in order to enhance the efficiency of its distribution network. Outsourcing a non-core labor-intensive function prevents Anheuser-Busch from requiring a resident team on its payroll. The savings in administration, labor, and overhead reduce the overall cost and enable Anheuser-Busch to maintain a good profit margin.

As an efficient supply chain which produces medium clock-speed products, Anheuser-Busch' core competence lies in its quality ingredients, sophisticated production process, well-connected distribution systems, and the reliability of its demand forecasting.

2.3.3 Efficient supply chain and slow clock-speed product: The steel industry

The steel industry is a slow-clock industry. Steel products have been used extensively for thousands of years and the steel production process remains fairly stable. The capital-intensive steel plant is estimated to have a life cycle of 20-30 years or even longer. Thus, an efficient supply chain is a well-accepted business model for the steel industry.

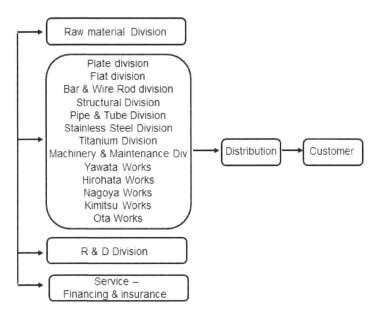

Fig. 2.7 Supply chains for Nippon Steel Corporation.

Nippon Steel Corporation is one of the world's largest integrated steelmakers. It produces steel bars, sheets, special steel, pipes, and other steel products. It is a vertically integrated company (Fig. 2.7). In 2012, Nippon Steel formally merged with Sumitomo Metal Industry and was renamed Nippon Steel & Sumitomo Metal Corporation.

Nippon Steel engages in everything from raw material supply to the distribution of finished products. It manufactures steel plates, sheets, pipes, and tubes, as well as specialty, processed, and fabricated steel products. The company's operations include engineering; construction; the production of chemicals, nonferrous metals, ceramics, and electronics; information and communications; and urban development. As a vertically integrated company, Nippon Steel even extends its service to include energy, finance, and insurance services.[8]

As an efficient supply chain which produces slow clock-speed products, Nippon Steel's core competence lies in its quality products, advanced production system, continuous product improvement, and customer service.

2.4 Service Industry

2.4.1 The book industry: Amazon.com

Amazon.com is a relatively new business model in the book industry. It sells books, music, and other items over the Internet. Founded in 1994 and based in Seattle, Washington, USA, Amazon.com started by filling all book orders using books purchased from a distributor. It gradually diversified its business to include selling CDs, DVDs, consumer electronics, handbags, footwear, and many other items. To make an online retailing business successful, the right product, in the right quantity, at the right time, and in the right place are the key ingredients. Order processing, a distribution network, inventory control, delivery management, and information system development are the five important supply chain functions that need to be integrated (Fig. 2.8).

One reason that Amazon.com has flourished is because it has no physical stores where customers can shop. Hence, it is able to take advantage of e-commerce technology via the Internet. Jeff Bezos, CEO of Amazon.com, indicated that the foundation for e-commerce is technology, as opposed to the foundation for retail commerce, which is real estate. As real estate gets more and more expensive, technology gets cheaper and cheaper. Amazon has taken full advantage of the Internet along with its effective inventory management policies that have saved them a lot of money.

This inventory management policy enables Amazon to turn its inventory over every two weeks (26 times a year). The average inventory

---

[8] Source: Date of access: 2013. www.nsc.co.jp.

turnover for the bookstore industry is about 2.6 times a year. Amazon.com differs from traditional bookstores in that it purchases directly from publishers and stocks books in the anticipation of customer orders. Amazon.com only stocks best-selling books, though it still gets other titles from distributors. It uses the U.S. Postal Service and other package carriers like the United Parcel Service (UPS) and FedEx to send books and other merchandise to its customers.

Configuring distribution facilities and fulfillment centers is a key supply chain linkage for an online retailing business. The order fulfillment goal is to ship the orders on the same day they are placed by the customers. In order to achieve this goal, Amazon.com has reconfigured its distribution centers every few years since its establishment in 1994 by closing down some warehouses and opening new ones to make it easier to locate, sort, and ship customer orders. By May 2013, Amazon operated 89 fulfillment centers that were strategically located across North America, Europe, and Asia; among them, 46 were in the US and 43 were outside North America (Wulfraat 2013a).

Amazon formed a unique sourcing strategy. It partnered with the Ingram Book Group, which ships single book orders directly to Amazon's customers when Amazon does not have the book in stock. In return, Amazon pays Ingram for any orders it has fulfilled. In a different partnership with Toys "R" Us, Borders, and Target, Amazon handles inventory and shipping duties in return for fees and a percentage of sales, and these partners pay inventory handling cost and assume all of the risks associated with any excess inventory.

As a responsive supply chain with a pull strategy, Amazon's competence lies in its ability to capitalize e-commerce technology, innovatively manage inventory, efficiently design distribution systems, and collaboratively forge strategic alliances and partnerships/ relationships with supply chain members.

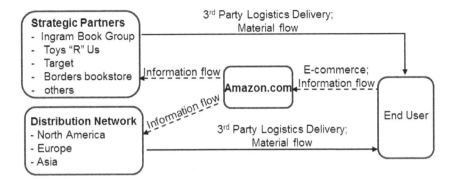

Fig. 2.8 (a) Amazon.com supply chain.

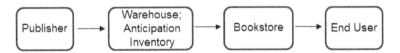

Fig. 2.8 (b) Traditional bookstore supply chain.

2.4.2 The retail industry: Walmart

Walmart is a retail chain built on providing unparalleled consumer value under the slogan: save money, live better. *Retail* is the sale of goods in small quantities directly to the consumer. Therefore, Walmart is the captain of its supply chain and essentially represents the interface between the consumer and the manufacturer in its supply chain.

Walmart has become a benchmark for creating a responsive supply-chain network capable of rapidly recognizing changes in customer demand and communicating these changes to the supplier. The level of response accelerates the turnover of inventory. Walmart's success lies in its inventory management, innovative logistics system, and distribution technique (Fig. 2.9). CPFR (collaborative planning, forecasting, and replenishment), cross-docking, and vendor-managed inventory (VIM) are a few examples of Walmart's achievements.

Walmart is one of the pioneers in creating the concept and process of collaborative planning, forecasting, and replenishment in supply chain management. As early as 1995, Walmart, along with Warner-Lambert, and SAP and Manugistics (two software companies) spearheaded an innovative CPFR project to create a supply chain process that would connect the consumer's demand to replenishment needs through the entire supply chain. The project tested the inventory of Listerine mouthwash kept in Walmart stores. The CPFR concept was conceptualized first and then was simulated using information technology and the Internet. The result was astounding: Warner-Lambert's in-stock inventory availability rose from 87% to 98%. Lead times shortened from 21 days to 11, and sales increased $8.5 million over the test period. Through implementing CPFR, Walmart compared its demand and sales projection with the manufacturer's order forecast. If a discrepancy occurred, the two supply chain trading partners would get together to decide on the replenishment quantity and would reconcile discrepancies. As such, Walmart had the right quantity of the right products for its customers, at the right time and in the right place. The supplier, on the other hand, could build the right products well in advance of receiving a promotional order, and could reduce safety stock, as well.

To reduce its logistics cost, Walmart pioneered the cross-docking method. Instead of using a warehouse to stock shipments and inventory, in a cross-docking operation shipments are first unloaded from an incoming truck trailer, and then sorted and consolidated at the dock according to the requests from various retail stores. Then, they are uploaded onto an outbound truck trailer. This practice reduces the cost of warehouse, labor, and other related overhead.

Walmart runs multiple supply chains with its massive distribution network. By the beginning of 2013, Walmart strategically operated 140 distribution centers in the US to distribute goods to the market. The company's distribution centers are categorized by facility types, states, and cities, such as regional general merchandise distribution centers, grocery and perishable goods distribution centers, import distribution centers, fashion distribution centers, Sam's Club distribution centers, and special distribution centers. By the fiscal year 2012, approximately 80 percent of the merchandise sold in Walmart stores was supplied by Walmart distribution centers (Wulraaf, 2013b). Fast-moving products are stocked close to the demand points and slow-moving items are kept at fewer warehouses further away from the retail stores. Stocking fast-moving items close to the demand points helps to reduce transportation costs, improve inventory turns, reduce the probability of inventory stock being out, and improve the customer service level.

Inventory management is a major strategic factor in Walmart's supply-chain system. Walmart has adopted the vendor-managed inventory (VMI) approach, in which vendors track their inventory regularly and replenish inventory when it is getting low. According to the company's inventory model, product supply is placed in a position of satisfying the retailer's specifications.

Walmart is the captain of its supply chain. It requires every supplier to submit a proposal which describes its targeted customers, its future market demand, the impact on related products currently sold at Walmart, and potential market share growth if Walmart sells the product. Additionally, potential suppliers are required to demonstrate financial stability, evidence of an insurance policy, lead-time and timely shipping capabilities, quality testing, industry knowledge and integrity, and basic technology such as UPC labeling. Suppliers should also be willing to join Walmart's Retail Link, EDI system, RFID initiative, and Transportation Link, to establish and maintain efficient supply management.

Walmart is recognized as having the best supply chain practice in the retail industry. Its core competencies lie in logistics management, distribution network design, inventory control, strategic partnership development, efficient customer relationship management, and information technology deployment.

2.5 Synchronizing the Supply Chain

2.5.1 Linking manufacturer to retailer: HP and Walmart

Walmart is one of Hewlett-Packard's fastest growing consumer accounts. In the mid-1990s, Walmart almost discontinued selling computer products due to a low profit margin. HP initiated a new marketing strategy to help Walmart sell PC products. In 1999, during the week after Thanksgiving, Walmart sold a few hundred truckloads of HP Pavilion PCs in an eight-hour period, coupled with HP scanners, printers, and ink cartridges.

Since 1996, HP and Walmart have jointly managed the HP inventory at Walmart stores. HP is involved in determining stocking levels for Walmart stores and warehouses, predicting the weekly demand at each store, and estimating HP production lead-time. Sales of HP printers and inventory turns at Walmart increased 3 times over a 9-month period. Product availability in stores improved from less than 80% to more than 95%. Based on the success of its retailer-manufacturer alliance, Walmart has asked HP to manage inventory for its entire electronic products category. Savings generated through high inventory turnovers enable HP to reduce the price for Walmart; then, Walmart is able to offer its Every Day Low Price to its customers.[9]

2.5.2 Linking suppliers to manufacturers: Covisint

Covisint is an Internet-based business-to-business exchange hub begun in 2000. It represents one of the most important developments in the support of business processes between manufacturers and their supply networks, as shown in Fig. 2.9. Covisint connects the auto industry in a virtual environment and collaborates with large powerful industry leaders to sponsor vertical industry e-marketplaces.

Covisint is a central hub in which original equipment manufacturers (OEMs) and suppliers of all sizes come together to do business in a single business environment using the same tools and the same user interface, with one user ID and password. Covisint has three major objectives: (i) promoting collaborative product development by harnessing the Internet's communications prowess; (ii) streamlining the procurement process for auto companies by setting up market

---

[9] Source: HP Invent (2003). "Case studies & white papers: Walmart", www.hp.com/country/us/eng/welsome.html.

mechanisms such as auctions; and (iii) streamlining the operations of the auto industry's supply chains. As networks of buyers and suppliers interact in the virtual space, the members of Covisint, such as General Motors, Ford, DaimlerChrysler, Nissan, and Renault, all hope that the auto industry's business processes will become more efficient and customer-friendly.[10]

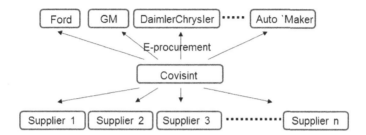

Fig. 2.9 (a) Covisint auto industry supply chain model.

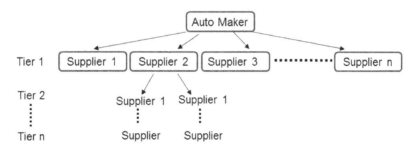

Fig. 2.9 (b) Traditional auto industry supply chain model.

General Motors (GM) has invested in many information technologies in order to improve its core competencies. Using the Covisint portal, GM is able to streamline the supply chain process using only one entry. Additionally, GM requests that its suppliers use the web-based exchange for all transactions regarding materials and parts, so as to reduce overall transactional costs.

---

[10] Source: e-biz Chronicle.com, May 1, 2001.

Covisint offers different features. For example, Covisint Fulfillment is a web-based direct material fulfillment service for the auto industry. It provides quicker responses to problems with real-time visibility of actual supply and demand.

The ultimate goal of Covisint is to optimize supply chain performance by exchanging all supply chain information through this web-enabled vehicle. Using Covisint, suppliers have access to real-time data so that they can optimize their own supply chains to serve their Covisint trading partners better. Some of the information exchanged includes inventory levels, usage history and demand patterns, forecasts, in-transit inventories, and other important information. Covisint speeds up decision making, eliminates waste, and reduces cost. When commenting on the benefits of Covisint, Robyn Meredith wrote in a *Forbes* article, "A car has 5,000 parts on average, and the auto industry has one of the world's most complex and antediluvian supply chains. A car giant processes one million invoices a year, at $150 a piece. Covisint cuts that to $15 a piece."

2.6 Lessons to Learn

2.6.1 Retail industry: K-Mart

K-Mart was once a leader in the US retail industry. Since its creation in 1962, Kmart's main strategy was to offer quality products at lower prices. As of January 2006, Kmart has 1,416 Kmart stores across 49 states in the US, Guam, Puerto Rico, and the U.S. Virgin Islands. As a discount department store chain, Kmart relies on reaching out to customers by expanding the number of its stores in the United States as well as in other markets, including Canada, Puerto Rico, the Czech Republic, Slovakia, Mexico, and Singapore. The market segment it targets is low- to middle-income class with an average annual income of $40,000. Kmart had a difficult time in the late 1990's and filed Chapter 11 bankruptcy in 2002. The following discussion focuses on Kmart's business performance during this period. Kmart's business strategy, which focuses on place, price, promotion, products, service, inventory management, and technology investment, did not evolve with the changing supply chain paradigm.

Place. Many Kmart stores are older than those of its competitors and are located in less-than attractive urban areas. This makes the stores less appealing to shoppers. It also makes it hard for trucks to deliver merchandise efficiently.

Price. Low price is supposed to be Kmart's competitive strength. But Kmart has not been able to match the prowess of Walmart's "Every Day Low Price."

Promotion. Kmart has kept the promotions-driven business model, which basically relies on special sales to attract customers to stores. This approach, along with a less-developed supply chain management system, has led to significant drops in demand for products.[11]

Product. Kmart signed exclusive deals with highly recognized brands like Martha Stewart, Jaclyn Smith and Sesame Street. To achieve growth through diversification, K-mart acquired Builders Square, Borders Group, Sports Authority, and 22% of Office Max. Also, an exclusive Disney line was added to its children's clothing line in 2001. Furthermore, historical data have not been adequately used to determine which products ought to be dropped. Consequently, the number of items offered at K-mart stores keeps broadening. As a result, Kmart has returned to Bluelight.com to promote its back inventory.

Service. With its assumption of being seen as a discount store, Kmart did not emphasize the importance of service. But service does have an effect on shopper satisfaction and loyalty.

Inventory. Kmart's inventory management has not been effective. It has had a hard time matching the merchandise pushed through its distribution system with the items it has been promoting through sales. There has been no rational link between local prices and local demand. The low price for promotion has led to early depletion of inventories before the season ended.

Kmart's inventory control system did not provide an easy way to view the data or help to provide the right information for decision-

---

[11] Source: Konicki, S. (2002). *"Now in Bankruptcy, Kmart Struggled with Supply Chain."* InformationWeek, Jan 28.

making on time. In 2000, Kmart's inventory turnover rate was 3.6 times, while Walmart had 7.3 turnovers, and Target 6.3 turnovers.

Information Systems. Kmart has continued to upgrade the technological infrastructure and information systems used in its stores, distribution centers, and headquarters. When it developed a supply chain execution expert (EXE) system for organizing the warehouse management system, Kmart chose to modify the existing system rather than to adopt the best of the breed. This technology decision means that pallets in a warehouse sometimes wait 24 hours before they are logged into a central tracking system.

Kmart considers low cost as its major competitive priority, based on the assumption that lowering prices can increase demand for its products. However, many of these strategies have not allowed Kmart to maintain its position as a leader among the discount retailers. A critical question has been asked by many: "What has led the company to such a decline?" Charles Conaway, the former CEO of Kmart, answered: "I believe the supply chain is really the Achilles heel of Kmart. Just fixing the supply chain could really turbo-charge Kmart."

2.6.2 The PC industry: IBM

IBM's experience in developing the personal computer through outsourcing and virtual integration is a worthy example of supply chain design. When IBM first introduced the personal computer, it was a fully vertically-integrated computer manufacturer. It produced a microprocessor, an operating system, application software, and accessories. It also controlled its own distribution channel and retail outlets. Meanwhile, IBM was facing a three-dimensional design challenge: creating a new product, developing a new manufacturing process to produce the new product, and developing a supply chain to supply parts and components for the newly developed product.

To speed up its new product introduction to market and to keep costs low, IBM chose a modular product design approach and outsourced its major components. During the early 80's, IBM outsourced its microprocessors to Intel and its operating system to Microsoft. IBM was able to deliver its first product to the market in 15 months. By 2000, the microprocessor had survived 10 generations (8088, 286, 386, 486, Pentium, Pentium-Pro, Pentium II, Pentium III, and Pentium IV). IBM has since been distanced in the PC industry by its two hand-picked suppliers (Intel and Microsoft). The two key components that IBM outsourced are the ones about which customers care the most: the power of a PC's processing speed and the architecture of its operating system.

IBM designed its PC with an open architecture that could use widely available components. The open architecture attracted many highly motivated third-parties that were able to develop hardware accessories and software applications and later assembled IBM-compatible computers. By forging a virtual supply chain for hardware, software, and distribution in the early 1980s, IBM reduced its R&D investment in PC development and was able to launch an attack on Apple Computer, a fast-growing computer company. By 1984, IBM owned 26% of the PC market, and by 1985, IBM owned 41% of PC business.[12]

It seemed to many people in the 1980s that the business model that IBM created for delivering the PC might offer a worthwhile approach for business in the future. But by 1995, IBM's PC market share was down to only 7.3%. IBM had been surpassed by many of its third-party suppliers and competitors. The decision IBM made to form a supply chain with Intel and Microsoft cost IBM its leadership position in the PC industry. Unfortunately, the painful lesson is "when designing your supply chain, whatever your industry, be aware of 'Intel Inside'.[13]" Today, Lenovo is the provider of IBM-branded personal computers, after it acquired IBM's PC business in 2005.

2.7 Summary

Based on a number of best practice case studies introduced in this chapter, we may conclude that the driver of the supply chain is globalization, the enabler is technology, the mechanism is collaboration, the way in which a supply chain does business is process management

---

[12] Chesbrough, H.W. and Teece, D.J. (2002), Organizing for Innovation: When is Virtual Virtuous?" *Harvard Business Review*, August, 5-11.
[13] Fine, C.H. (1999). Clockspeed. (Perseus Books, Reading, MA).

and order fulfillment, and the objective is revenue management and customer service.

Dell and Walmart are the captains of their respective supply chains. Dell's supply chain excellence lies at the core of its consumer-direct model, which is based on a pull-style assemble-to-order manufacturing strategy, effective supplier management, just-in-time processes, and the use of technology to integrate with customers and suppliers. Walmart's supply chain excellence lies in its everyday-low-price strategy, realized through consistently wringing greater efficiency from its supply chain, cutting-edge technology applications, and innovative logistics methods, distribution strategy, and inventory policy.

Supply chain models are the key to success in today's global market. Therefore, how a supply chain is formed, where the plants and warehouses are located, what degree of flexibility each supply chain has, and what capacity each plant needs to maintain are the central issues to be considered during the process of designing a supply chain. Supply chains are not static. Thus, supply chain design needs to be fine-tuned constantly to match evolving industry dynamics and changing business paradigms.

Questions for Pondering

1. Today, Dell purchases its microprocessors from Intel and its operating system from the marketplace, just as IBM did in the early 1980s. Why is Dell a successful example of supply chain management while IBM is not? If you were able to travel back to early 1980s and had the opportunity to be the CEO of IBM, what would you do differently?
2. What supply chain decisions make the difference between Wal-Mart, Target, and Kmart?
3. What advantages does selling books and music via the Internet provide over a traditional bookstore? Are there any disadvantages to selling books and music via the Internet?
4. For which products does the e-commerce supply chain channel offer the greatest advantage? What characterizes these products?

References

Atkinson, H. and Mongelluzzo, B. (2002). "King of the Jungle: Mass Retailers Dictate Terms for Suppliers and Transportation Providers, but Inventories Still Offer Huge Potential for Savings." *JoC Week*, Feb 4, 3(5), pp. 9-11.

Cooper, M and Gardner J. (1993). "Building good business relationships – more than just partnership or strategic alliances." *International Journal of Physical Distribution and Logistics management*, 23(6), pp. 14-26.

Fine, C.H. (1999). Clockspeed. (Perseus Books, Reading, MA).

Kestelyn, J. (2000). "Delivering the Goods." *Intelligent Enterprise Magazine*, March, 3(1).

Kinsey, J. (2000). "A Faster, Leaner, Supply Chain: New Uses of Information Technology." *American Journal of Agricultural Economics*, 82(5), pp. 1123.

Lebhar-Friedman, Inc. (2001). "Vendor Partnerships Enhance Product Quality and Pipeline Efficiency." *DSN Retailing Today*, June, pp. 14.

Magretta, J. (1998). "The power of virtual integration: An interview with Dell computer's Michael Dell." *Harvard Business Review*, March-April.

Meredith, Robyn (2001). "Harder than the Hype." *Forbes*. April 16, 2001.

Mulani, N., Lee, H. (2002). New Business Models for Supply Chain Excellence, (5/15/2002) *ASCET*, Vol 4, www.ascet.com

Neef, D., 2001. e-Procurement: form strategy to implementation. (Prentice Hall, One Lake Street, Upper Saddle River, NJ).

Nippon Steel Tries SRM by Editorial Staff, www.isourceonline.com

Reeve, J.M and Srinivasan, M.M. (2005). "Which supply chain design is right for you?" Supply Chain Management Review, May / June, pp. 50-57.

Tang, C.S. and Zimmerman, J.D. (2009). "Managing New Product Development and Supply Chain Risks: The Boeing 787 Case." Supply Chain Forum: International Journal, 10 (2), pp. 74-86.

Troy, M. (2001). "Behind-the-Scenes Efficiency Keeps Growth Curve on Course." DSN Retailing Today, 40(11), pp. 80.

Welch, D. (2000). E-Marketplace: Covisint, *Business Week* On-line, June 5.

Guan, W. and Rehme, J. (2012). Vertical integration in supply chains: driving forces and consequences for a manufacturer's downstream integration. *Supply Chain Management: An International Journal,* 17(2), pp. 187-201.

Wulfraat, M. (2013a). Amazon.com Distribution Network. MWPVL International Inc. Date of access: June 28, 2013. www.mwpvl.com.

Wulfraat, M. (2013b). Retail Distribution - US Network. MWPVL International Inc. Date of access: June 28, 2013. www.mwpvl.com.

Part 2

Purchasing, Procurement, and Supply Relationships

Chapter 3
Purchasing and Procurement

Chapter 4
Choosing the Right Supply Chain Partner

Chapter 3

Purchasing and Procurement

3.1 The Role of Purchasing

3.1.1 Introduction to purchasing

The role of purchasing is to obtain raw material, components, parts, and information that are needed for the production of goods or for the providing of services. The purchasing process includes many aspects, such as the request for quotation (RFQ), the supplier market analysis, supplier selection, the contract negotiations, and the purchase plan implementation.

The purchase function serves as the connecting link between the various departments within the organization and the numerous suppliers outside the company. The purchase goal is to develop and implement a purchasing plan that supports the company's daily operation and overall strategic goal.

It is estimated that, in the manufacturing sector, the purchased material cost accounts for 60% of the total product cost. In the retail and wholesale environments, the cost of a purchased commodity or material can be as high as 90%. According to the US Census Bureau's 2010 manufacturing research report,[1] the total cost of materials exceeded the amount of the value-added portion in the US manufacturing section in 2010. This shows clearly that the effective management of purchasing and sourcing can enhance a firm's competitive advantages.

---

[1] Source: U.S. Census Bureau (2010). Annual Survey of Manufactures, http://www.census.gov/econ/manufacturing.html.

For a long time, purchasing was regarded as a supporting function in an organization. Today, in the age of supply chain management, the purchasing function plays an important role in implementing a company's overall business strategy. Important aspects of supply chain management include outsourcing, searching for better quality products, and emphasizing lean and profitable production. The introduction of Internet technology, e-commerce, online auctions, and vendor-managed inventory has significantly influenced the purchasing relationship between the buyer and supplier.

Prior to the 1980s, it was common to have purchasing and logistics functions housed in the same department. However, as the role of purchasing becomes increasingly important in supply chain management, purchasing and logistics functions are being separated. For example, Procter & Gamble had its purchasing and logistics functions in the same department in the 1970s and 1980s. Then, during the late 1980s and early 1990s, the two functions were separated. The department responsibilities were re-established by the late 1990s. In general, logistics tend to be operational; managing the flow of the goods is its main task. The purchasing and sourcing, on the other hand, are more attuned. Staff members in the purchasing and sourcing section make certain supplier selections to reflect a company's goals in terms of cost control, longer-term production capacity, product quality, and other pertinent objectives.

3.1.1.1 Commercial purchasing and industry purchasing

Purchasing can usually be divided into two categories: commercial purchasing and industry purchasing. Wholesalers engage in commercial purchasing, which enables the process of retail sales. The commercial purchase takes advantage of large quantity discounts, then breaks down the large quantities into to smaller quantities for retail sales. This process provides material management services to retailers and end users. Industry purchasing, in contrast, buys raw material, components, parts, etc. for the purpose of manufacturing products. Industry purchasing may also include acquiring indirect materials for the purpose of maintenance, repair, and operation (MRO).

3.1.1.2 Purchasing and procurement

The terms "purchasing" and "procurement" are often used interchangeably, although procurement tends to be at the tactical level and purchasing at the clerical level. Purchasing's main responsibility is to acquire materials or commodities. Procurement, on the other hand, consists of a wider range of activities, including purchasing, development of service requirements, supplier selection, supplier quality management, and market analyses.

This chapter focuses on purchasing and procurement, while supplier market analysis, supplier selection, and outsourcing are discussed in Chapter 4, Collaborative Relations and Strategic Sourcing.

3.1.2 Evolution of purchasing and supply chain management

The evolution of purchasing and supply chain management can be categorized into seven periods according to the National Association of Purchasing Management[2] in the US, and Monczka, Trent, and Handfield (2005).[3] Based on these two sources, the evolution of purchasing and supply chain management is illustrated in Table 3.1.

The history of purchasing can be traced back to the 19th century. One of the first books that mentioned the purchasing function is "*On the Economy of Machinery and Manufacturers*" by Charles Babbag[4] in 1832. In the book, the purchasing function is discussed. The significant growth of the early years occurred after 1850 when railroad companies first recognized the purchasing function as an independent department. By 1866, the Pennsylvania Railroad in the US gave the purchasing function department prime status under the title of Supplying Department. The head purchaser reported directly to the president of the company. Since

---

[2] www.napm-centraltexas.org/History/ISM_History.htm.

[3] Monczka, R. Trent, R. and Handfield, R. (2005). "Purchasing and Supply Chain Management," 3rd edition, pp. 20-24.

[4] Charles Babbage (1832). "On the Economy of Machinery and Manufacturers." (Charles Knight Publishing, London).

the chief purchaser played an important role in the company's overall business, he was granted top managerial status.[5]

In the purchasing procedure's refining years (1900-1914), the industrial purchasing function came into view. Qualified purchasing agents and material specifications were discussed in industrial magazines. *The Book on Buying* was published in 1905 to introduce the principles of buying. Nevertheless, purchasing was regarded as a clerical job.

During the war years (1914-1945), the importance of the purchasing function increased due to the need to obtain materials and supplies for military missions. Additionally during this time, Ford Motor Company introduced mass production which consumed a large amount of raw material and parts. Purchasing became an important component of the large scale manufacturing production.

Throughout the quiet years (late 1940s - mid-1960s), the purchasing function became more refined and the number of trained purchasing professionals increased. The main responsibilities associated with purchasing included records management, vendor selection, purchase order implementation, and interaction with vendors.

The age of materials management (mid-1960s - early 1980s) introduced the concept of materials management. In the late 1960s, George Plossl and John Orlicky pioneered an effort to develop a Material Requirement Planning (MRP) system. Later, MRP evolved into MRPII (Manufacturing Resource Planning) to include financial and other resources. Meanwhile, Just-in-Time (JIT) production methods were popularized, which had an emphasis on the supplier relationship. The purchasing function became a more tactical than clerical activity and evolved from pure purchasing to procurement.

The age of globalization and e-commerce (late 1980s-2000) is the period in which purchasing became more integrated into the overall corporate strategy. The 1990s continued to move purchasing into the

---

[5] Fearon, H. (1968). "History of Purchasing," *Journal of Purchasing*, February, p. 44-50.

Table 3.1 History of purchasing.

Period	Evolution Stage
The Early Years (Early 1800s - 1900)	After the industry revolution, mass production made purchasing a necessary function of organizations. Railroad companies in the US were the first ones to grant the purchasing function department status.
The Purchasing Procedure Refining Years (1900 - 1914)	Purchasing procedures and ideas were refined and published. However, purchasing was considered a clerical task.
The War Years WWI - WWII (1914 - 1945)	The importance of the purchasing function was increased due to the need to obtain war materials and supplies. Additionally, mass production initiated by Ford Motor made purchasing an important function.
The Quiet Years (Late 40s - mid 60s)	The purchasing function became better refined as the number of trained professionals increased.
The Age of Materials Management (Mid-1960s - early 1980s)	A Material Requirement Planning (MRP) System was introduced in the late 1960s. The purchasing function became more managerial-oriented. MRP evolved into MRPII to include more than the factory production and material needs. During the 1980s, JIT production methods were popularized, which emphasized the supplier relationship. Purchasing evolved to procurement during this time.
The Age of Globalization and e-Commerce (Late 1980s - 2000)	The advancement of technology and the Internet changed the way purchasing operates. Business-to-Business (B2B), Business-to-Consumer (B2C), and Consumer-to-Business (C2B) became new business transaction models. The supply network expanded to include a more global market. Mom and Pop stores were replaced by super retail stores such as Home Depot and Walmart.
The Age of Integrated SCM (2000 & beyond)	Increasing integration with supply networks and information technology causes yet more changes. Process reengineering, which is influenced by advanced technology, becomes strategically important.

computer age. Requisitions were computerized and purchase orders were electronically delivered daily. E-commerce narrowed down the physical distance between countries and regions. Mom and Pop stores were replaced by retail giants such as Home Depot and Walmart, which further transformed purchasing into procurement. As a result, global sourcing became a common practice.

The age of integrated supply chain management (2000 and beyond) has witnessed even more changes. Small supply stores and manual typewriters are becoming history. Furthermore, purchasing is experiencing increased integration with supply networks and information technology. The purchasing function has evolved from being a tactical function to being a major part of the strategic supply chain management team. In addition to purchasing and procurement activities, strategic sourcing is involved into long-term acquisition plan development, continuous improvement, supplier development, and corporate strategy formulation.

The results of over 150 years' evolution in purchasing include the formalization of purchasing departments, the professional growth of purchasing and procurement personnel, the involvement in cross-functional teams internally, and the creation of supply chains with external trading partners.

3.1.3 Commodity types and procurement strategy

The procurement strategy is determined according to the nature of the commodity. The objectives for an effective procurement strategy for each major commodity include: defining a strategic vision for the commodity which supports overall business objectives, developing a sourcing strategy for each commodity based on assessments of the commodity profile, and the total cost of acquisition and possession. There are four kinds of commodities: non-critical commodity, leveraged commodity, key commodity, and strategic commodity. The commodity map illustrated in Fig. 3.1 is a two dimensional matrix. One dimension reflects the impact of the commodity usage on business and the other the complexity of the supply sources. When formulating commodity-sourcing strategy, the overall business strategy ought to be considered and the supply market should be analyzed. The sourcing strategy should be in line with the company's overall business strategy. Example problem 3.1 provides a case of utilizing the commodity map.

Key Commodity in Fig. 3.1 shows a low impact on business and a high supply challenge. This type of product has a complex manufacturing process and a long lead time. There are a few alternative products and qualified suppliers. The objective of managing this type of commodity is to ensure item availability and to minimize the number of items in this category. Purchasing strategy includes a long-term contract, management of the whole supply chain, and new supplier development.

Strategic Commodity has a high impact on business and supply management. A strategic commodity has complex product design specifications and tends to have an important impact on a firm's profitability. Product quality is very important. The objective of this type of commodity is to create product differentiation. There are very few qualified suppliers. Procurement strategy includes long-term agreement, product design collaboration, and seamless supply chain processes between the trading partners. A contingency plan is also necessary for this type of commodity.

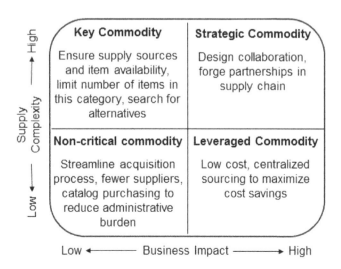

Fig. 3.1 Commodity characteristics and purchasing strategy.

Leveraged Commodity has a high impact on business and a low supply challenge. This type of product generally has high volume expenditures and is bulk-purchased (such as maintenance, repair, and operating (MRO) items). The supply source is rich, and alternative suppliers are available. The purchasing strategy includes competitive bidding, centralized procurement to achieve volume discount, and a value-added service package from suppliers.

Non-critical Commodity has a low impact on business and a low supply challenge. This type of commodity has low value. There are many existing supply sources on the market. The sourcing strategy includes simplifying the acquisition process to achieve efficiency and cost reduction. Long-term contracts, vendor-managed inventory, and catalog purchasing can be considered.

3.1.4 Centralized purchasing vs. decentralized purchasing

Centralized purchasing vs. decentralized purchasing is a choice many companies have to make because very few companies employ a pure centralized purchasing strategy or a pure decentralized purchasing strategy. Centralized and decentralized sourcing approaches each have specific advantages and disadvantages. In addition, sourcing decisions can have significant implications for the control of the supply chain and can impact the firm's overall performance.

Centralized Purchasing consolidates the entire company's purchasing needs. A purchasing department identifies potential suppliers, negotiates contracts, and implements the purchasing plan. The advantages of centralized purchasing include greater purchasing specialization, buyers' influence, and a possible quantity discount due to a large volume purchase. Increased purchasing quantity created by combining orders also can mean obtaining better service, ensuring long-term supply sources, and developing new supplier networks. Large Quantity Centralized Purchasing tends to have fewer orders. But one disadvantage of centralized purchasing is losing control at the department or division level. The lead-time associated with centralized purchasing is longer than that with the decentralized purchasing approach. In general, centralized purchasing is a choice for a leveraged commodity, as mentioned in Fig. 3.1.

Decentralized purchasing gives the local business unit more power to choose the best group of suppliers and also to use local resources more effectively. The advantages of decentralized purchasing include a better understanding of the user's needs and product specifications, easier communication and coordination, and a shorter sourcing lead-time. The shortcomings of decentralized purchasing include the loss of the quantity discount or a whole truckload freight rate. The decentralized sourcing approach can be a choice for a key commodity, as mentioned in Fig. 3.1.

Considering the advantages and disadvantages of centralized and decentralized purchasing, a hybrid purchasing system that integrates both centralized and decentralized purchasing is ideal for organizations that have different divisions and business units. The hybrid approach can take advantage of both centralized and decentralized purchasing needs. For example, firms can employ the centralized sourcing approach to purchase large quantity items and leveraged commodities, and can utilize a decentralized sourcing approach when purchasing key and strategic commodities.

Example problem 3.1:

A university bookstore sells textbooks, magazines, greeting cards, gum, and university reminiscence items such as mugs, hats, T-shirts, reference books, etc. Use the purchasing metrics discussed in Fig. 3.1 to determine the sourcing strategy and partnership relationship for each item.

Solution

To a university bookstore, textbooks are the strategic items, as illustrated in Fig. 3.2. Publishers and bookstores usually forge a strategic partnership. Publisher's representatives keep close contact with professors and with the university bookstore to promote new textbooks and to learn of the specific educational needs and curriculum requirements at the university. Extensive services are provided to ensure that the right textbooks are provided at the right time in the right quantities.

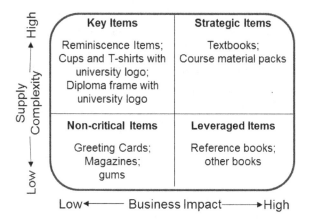

Fig. 3.2 Commodity characteristics of a university book store.

Reference books such as dictionaries and GRE and GMAT study guides are the leveraged items to a university bookstore. Many universities outsource their bookstores to retail chains such as Follett Higher Education Group which managed more than 960 bookstores in the US in 2013. Leveraged items such as GRE review books are adopted by all schools without any customization. Centralized purchasing is a common sourcing strategy for this type of commodity. A contract is usually negotiated at the corporate level to achieve large volume quantity discount and better service.

University mugs and T-shirts are reminiscence items. Since these items have specific and localized requirements, a decentralized sourcing approach must be taken. Reminiscence items can be outsourced to local vendors who have specific techniques or who can provide accommodating services that the bookstore is looking for.

Magazines, backpacks and bags, gum, and chocolate are non-critical commodities to a university bookstore. The supplier relationship is arm's-length oriented. The purchasing process should be simplified to reduce the administrative cost.

3.2 Procurement Procedure

3.2.1 Supplier market analysis

Supplier Market Analysis provides important information for procurement decisions. For example, it provides the number of available suppliers, the supplier's technical capability, the supplier's geographic location, and so on. After conducting a supply market analysis, the buyer will have a better understanding of the market.

3.2.2 Types of request

There are a few approaches to soliciting offers from potential suppliers: a Request for Quotation (RFQ), a Request for Proposal (RFP), and a Request for Bid (RFB).

A Request for Quotation (RFQ) is applied when the buyer is able to articulate the need. For example, when purchasing work gloves, the buyer is able to specify the quality of the material and what sizes are needed. As the buyer receives the quotes from various suppliers, he will decide with whom he is going to do business.

A Request for Proposal (RFP) is applied when the buyer has complicated requirements and is looking for technical expertise. The buyer usually cannot articulate detailed specifications. Negotiating for price, quality, the delivery schedule, and service are appropriate activities. For example, when purchasing a maintenance package, the buyer may specify various maintenance schedules for each different functional area and negotiate for price and service standards.

A Request for Bid (RFB) is similar to a RFP in terms of looking for specific packages. A RFB is appropriate when the buyer is looking for competitive bids for the lowest price (or other specifications), and the lowest offer will be accepted without negotiation. Other issues that need to be considered are whether it is a sealed offer, or whether there will be opportunity for negotiation after the bid is submitted.

3.2.3 Purchase plan implementation

The purchasing process is the passing of the material requirement information from the user to the purchaser, and then from the purchaser to the supplier. After the purchasing information is passed on to the appropriate supplier, the materials purchased are delivered to the user and the invoice is sent to the accounting department. Meanwhile, quality and quantity of the purchased items is verified and checked. In general, there are six steps involved in the purchasing process, as illustrated in Fig. 3.3.

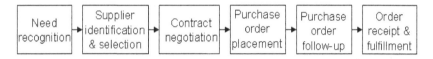

Fig. 3.3 Purchasing process.

Step 1 <u>Need Recognition</u> – Purchasing starts from the recognition of need from an individual or a department of the company. The request may include the kind of material, quantity, delivery time, and quality standards.

Step 2 <u>Supplier Identification and Selection</u> – Supplier selection is extremely important to a company. After the user communicates the need to the purchaser, the purchaser conducts an analysis of the price trend, supplier availability, and market condition. In general, cost is one of the important competitive factors. Other factors considered include material quality, on-time delivery, service, and so on. Section 4.2 provides a detailed discussion of supplier selection.

Step 3 <u>Contract Negotiations</u> – Before negotiating a purchasing contract, the purchasing personnel divide the items they want to purchase into various categories using the commodity map described in section 3.1.3 or the ABC analysis method.

ABC analysis divides all materials or inventories obtained by a company into three categories: A, B, and C. Category A items usually account for 20% of the usage and 80% of the total purchasing dollar value. Category B items account for about 30% of item usage and 15% of the total purchasing dollar value. Category C items usually account for 50% of the usage and 5% of the total purchasing dollar value. For example, when a purchaser negotiates a contract for C items, he signs a long-term contract with suppliers and negotiates for a quantity discount and a product delivery schedule because C items are high usage and low dollar value commodities. For category B items, the purchaser or company orders one item at a time using the centralized purchasing approach to consolidate the volume from different facilities. The usage of category A goods is very low, so the department that has initiated the need can directly contact the supplier when there is a need for it to ensure that specifications are clearly communicated to the supplier.

Step 4 Purchase Order Placement – The purchaser issues the purchase order after the purchaser and supplier have signed the purchasing contract. The purchase order form includes information such as the purchased product, quantity, unit price, total cost, company address, delivery arrangement, payment provision, free on board (FOB) provision, and other relevant information. Once the supplier receives the order form from the buyer, the purchase order form becomes an effective legal document.

Step 5 Purchase Order Follow-up – The purchaser should keep track of the order status after the supplier receives the order form to be certain that the order is promptly fulfilled. If there is any change in quantity or delivery date from the user's side, the purchaser should contact the supplier immediately.

Step 6 Order Receipt and Fulfillment – When the buyer receives the order, the quantity and quality should be verified and checked. If the quantity or quality does not match the description on the purchase order, any errors should be corrected immediately. When the delivery meets the stipulation on the purchase order, the order is fulfilled.

3.3 Procurement in a Digital World

3.3.1 Electronic integration in purchasing

Business-to-business electronic commerce describes a broad array of applications that enable an enterprise or business to form electronic relationships with its distributors, supplier, and other partners. Business-to-business (B2B) electronic commerce implies that both buyers and suppliers are business entities, while business-to-customer (B2C) electronic commerce implies that the buyers are individuals.

E-procurement uses web-based technology in order to streamline order processing and enhance purchasing administrative functions. However, e-procurement is more than just making purchases online. A properly implemented e-procurement system links organizations and their business processes with those of their suppliers and manages all interactions between them. This includes making bids, quoting prices, sending emails to participants, and communicating electronically with suppliers and customers. Typically, e-procurement websites allow qualified and registered users to look for buyers or sellers of goods and services. Depending on the approach, buyers or sellers may specify prices or may invite bids.

The benefits of an e-procurement system to a buyer include: availability of relevant information, well organized data, standardized transaction processes, improved contract compliance, less inventory, and reduced material and process costs. The benefits of e-procurement to a buying company mean more choices of suppliers, easier access to the seller's product list, faster ordering, lower transaction costs, less paperwork, and increased efficiency. The benefits of e-procurement to a seller include increased sales volume, reduced operating costs, more collaboration between the buyer and seller, better communication with customers, and improved performance.

There are some shortcomings associated with e-procurement: system-to-system integration and compatibility, initial investment in hardware and software, system maintenance, information security, data accuracy, and reengineering the procurement process.

3.3.2 Vertical and horizontal partnerships

Supply chain partners can be categorized into two groups: vertical partners and horizontal partners. Vertical partners have complementary, non-overlapping skills and are relatively equal in their contribution to the value-added efforts. Horizontal partners, on the other hand, usually have overlapping capabilities.

Table 3.2 shows the direction of supply chain partnerships. A horizontal partner is a partner at the same level or at the same echelon of a supply chain. Partners' skills and expertise may overlap. For example, two transportation carriers, DHL and US Postal Service, forge partnerships in order to reduce distribution costs, ease delivery scheduling complexity, and offer better geographic coverage. In this case, the carriers' expertise overlaps.

A vertical partnership does not have an overlap in capability and technical expertise. An example is The Limited's partnership with its fabric and garment supplier, Li & Fung in Hong Kong. The Limited provides point-of-sale information and apparel design requirements to Li & Fung. Li & Fung, a company in the upstream of the supply chain, contacts raw material producers, schedules production, and delivers the shipments to The Limited stores. Vertical partnership reflects the trend toward integration in many supply chains.

A hybrid partnership integrates both horizontal and vertical partnership practices. The expansion of capability and expertise of both partners occur both horizontally and vertically.

Table 3.2 Direction of partnerships.

Partnership Direction	Description
Horizontal partnership	Partners are at the same level or at the same echelon of a supply chain.
Vertical partnership	Partners are at different levels or echelons of a supply chain.
Hybrid partnership	Partnership integrates both horizontal and vertical relationship and expands the capability and expertise horizontally and vertically.

3.3.3 One or many relationships

One or many relationships in a supply chain reflect the relative strength of each partner and the number of partners available for collaboration.

Table 3.3 uses data management terms to show the partnership relationship. In Column 1 of Table 3.3, the supply relationship is identified and the available suppliers and choices are indicated in the second column.

Many-to-Many Relationship. In this scenario, a company has a pool of potential candidates for partnership. None of the partners is currently a dominant company. The apparel industry fits this category. There are many companies specialized in garment production such as Li & Fung in Hong Kong, the Berne Apparel Company in Berne, Indiana, USA and many other garment producers in Pakistan, Bangladesh, and South America. At the same time, there are many apparel retailers that sell clothing, such as Macy's, Nordstrom, Target, and Talbots.

Table 3.3 One or many relationships.

Supply Relationship	Description
Many-to-many	A single company has many partner candidates from which to choose. Neither partner is currently a dominant company.
One-to-many	This group is characterized by large companies with many available suppliers.
Many-to-one	A company with low market share competes with many companies for the business of the strong partner.
One-to-one	This is a peer relationship with dominant partners on each side. There is little choice for partner selection.

One-to-Many and Many-to-One Relationship. In the commercial airline industry, Airbus is a "one-to-many" company. It has many suppliers. On the other hand, a supplier to Airbus is a "many-to-one" company. A "one-to-many" company has a lot of power in sourcing, while a "many to one" company might have a tougher time competing for orders.

One-to-One Relationship. A One-to-One relationship is not very popular in the market place; it presents a risk to businesses, should anything unexpected happen. For example, Deere & Company is one of the world's major providers of agricultural equipment, with manufacturing facilities and offices in 160 countries. Excelsior is one of very few manufacturers of tractor attachments. Deere purchases tractor attachments from Excelsior. Deere's business accounts for 95% of Excelsior's revenue. On the other hand, Excelsior owns the design of the attachments that it builds for Deere.[6] When Deere wanted Excelsior to invest in a new manufacturing process, Excelsior was hesitant to do so because of the investment cost. If the two companies broke their relationship, the cost would be enormous to both. Deere would have a difficult time finding a replacement, and Excelsior would lose its business.

3.3.4 e-Marketplace

The e-marketplace or e-hub displays a supplier's goods or services on the Internet in the same way that a catalog does in a hard copy or printed form. By using the e-marketplace, companies are able to identify new suppliers, negotiate for services, and streamline their supply chains.

3.3.5 Supplier-oriented marketplace

The most common B2B model is the supplier-oriented marketplace. In this model, both individual customers and business buyers use the same supplier-provided marketplace. Thus, suppliers are able to focus on their most lucrative trading partners and contracts.

Companies like Dell Inc., Intel, Cisco, and IBM have successfully implemented the supplier-oriented business model. It is reported that Dell Inc. sold 90 percent of its computers to business buyers, and Cisco sold $1 billion worth of routers, switches, and other network interconnection devices in 1998 mostly to business customers or industry buyers through its Internet e-marketplace.

The supplier-oriented business model is successful as long as the e-marketplace has a sound reputation and loyal customers. This model is not always efficient for large and repetitive business buyers, because the

---

[6] Source: Forman, H., (2001). "Supplier development at Deere & Company." Penn State University, 2001 Case Writing Workshop.

large buyers' information is stored on the suppliers' servers. Under a supplier-oriented marketplace platform, the buyer's procurement department must manually enter the order information into its own corporate information system. In addition, searching e-stores and e-malls to find suppliers and comparing suppliers and products is time consuming and can be costly to companies who purchase thousands of products on the Internet.

Another application of the supplier-oriented marketplace can be seen in proprietary auction sites like computer reseller Ingram Micro. These sites are accessible only to existing customers. The sites are designed to forge strong business relationships between the company and its regular buyers. Promotion and sales of surplus goods are easily facilitated in this kind of e-marketplace site, which enables business customers to realize deep discounts.

3.3.6 Buyer-oriented marketplace

Big buyers often wish to open their own marketplaces where they can invite potential suppliers to bid on the announced Request for Quote (RFQ). For example, Walmart's e-Marketplace invites proposals from potential vendors. In this case, the buyer's procurement department needs to define the scope of products to buy and to invite vendors to bid.

As more companies move to this model, it will become increasingly difficult to trace all buyer-oriented web sites. This situation can be improved by providing online directories that list the open RFQs. Another way to address this problem is via the deployment of software agents that can reduce the human effort in the bidding process.

3.3.7 Intermediary-oriented marketplace

An intermediary-oriented platform features an electronic intermediary company that runs a marketplace where business buyers and sellers can meet. This concept is similar to intermediary-based e-stores and e-malls.

An example of an intermediary-oriented marketplace is Covisint, the automotive trade consortium formed by GM, Ford, Daimler-Chrysler, Renault, and Nissan. In the airline industry, Boeing's PART (part analysis and requirements tracking) serves as an intermediary marketplace. Boeing's PART links over 500 airlines with 300 key suppliers of Boeing's maintenance parts. Customers of PART place orders online and the orders can be shipped on the same day or next day. The paperless e-procurement transaction is fulfilled at a significantly lower cost than the cost of paper purchasing orders, faxes, and telephone calls.

Auctions on the Internet, which began in 1995, create an intermediary-oriented marketplace. A host site such as e-Bay acts like a broker; it offers a service that allows sellers to post their goods for sale and allows buyers to bid on those items. Most auctions open with a starting bid, the lowest price the seller is willing to accept. Detailed information for each item is posted to the site. Bidders look at the descriptions and then start bidding by sending an e-mail or by filling out an election form. The bidding, which may last several days, is shown on a page at the host's web site and is continuously updated to show the current high bids.

3.3.8 Disintermediation and reintermediation

To *disintermediate* is to reduce one or more steps in a supply chain by cutting out one or more intermediaries. For example, Dell Computer is well known for selling computers and other PC related electronic appliances online to businesses and individual customers. Through its application of the Direct Model, Dell Computer cuts out the retail function from its supply chain.

To *reintermediate* is to introduce a new intermediary to the supply chain. For example, to inject a fee-for-transaction website into a supply chain is to introduce a new intermediary. The web-based travel agency Travelocity.com consolidates and filters information on hotels, resort areas, airline flights, car rental, local attractions, etc. Customers can arrange their entire trips on-line. In this case, Travelocity.com serves as a new intermediary in the tourism supply chain.

Another example of reintermediation is the introduction of a third party escrow service to the value chain of the online auction. Customers who have conducted auctions online have complained that the items they received were materially different from the seller's representations. When Amazon.com promoted its auction service, it ensured customers by offering a guarantee, promising satisfaction or their money back on items valued at $250 or less. A third party escrow service is recommended for items that are more valuable. The escrow service provider is a new party in the online auction supply chain.

3.4 Green Purchasing and Supply Chain Management

Rapid environmental deterioration over the last few decades has dramatically increased corporate awareness of environmental responsibility. A growing number of companies, such as Du Pont, Coca-Cola, PepsiCo, Procter & Gamble, and H.J. Heinz, are developing environmentally "green" products.[7]

Formulation of a green purchasing strategy is challenging because green purchasing may result in increased material cost and fewer qualified suppliers. A survey conducted in the US on the issue of green purchasing identified three strategies that could be used to reduce the sources of upstream waste. The three strategies are (i) reducing the purchased volume of items that are difficult to dispose of or are harmful to the ecosystem; (ii) reducing the use of hazardous virgin materials by purchasing a higher percentage of recycled or reused content; and (iii) requiring that suppliers minimize unnecessary packaging and use more biodegradable or returnable packaging.

Recycling and reuse are important components of both green purchasing strategies and waste management programs. Recycling is the most popular method of reducing waste. Recycled commodities include soft drink cans, newspaper, cardboard, aluminum, plastics, and ferrous metal. To effectively implement a recycling strategy, buying firms need to specify their recycling policy and involve collection, separation, storage, transportation, reprocessing, and remanufacturing. Green purchasing professionals should identify items that are recyclable, figure

---

[7] Hokey Min & William P Galle (1997). "Green Purchasing Strategies: Trends and Implications." *International Journal of Purchasing and Materials Management.* 33(3), pp. 10-17.

out how recyclables are sorted, and find places where recyclables are sold back or remanufactured.

Reuse is different from recycling. Reuse may result in "non-durable" products or unreusable parts. As such, reuse seems to be restricted to commodities that are more durable, such as pallets, cardboards, and paper.

Current green purchasing strategies seem to be reactive in that they try to avoid violations of environmental statutes, rather than embedding environmental goals within a long-term corporate policy. The linkage between green purchasing and supplier quality assurance is still weak. Chapter 10 provides more detailed discussions on this topic.

3.5 Total Cost of Ownership Analysis in Procurement

Total cost of ownership is a financial estimate conducted during the acquisition of any capital investment, such as machines, enterprise information systems, and computers that assists supply chain managers to evaluate the possible direct and indirect costs related to the purchase. A total cost assessment provides a comprehensive statement which not only reflects the initial purchase cost but also considers the further use and maintenance of the equipment, device, or system considered. This consideration includes repairs, maintenance, upgrades, service and support, networking, security, user training, and software licensing, among other expenses.

The Total Cost of Ownership (TCO) analysis originated with the Gartner Group in 1987. Since then, the concept has been broadly applied. For example, the total cost of an automobile includes the cost of purchasing the vehicle, insurance, gas consumption, maintenance, and finally its resale value. A comparative cost analysis that studies various car models helps consumers choose a car to fit their needs and budget.

In general, the total cost analysis has three cost categories: (i) acquisition costs, (ii) ownership costs, and (iii) post-ownership costs. Acquisition costs may consist of purchasing costs, quality costs, financial costs, transportation costs, taxes, etc. Ownership costs are the costs after the initial purchase, and may include maintenance costs, conversion costs, cycle time costs, etc. Post-ownership costs usually include warranty costs, product liability costs, salvage value of a durable equipment, disposal costs, etc.

Total cost of ownership studies can serve as the basis to make decisions such as make-or-buy decisions, supplier selection decisions, and buy-or-lease decisions. To determine TCO, all of the important cost drivers should be identified, especially some hidden costs, such as administrative costs, upgrade costs, technical support costs, end-user operation costs, and so on.

Example problem 3.2: Total cost ownership

A buyer receives bids from two suppliers for a specially designed motor for its latest production. Use the information given below to determine which supplier should be chosen. The cost of working capital is 10% per year. Assume that there are 360 days in a year.

	Supplier A	**Supplier B**
Motor purchase price	$1,000/unit	$1,200/unit
Terms	2/10, net 30	1/15, net 30
Number of motors needed	20	20
Weight per motor	55lb	58lb
Transportation cost	$5.00/ton-mile	$4.50/ton-mile
Distance	200 miles	150 miles
Installation fee	$3,000	no charge

Notes: per ton-mile = 2,000 lb. per mile.

Solution

Table 3.4 presents the results. The cash discount term from supplier A (2/10, net 30) means that Supplier A will give 2% off of the total purchase cost if the buyer pays the bill within 10 days after he receives the invoice. Otherwise, the buyer should pay the full amount on the 30th day after receiving the invoice. Additionally, the buyer will gain 10 day's interest if he pays the bill on the 10th day with an annual 10% working capital cost. Transportation cost is based on ton/mile. Twenty

(20) motors each weighing 55 pounds will be 1100 pounds, which is 0.55 ton (1100/2000 = 0.55 ton). Five dollar per ton for 0.55 ton and for 200 miles is $550 ($5 * 0.55 * 200 = $550). Supplier A charges $3,000 for installation. The total cost is $23,094.44.

Supplier B offers the term: 1/15, net 30. This means Supplier B will give 1% off if the buyer pays the bill within 15 days after receiving the invoice. Otherwise, the buyer will pay the full amount on the 30th day after receiving the bill. Supplier B does not charge an installation fee. According to the result from the total cost analysis, the buyer should purchase motors from Supplier A, who offers a lower total cost package than that of supplier B. The amount of savings is $957.06.

Table 3.4 Total cost ownership.

Item	Description	Supplier A
Motor Purchase Price	20*$1000	20,000.00
Cash Discount	$20,000*[(10%*(10/360))+2%]	455.56
Transportation Cost	$5.00*((55lb.*20 motors)/2000lb.)* 200miles	550.00
Installation		3,000.00
		$23,094.44
		Supplier B
Motor Purchase Price	20*$1200	24,000.00
Cash Discount	$24,000*[(10%*(15/360))+1%]	340.00
Transportation Cost	$4.50*((58lb.*20motors)/2000lb.) * 150mile	391.50
Training Cost		0.00
		$24,051.50

3.6 Enhancing Value through Purchasing and Procurement

In recent years, e-Procurement has added value to supply chain management. Since 1996, General Electric Lighting has forged strategic partnerships with its suppliers and has piloted its Trading Partner Network (TPN) to conduct online procurement.[8] Requisitions are sent electronically to the sourcing department from internal

---

[8] Source: Date of access: June 2007. http://tpn.geis.com.

customers; then Request for Quotation (RFQ) packages are sent out electronically to would-be-suppliers. The Internet provides the GE Lighting sourcing department with access to suppliers around the world. The system is capable of automatically attaching accurate drawings to electronic requisition forms. Suppliers are notified within two hours of the time that the sourcing department begins the process via e-mail, fax, or EDI that an RFQ is on its way. Suppliers are given a seven-day window for bid preparation and for sending that bid back to GE Lighting. The bid is then routed to the proper evaluator, and a contract can be awarded the same day.

General Electric Lighting purchased over $1 billion in goods and services over the Internet during 1997. The estimated annual savings through this streamlining the procurement process is about $500-$700 million. The benefits of e-Procurement gained by GE and its suppliers include:

1. *Labor cost reduction.* The amount of labor involved in the procurement process has declined by 30 percent. At the same time, material costs have declined 5 to 20%, due to an increased ability to reach a wider supplier base.
2. *Value-added activities.* Of the staff involved in the procurement process, 60% have been redeployed. The sourcing department has at least 6 to 8 more days a month to concentrate on strategic activities. These are days that were previously utilized in performing manual processing activities.
3. *Procurement cycle time reduction.* It once took 18 to 23 days to identify suppliers, prepare a request for bid, negotiate a price, and award a contract to a supplier; today, it takes 9 to 11 days.
4. *Invoice and purchase order reconciliation.* Since the transactions are handled electronically from beginning to end, invoices are automatically reconciled with purchase orders, reflecting any modifications that occurred along the way.
5. *A better supplier pool.* GE procurement departments across the world now share information about their best suppliers. In February 1997 alone, GE Lighting found seven new suppliers using the Internet, including one that charged 20 percent less than the second lowest bid.

The benefits of strategic partnership extend far beyond the confines of GE. Suppliers have also reaped significant benefits. For example, exposure to other units of GE has helped GE's suppliers to be introduced to other potential customers in GE and in other companies.

3.7 Purchasing Performance Metrics

Establishing key performance indicators for purchasing helps to benchmark purchasing activities with the firm's overall goal, to identify gaps, and make continuous improvement. In general, purchasing performance metrics can be classified into two categories: efficient and effective.

3.7.1 Metrics for measuring purchasing efficiency

Efficient metrics try to describe how efficient the purchasing process is. This effort usually is based on the total dollar volume of purchases and the total dollars spent for departmental operating expenses.[9] The following are a few metrics:

(i) Purchase dollar as a percent of sales dollars
(ii) Purchase operating expenses as a percentage of purchase dollars
(iii) Purchase operating expenses as a percentage of total sales dollars
(iv) Purchase operating expenses per purchasing employee.

Comparing the results of the above metrics with the previous period's results and the industry average will provide some insight into the efficiency of the purchasing function.

When examining purchasing costs and prices, external market and economic conditions should be considered. The purchasing price should be compared with (i) standard costs that are applied by accounting methods; (ii) quoted market price; and (iii) target costs as determined by market index price (reflecting changes for the material and

---

[9] CAPS Research. Date of access: August 2004. www.capsresearch.org.

commodities). However, these numbers do not provide information on purchasing function effectiveness.

3.7.2 Metrics for measuring purchasing effectiveness

Effective metrics try to explain how well purchasing is done. These measures include the quality of the items purchased, on-time delivery, customer satisfaction, faster time-to-market, contribution to the firm's overall profit, increased sales, etc.

Some inventory investment measures can be used as surrogate measures to evaluate purchasing performance. Measures such as days of supply, ratio of inventory dollar investment to sales dollar volume, and number of inventory turnovers are useful calculations when evaluating effectiveness in purchasing.

Purchasing's and suppliers' collaborative activities can provide useful information to measure purchasing. These measures can be the percentage of on-time deliveries, the percentage of cost reduction, the number of change orders issued, the number of requisitions received and processed, employee workload and productivity, the reduction in the number of out-of-stock cases, and cycle service levels.

Effective measures require examining the relationships from both the buyer's and seller's sides. If purchasing is to contribute to the competitiveness of the firm, it must focus on quality, flexibility, cost, service, cycle time, and on-time delivery.

3.8 Summary

In this chapter, we have discussed the evolution of purchasing and the emergence of e-Procurement. Traditionally, purchasing was considered as a clerical function that did not contribute significantly to a firm's overall business strategy. However, in recent decades, the purchasing function has evolved into an integral part of supply chain management and adds significant value to a firm's overall performance, as well as to the performance of the supply chain itself.

The commodity and purchasing strategies described in this chapter can be applied to analyze the characteristics of various products and can be used to develop appropriate sourcing strategies. The Total Cost of Ownership model, on the other hand, considers the total cost of purchasing and takes other qualitative and quantitative factors into consideration.

Questions for Pondering

1. Relate the objective of purchasing to
   (1) a large fast-food restaurant chain
   (2) a hospital emergency room
   (3) a government division.
   What are the strategic, leveraged, key, and non-critical items?
2. Discuss the challenges faced by a supply manager working in (i) a highly centralized organization structure, and (ii) a highly decentralized organization structure.
3. The Walmart retail chain purchases thousands of items from suppliers and enjoys great purchasing power. Limited Brands, on the other hand, owns Mast Industries, which produces fashion items, sold in The Limited stores. Compare and contrast the purchasing and sourcing strategies of the two retail giants. Why do they employ different purchasing and sourcing strategies?
5. Explain how and when equipment purchasing might be strategic.
6. Describe your own experience in purchasing online. What factors make you prefer online purchasing? What factors deter you from buying online? Why would you hesitate to buy online?
7. Find three e-Procurement examples on the Internet. Describe the objectives, the implementation mechanisms, and the performance outcome of the three examples.
8. Based on the Commodity Map presented in Figure 3.1, give an example for each quadrant, and discuss its commodity characteristics and purchasing strategy.

Problems

1. Given the information below, use total cost analysis to determine which supplier is more cost-effective. The cost of working capital is 12% per year. Assume that there are 360 days in a year.

	Supplier A	Supplier B	Supplier C
Equipment purchase price	$65,100/unit	$71,200/unit	$68,500/unit
Terms	2/10, net 30	1/15, net 30	3/10, net 20
Number of motors needed	10	10	10
Weight per motor	150 lbs.	130 lbs.	170 lbs.
Transportation cost	$10/ton-mile	$9/ton-mile	$12/ton-mile
Distance	200 miles	150 miles	120 miles
Installation fee	$2,000	no charge	$1,500

Notes: per ton-mile = 2,000 lbs per mile.

2. Table 3.5 presents various costs associated with four car models. Conduct a Four-Year Total Cost Analysis based on the cost information given in Table 3.5. Suppose the user purchases the car with cash and drives 10,000 miles a year. The cost of working capital is 10% per year. Assume that there are 360 days in a year.

	Honda Accord LX	Toyota Camry LE	BMW 525 Xi	Mercedes Benz E350
Price	$20,825	$20,500	$45,395	50,825
Maintenance	3 yrs / 45000 miles	3 yrs / 36000 miles	48 mon. / 50000 miles	48 mon. / 50000 miles
Gas / mile City/highway	24/34	28/36	20/30	19/27
Resale value after 4 yr.	$10,000	$10,000	$30,000	$32,000
Color Choice	6 colors	8 colors	11 colors	15 colors
Wheelbase in inches	107.9	109.3	113.7	112.4

a. Which car should the user purchase?
b. Identify other hidden factors that might be important to the user in choosing a car.
c. Reconsider the choice of the car including the costs in Table 3.5 and the hidden factors.

References

APICS (1998). Dictionary, 9th edition (Falls Church, VA).

Ayers, J.B. (2001). Handbook of Supply Chain Management (The St. Lucie Press, New York).

Chen, I.J. and Paulraj, A. (2004). Understanding supply chain management: critical research and a theoretical framework. *International Journal of Production Research*. 42(1), pp. 131-163.

Chesbrough, H.W. & Teece, D.J. (1996). "Organizing for innovation: When is virtual virtuous?" *Harvard Business Review*, pp. 6.

Chopra, S. and Meindl, P. (2002). Supply Chain Management (Prentice Hall, New Jersey).

Ellram, L.M. and Siferd, S.P. (1998). "Total cost of ownership: a key concept in strategic cost management decisions", *Journal of Business Logistics*, 19(1), pp. 55-84.

Leenders, M.R., Johnson, P.F., Flynn, A.E., Fearon, H.E. (2006). "Purchasing and Supply Management," (McGraw-Hill/Irwin, New York).

Monczka, R. Trent, R. and Handfield, R. (2005). "Purchasing and Supply Chain Management," 3rd edition (South Western, Ohio).

Neef, D. (2001). "e-Procurement: From strategy to Implementation." (Prentice Hall, New Jersey).

O'Brien, K. (2006). "Value-Chain Report -- Strategic Sourcing." Date of access: Feb. 17, http://www.industryweek.com.

"Purchasing Activity Analysis." Date of access: Feb. 17, 2006. http://www.strategicpurchasingservices.com

Schneider, Gary P. (2004). "Electronic Commerce: the Second Wave," 5th edition. (Thomson Course Technology, Canada).

Date of access: June 2009.
   http://en.wikipedia.org/wiki/Total_cost_of_ownership
Date of access: June 2009. www.ingram.com

Chapter 4

Choosing the Right Supply Chain Partner

4.1 The Basics of Supply Relationships

No matter how big and powerful a company is, suppliers and partners will be an integral part of its business. In this sense, supply chain relationships are perhaps the most difficult aspect of supply chain management. The term *supply chain* implies that a firm is seeking outside suppliers or partners to better sustain its operations and to fulfill customer orders. Well-established partnerships can offer significant opportunities in most supply chains and can quicken the pace of new product development, manufacturing, and delivery of products to market. On the other hand, poorly executed supplier relationships can have a negative impact on the company and on the supply chain as well.

4.1.1 Types of supply relationships

While many companies are interested in decentralizing, downsizing, and forging alliances to develop and produce products or deliver services, the decision of whether to outsource or to establish virtual integration with suppliers should be based on the nature of the product that the company produces and on its production system. When a product can be developed without relying on suppliers, vertical integration and autonomous divisions are good choices. However, when a product can be produced only in conjunction with related suppliers and complementary parts and components, alliances and virtual integration are a better choice.

As a company moves toward self-sustained centralization and relies less on its suppliers, its ability to coordinate activities and to settle conflicts increases, while its incentive to take risk decreases. Furthermore, when a company chooses to outsource most of its operations, its ability to manage market competition increases. Table 3.1 presents six possible supplier relationships. Vertical integration, autonomous division, arm's length relationship, joint venture, strategic alliances, and virtual integration are all ways that a product can be produced or a service can be delivered.

Vertical Integration: This describes the degree to which a firm has decided to directly control multiple value-added stages, from raw material production to the sale of the product to the ultimate consumers. The more steps in the sequence, the greater the vertical integration. A manufacturer that decides to begin producing parts and components that it normally purchases is said to be backward-integrated. Likewise, a manufacturer that decides to take over distribution and perhaps sales to the ultimate consumer is considered forward-integrated.[1] Perdue Farms (a company discussed in Chapter 1) is an example of a vertically integrated company.

Autonomous Divisions: Between the vertically integrated corporation and the joint venture is the autonomous division. In this scenario, the product can be manufactured independently from its parts and components produced within the division of a large corporation. Nippon Steel Corporation, one of the world's largest integrated steelmakers, (discussed in Chapter 2) is an example of a company with autonomous divisions.

Arm's length: Arm's length is a transactional relationship. The seller usually offers standardized products to a wide range of customers. Negotiation focuses on low price. When the transaction is complete, the relationship ends.

Joint Venture: A joint venture is an agreement between two or more firms to share risks in equity capital in order to achieve a specific business objective.[1] Boeing has joint venture relationships with its large-account customers' native countries. For example, Japanese companies such as Mitsubishi Heavy Industries (MHI), Kawasaki Heavy Industries

---

[1] APICS Dictionary, 9th edition, Editor (1998). (Falls Church, VA).

(KHI) and Fuji Heavy Industries (FHI) have joint venture projects with Boeing and have supplied Boeing for more than 30 years.

Strategic Alliances: A strategic alliance is a long-term, goal-oriented partnership between two companies who share both risks and benefits. For example, instead of pushing for a price cut, Toyota builds strategic alliances with suppliers and focuses on a value-based supply relationship. By doing this, Toyota has been a top-selling automaker in the market place.

Virtual Integration: Virtual companies coordinate much of their business through the marketplace, where free agents come together to buy and sell one another's goods and services. Thus, virtual companies can harness the power of market forces to develop, manufacture, market, distribute, and support their offerings in ways that fully integrated companies cannot duplicate.[2] Dell Inc.'s direct model is an example of virtual integration.

Table 4.1 Types of supply relationships.

Supply Relations	Organizational Structure	Commitment
Vertical Integration	Centralized organization	Directly owns multiple value-added stages within the company
Autonomous Division	Moderately Centralized	Between vertically integrated corporation and joint venture
Arm's length	No joint commitment or operations between the seller and buyer	When the transaction completes, relationship ends
Joint Venture	Certain level of commitment	Agreement to share risks in equity capital
Strategic Partnership	Higher level of commitment	Long-term relationships, sharing both risks and benefits
Virtual Integration	Decentralized organization	Coordinate much of the business through the marketplace

---

[2] Chesbrough, H.W. & Teece, D.J. (1996). "Organizing for innovation: When is virtual virtuous?" *Harvard Business Review*, pp. 6.

4.1.2 Strategic sourcing

Strategic sourcing goes beyond just purchasing and e-procurement. Strategic sourcing plays a proactive role in implementing a firm's overall goals and business objectives. The long-term focus is to establish cooperative supplier relationships to match the firm's competitive stance. Sourcing performance is measured in terms of contributions to the firm's overall success.

Strategic partners involved in strategic sourcing usually have a high degree of understanding between trading partners with respect to each other's goals and business practices. There is a high degree of confidence and willingness between the trading firms, which follow an agreement regarding matters of benefits and risk. Strategic partners have a high degree of compatibility in their activities, resources, and goals. The communication process between strategic partners tends to be timely and credible. Activities are smoothly coordinated between the partners.

Strategic sourcing affects every function of an organization. Firms need to think about their relationships with their suppliers and reconsider their entire supply chain, from supplier to customer. The complicated nature of strategic sourcing causes companies to rethink what materials and services to purchase, outsource, or produce in-house. Once these decisions are made, the appropriate computer systems needed to accommodate sourcing activities can be selected accordingly.

Strategic sourcing has also been popularized in the service industry. For example, Alabama Power has made alliances with some of its key suppliers, including those that give the utility priority when it needs material. They have established a coalition group called Mutual Emergency Material Solutions (MEMS). Members of MEMS collaborate during emergencies and share information on material sources.

4.1.3 Supply base development

The supply base refers to a list of suppliers that a firm uses to purchase materials, services, or information. Many organizations have come to realize the importance of having a supplier base that they can rely on to provide materials and services that meet the design specifications, in order to consistently offer competitive prices and to deliver products on time. This supplier base relies on strategic partnerships. The partners are not only willing to go the extra mile for each other, but also are truthful about quality, prices, promises, and due dates. This relationship forges loyalty among the partners and creates financial success in the supply chain.

Many companies have come to realize that if they purchase a large quantity from a smaller supplier base, it will enable them to achieve volume discounts, reduce administration costs, and cooperate on product development. There is reported evidence of the advantages of supply base reduction. For example, world-class manufacturers in the automotive sector have reduced their supplier base typically by 50% and have moved to single-sourcing and one supplier per part throughout the mid-1990s.[3] In the 1980s, Xerox reduced its supply base by 90% to consolidate volume into a few suppliers.

Toyota is well-known for its supplier based management. Unlike some large manufacturers who put pressure for cost cutting disproportionately onto their suppliers' shoulders, Toyota concentrates on a value-based supplier base management in order to build and maintain a collaborative supplier strategy. By doing this, Toyota is more competitive in the marketplace.

Aiming at cost- and quality-control at the process level, Toyota recognizes that fulfilling the enterprise potential of the Toyota Production System requires a substantial cultural shift toward supplier collaboration and continuous improvement. For instance, Toyota's $800 million facility in Texas assembles the full-sized Tundra. Supplier proximity was a concern that was solved by incorporating an on-site supplier park that accommodates 21 suppliers.[4] Toyota has demonstrated a commitment to strengthening its supplier relationship. When Visteon and Delphi were separated from Ford and GM, Toyota continued its

[3] Asmus, D. and Griffin, J. (1993). "Harnessing the Power of Your Suppliers," *The McKinsey Quarterly*, No. 3 (1993), pp. 63-78.
[4] John Teresko (2006). "Learn from Toyota again." IndustryWeek.com, Feb. 1, 2006 http://www.industryweek.com/PrintArticle.aspx?ArticleID=11301.

commitment of close collaboration with the two companies, and even increased its equity position in the suppliers.

Cultivating a successful supplier base requires a firm to have a good understanding of its core competence and to conduct a baseline analysis of its business. After the core competence has been identified, a firm is able to determine what should be outsourced and what should be produced in-house. Then, an analysis of business activities can be conducted to determine the baseline cost and performance. For example, Starwood Hotels & Resorts Worldwide is a leader in the hospitality industry. Its competitive success is dependent upon its ability to attract and retain guests. After analyzing its core competency, Starwood Hotels & Resorts Worldwide realized that IT infrastructure was not its core business. Therefore, Starwood turned to HP to form a partnership. The two companies pooled resources and expertise to build a new global reservation system that is managed by HP. Because of this collaboration, Starwood experiences a substantial savings on operating costs and has gained increased agility. It even re-designs, deploys, and manages the new reservation system, based on HP servers. Built to handle millions of guest transactions each year, the new solution appears in all of Starwood's distribution channels, including its world-class global customer contact centers, its web sites, and its 750 hotels worldwide.[5]

Setting a realistic objective for partnership is an important step in managing a supplier base. The objective of the McDonald's restaurants partnership with Coca-Cola is to improve each partner's market presence. McDonald's is Coca-Cola's largest customer, and Coca-Cola is McDonald's' largest supplier of beverages. When McDonald's opened new restaurants in India, Coca-Cola India created iced tea and cold coffee exclusively for McDonald's under the brand umbrella of "Georgia Gold."[6] Coca-Cola India R&D developed the equipment. The Georgia Gold brand is the first vending solution in iced tea and cold coffee that Coca-Cola developed for McDonald's across the system worldwide.

---

[5] Susan Twombly (2004). "HP wins in strategic outsourcing." Date of access: Nov. 2004 www.hp.com.

[6] McDonald's, Coca Cola ready ice tea & cold coffee, Date of access: June 2013. http://www.indiantelevision.com/mam/headlines/y2k4/may/maymam100.htm.

This brand has been in the Japanese market for over two decades and enjoys the highest share in the Japanese ready-to-drink coffee market. In India, Georgia Gold Roast and Ground premium hot coffee was launched in India exclusively with McDonald's in July 2002, and has been deemed a success.

McDonald's seeks to leverage the diversity within its supplier community through growing its existing supplier base, even as it is developing new supplier relationships. The more diverse McDonald's customers become, the more important it is to have a group of diverse suppliers in order to channel wealth back into those respective communities.

McDonald's buys from dedicated suppliers. J.R. Simplot, McDonald's leading potato producer, is an excellent example of this. When J.R. Simplot developed a better process to freeze potatoes, McDonald's rewarded the company with a better contract and shared the technology with the rest of their suppliers. This practice created a sustainable partnership that improved both products and each partner's financial status.[7]

4.2 Supplier Selection

Supplier selection involves the responsibility of the various functional areas of an organization. The procurement manager needs to team up with engineers, the production manager, the marketing manager, and the shop floor supervisors to select suppliers.

The selection process is usually based on well-established criteria such as price, quality, delivery promise, and service. Nevertheless, sometimes qualitative criteria such as communication convenience and the quality of relationship are considered to be more important than price. Therefore, a balanced approach should be taken when considering suppliers.

---

[7] Date of access: June 2013. http://www.mcdonalds.com.

4.2.1 Value analysis

Value analysis in the supply chain is the systematic analysis of the entire business process to improve both product and service performance through cost reduction, quality improvement, and customer service enhancement.

Value analysis addresses issues that are related to a firm's or a supply chain's strategic goals. Issues raised include:

- What are the core and non-core supply chain activities?
- What is the role of a certain function in the supply chain?
- Does the function add value to the manufacturing or service process?
- Can the process be simplified?
- If yes, what tasks can be reduced or outsourced?
- Can a certain component be produced more efficiently?
- Can lower-cost standard components be identified to substitute the ones that are used now?

Value analysis is the continuous improvement process of a supply chain and aims at improving supply chain performance.

Value analysis can focus on either internal supply chain or external supply chain management. The level of supplier involvement in value analysis may vary – from making minor material alteration ideas to providing major process reengineering suggestions. For example, Motorola includes suppliers in the early development stages of new product development. The buyer and suppliers jointly find solutions to design issues, product development speed, material problems, and manufacturing processes. Through information sharing, both the buyer and the suppliers are able to forecast demand more accurately, develop production plans more effectively, and replenish materials more efficiently.

The *20-80 Rule* is a convenient approach used by industries to determine sourcing and procurement. The rule states that about 80 percent of what a business purchases represents 20 percent of the total purchase value and about 20 percent of items accounts for 80 percent of the purchase value. Large usage volume / low value items can be procured by using a centralized purchasing contract to negotiate for price discount, on time delivery, and better services. High value / low usage items should be purchased at the division level. Therefore, the user can communicate the specific requirement directly to the vendors.

4.2.2 Decision model for choosing the right supplier

4.2.2.1 Preference matrix for vendor rating

Very often, multiple criteria are used to evaluate a supplier. In this case, the multiple performance attributes need to be converted to a single score to compare a few suppliers. The preference matrix is the method of choice used to convert multiple criteria to a single measure.

A preference matrix is a table that can be used to rate a supplier according to several performance attributes. The performance attributes can be scored on any scale, such as from 1 to 7, one being the poorest and seven being the best. Each performance attribute is weighted according to its perceived importance. The total of the weights usually adds up to 100. The total weighted score is obtained by multiplying the weight by the score for each performance attribute. The following is an example.

Example problem 4.1:

Mac, Inc. is seeking an IT service provider. The following is the rating for the three vendors that Mac has contacted. Performance attributes are rated from 1 to 5, one being the poorest and five being the best. Additionally, the weight can determine each attribute based on historical experience. Which one should Mac choose as its IT supplier? Use the preference matrix method to solve the problem.

Solution

Column A presents the weight for each attribute (see the table above). The sum of all weights equals 100.

The quality score for Vendor 1 is three and its weight for quality is twenty. Vendor 1's weighted score for quality is 3*20 = 60. Continue this computation for all the vendors. Finally, sum up the weighted scores by each vendor. The total weighted score for Vendor 1 is 400, which is the highest among the three. Therefore, Vendor 1 should be selected as the supplier for Mac, Inc.

Performance Attribute	Column A	Column B		Column C		Column D	
	Weight	Vendor 1		Vendor 2		Vendor 3	
		Score	A*B	Score	A*C	Score	A*D
Quality	20	3	60	3	60	5	100
Flexibility	30	5	150	3	90	2	60
Supply chain cost	20	2	40	1	20	5	100
Asset utilization	10	5	50	5	50	4	40
Responsiveness	20	5	100	3	60	2	40
Total Weighted Score	100		400		280		340

The advantage of this method is that it can be applied to compare the qualitative attributes of suppliers.

4.2.2.2 Make-or-buy decision for making outsourcing decision

The breakeven analysis is a convenient method to determine when the outsourcing of a component or function should be considered. The breakeven point is the point at which total revenue equals total costs. The computation formula is as follows:

$$Q = \frac{F}{p-c}$$

(4.1)

Total cost = F + cQ
Total revenue = pQ

Where:

p = unit price
c = unit variable cost
F = Annual fixed cost
Q = Annual production or sales volume

Example problem 4.2:

July Cox, the owner of Cox Products, is evaluating whether a) to outsource a new innovation to a supplier or b) to make the product in-house. After an analysis of the production cost, she estimates that the annual fixed cost is $75,000, the unit variable cost (which includes material and labor costs) is $20, and the product will sell for $35 per unit. Should July Cox outsource the new innovation?

Solution

$$Q = \frac{F}{p-c} = \frac{75000}{35-20} = 5{,}000 \text{ units}$$

Total cost = 75,000 + 20(5,000) = $175,000
Total revenue = 35(5,000) = $175,000

The breakeven point is 5,000 units, which is the breakeven quantity at which total cost equals total revenue. If Cox Products is able sell 5,000 units or more, the new innovation can be made in-house. However, if Cox's annual sales volume will be fewer than 5,000 units, it is better to consider outsourcing.

4.2.2.3 Decision tree for sourcing strategy

The decision tree is a schematic model of the alternatives available to the decision maker, along with their possible consequences. A simple decision tree model is shown in Fig. 4.1. The meaning of the model notations is as follows:

- Square node: representing decision points and the branches representing alternatives.
- Round node: representing event. The probabilities for all branches leaving a round node must sum to 1.0.
- The conditional payoff: the payoff for each possible alternative. Payoff is shown at the end of each combination.

After drawing the decision tree from left to right according to the given information, the problem is solved from right to left, calculating the expected payoff for each node.

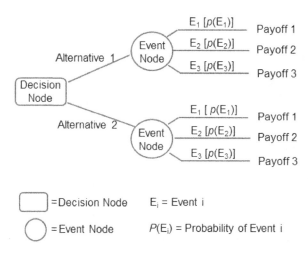

Fig. 4.1 A decision tree model.

Example problem 4.3: Supplier selection

The general manager of Tower Light needs to decide whether to hire one supplier or two. If one supplier is hired and demand proves to be excessive, the second supplier can be hired later. If the second supplier is hired later, some sales will be lost because the lead time for producing the special lights is five months.

The cost of hiring two suppliers at the same time would be lower because the fee was charged only once by the hiring consulting firm.

The probability of low demand is estimated to be 30% and high demand is estimated to be 70%.

Hiring one supplier at the beginning, the manager will consider the scenarios associated with high and low demand as illustrated below.

If demand is low (i.e. 30%): one supplier is hired, the net present value is $240,000.

If demand is high (i.e. 70%): the manager has three options:

(i)   Doing nothing has a net present value of $240,000;
(ii) Hiring the second supplier, the payoff is $280,000;
(iii) Subcontracting, the payoff is $320,000.

Hiring two suppliers at the beginning: The net present value of hiring two suppliers together is $180,000 if demand is low (i.e. 30%) and $360,000 if demand is high (i.e. 70%).

a. Draw a decision tree for this problem.
b. Should the company hire one or two suppliers initially? What is the expected payoff of your choice?

Solution

Answer to (a). Graph the decision tree for this problem from left to right using information provided in the problem.

Answer to (b). Decision Node 4: Comparing the three options, 'doing nothing' and 'hiring 2nd supplier' yield a lower expected return than the 'subcontracting' option. Therefore, prune the options of doing nothing and 2nd supplier and keep the 'subcontracting' option which has the highest net present value.

Next, we will evaluate the two event nodes (Node 2 and Node 3). When computing the value for the event nodes, the probability for each branch should be considered.

Event Node 2: (240,000*0.3 + 320,000*0.7)
          = (72,000 + 224,000) = $296,000
Event Node 3: (180,000*0.3 + 360,000*0.7)
          = (54,000 + 252,000) = $306,000

Decision Node 1: Comparing the result from Event Nodes 2 and 3, we should hire two suppliers initially. The expected net present value is $306,000.

The tree solution is provided in Fig. 4.2.

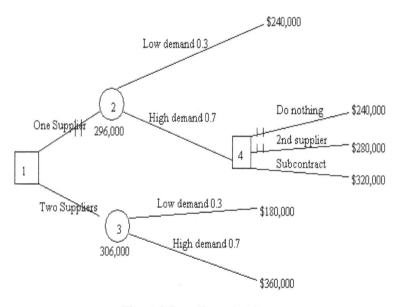

Fig. 4.2 Supplier selection.

4.2.3 Supplier certificate — ISO 9000 family of standards

The most popular supplier certificate is the ISO 9000 family of standards. ISO 9000 is a set of international standards on quality management and quality assurance that was first established in 1986 by the International Organization for Standardization (ISO).[8] Since then, ISO 9000 standards have been updated and revised a few times by ISO standing technical committees and advisory groups.

Many companies around the world require their suppliers to be ISO 9000 certified to ensure that the product they purchase meets a unified standard. ISO 9000 standards require firms to document their quality control systems at every step (incoming raw materials, product design, in-process monitoring, and so forth) so that they will be able to identify those areas that are causing quality problems and correct them in a timely manner.[9] According to the ISO 2011 Survey, by December 2011, there were 1,111,698 organizations worldwide certified with ISO 9001 (Quality Management Systems – Requirements).

ISO is not an organization that issues certificates. Many third party audit bodies exist. These audit bodies inspect and audit firms that made a request for certification; and those firms that meet the quality standards will be granted ISO 9001 certificates.

When an organization feels that its quality system is good enough, it may ask an accredited registrar or other third party audit team for pre-assessment. The final audit begins with a review of the company's quality manual, which the accredited registrar or third party audit team typically uses as its guide. The audit team checks to see that the documented quality system meets the requirements of ISO 9001 and that the organization is practicing what it has documented. When the registrar is satisfied with the favorable recommendation of the audit team, it grants registration and issues a registration document to the company. Companies are required to document everything that affects the quality of their goods and services.

In past years, the ISO has broadened the scope of its standards to include managerial and organizational practices, such as the ISO 14000 standards, which assess a company's environmental performance in three major areas: management systems, operations, and environmental

---

[8] ISO 9000 extended from British Standards 5750 series issued by British Standards Institution (or BSI), which is an organization that has issued certificates of quality management systems for organizations since 1978.

[9] Date of access: July 2013. www.iso.org.

systems. According to ISO, it plans to offer new standards addressing a wide range of emerging issues in the supply chain, such as the carbon footprint of products, asset management, energy savings, human resource management, natural gas fuelling stations for vehicles, outsourcing, and more, during the next few years.[9] Additionally, the ISO has collaborated with the World Trade Organization (WTO) to promote a free and fair global trading system, which is important to the development of global supply chain management.

4.2.4 Trust and commitment of supply chain partners

The supply chain relationship is built on a foundation of trust and commitment. Being an effective competitor in the global supply chain requires one to be a trusted cooperator. The supply chain relationship cannot exist without trust and commitment between trading partners. A good supply chain relationship will serve as the basis for the development of trust between supply chain partners and will serve as the grounds for a long-term commitment to supply chain collaboration. Trust and commitment often occur hand-in-hand. For example, once trust is established, a manufacturer may make a commitment to keep a long-term relationship with its supplier.

Trust is conveyed through faith, reliance, honesty, credibility, or confidence between the supply partners and is viewed as willingness to forego opportunistic behavior. Trust, which can make dyadic partners open to each other, has various forms, such as calculative trust, relational trust, inter-organizational trust, etc.

Calculative trust, which considers the cost and the benefits of the courses of action of the buyer and supplier, has a significant impact on both buyer-supplier relationships and supply chain performance.

Relational trust does not have a formal contract and can be an efficient governance mechanism that reduces transaction costs by minimizing searching, contracting, and monitoring, and enforces costs over the long term.

Inter-organizational trust can enhance supplier performance, lower the costs of negotiation, and reduce conflict.

Commitment, on the other hand, implies that the trading partners are willing to devote resources to sustaining the partnership relationship. Commitment can be described as a buyer's long-term orientation toward a business relationship that is grounded in both emotional bonds and the buyer's conviction. With commitment, supply chain partners become integrated into their major customers' processes and become more tied to their goals. Commitment tends to have a direct and positive impact on performance.

4.3 Outsourcing

Outsourcing is allowing an outside contractor to produce a certain part or component, or to provide certain services, which they may specialize in, such as software development.

Business process outsourcing (BPO), on the other hand, involves more than just allowing a partner to produce parts and components. A BPO service provider brings a different perspective, knowledge, experience, and technology to the existing function and will work with the firm to reengineer its process into a new or an improved process. Business process outsourcing is an outcome-based result, not just a pure cost-reduction issue. The new process will interact or will be integrated into the company in a way that can bring value to customers.

4.3.1 Creating outsourcing vision

When an organization outsources its business applications or its IT infrastructure, it uses outsourcing to reshape the way it does its business and it hopes to achieve better business performance. An outsourcing initiative that aims at business transformation will offer the greatest opportunities for radical improvement through the rethinking of critical management processes.

However, outsourcing is not driven by the same vision in all businesses. The pursuit of value through outsourcing takes two significantly different paths:

(i) Organizational strategic transformation;
(ii) Production efficiency.

Industry on the strategic transformational path typically approaches outsourcing as a tool to implement a strategic agenda. For example, Cisco Systems outsources its entire logistics function to UPS Logistics. UPS Logistics coordinates Cisco's manufacturing interfaces, inbound and outbound shipments, and customer order fulfillment. In this case, the outsourcing initiative is more complex and more mature, and both parties expect high potential value.

Conversely, business on the production efficiency path primarily views business applications and IT infrastructure outsourcing as a tool for achieving cost reduction and increasing productivity. For example, Anheuser-Busch outsources its logistics program to third-party logistic providers, thereby boosting the efficiency of its distribution network. Outsourcing a non-core labor-intensive function prevents Anheuser-Busch from requiring a resident payroll team. The savings on administration, labor, and overhead cost enable Anheuser-Busch to maintain a good profit margin.

Businesses outsource for a broad range of reasons, such as the need to provide existing and additional services, lack of available expertise to produce certain products, and the ability to reduce operating expenses. Whatever the reason, outsourcing is used not only to reduce cost, but also to deliver increased value.

4.3.2 Model for implementing outsourcing

To be successful in implementing outsourcing tasks, a mechanism should be created to facilitate all of the steps involved. Fig. 4.3 illustrates a four-step outsourcing model:

(i)   motivation for outsourcing;
(ii)   compatibility of the organizational characteristics of buying and selling companies;
(iii)   outsourcing implementation components; and

(iv)   outsourcing outcome measurement. The model suggested here is adapted from Lambert's partnership model.[10]

Outsourcing motivation is the first step, which examines the compelling reasons to outsource business functions or products. For example, if the reason for outsourcing a non-core function is to be able to focus on core competences, then the two different outsourcing paths (organizational strategic transformation or production efficiency) should be determined.

The second step is the compatibility of the organizational characteristics of the two companies involved in outsourcing. Supportive factors include but are not limited to corporate compatibility, managerial philosophy, benefit and risk sharing, close proximity, and shared customers. If the corporate environment does not support the partnership relationship, the potential benefits of outsourcing or partnership will be reduced. The strength, weakness, opportunity, and threat (SWOT) model can be applied here to determine the compatibility of partners.

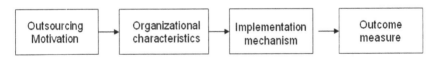

Fig. 4.3 Outsourcing model.

The third step is the implementation mechanism, which consists of managerial activities and procedures that are applied to create and sustain the outsourcing relationship. Planning, operational control, communication, risk and reward sharing, and contract negotiation are all components of the implementation mechanism.

The final step is the outcome measure that assesses the result of outsourcing. The metrics of outsourcing can be return on investment, asset utilization, inventory turnover, inventory holding costs, customer satisfactory level, etc.

---

[10] Lambert, D.M, Emmelhainz, M.A., and Gardner, J.T. (1996). "Developing and implementing partnerships." *The International Journal of Logistics Management*, 7(2), pp. 3.

This model can be applied to assess a potential outsourcing project, as well as to diagnose an existing outsourcing relationship. The dynamics of any supply chain change over time. Therefore, outsourcing projects should be evaluated accordingly. Through re-assessing the outsourcing motivation, organizational characteristics, and implementation mechanism, buyers and sellers can determine whether the supply chain is strong enough to stay competitive in the market, can identify the weak link of the supply chain, and can strengthen the relationship.

Example problem 4.4: University bookstore

Consider the university bookstore discussed in Chapter 3. The outsourcing model in Fig. 4.3 can be applied to analyze the strategic item, which is the textbook, in this case. To the bookstore, the motivation of the partnership with publishers is to ensure that all the textbooks will be available before school starts and that the book chosen best reflects the course curriculum. To the publisher, the motivation of partnering with the bookstore and the professors is to ensure that its textbook selection is current and meets market needs. Furthermore, the publisher would like to sustain and expand its market.

The organizational characteristics of the bookstore and the publisher should be compatible. The publisher should have a commitment to publishing textbooks that meet the university's teaching needs and should provide services to the university bookstore to support the partnership relationship.

The implementation process includes contract negotiation between the university bookstore and the publisher. Additionally, demand forecast, production planning, transportation and delivery, operational control, and timely communication between the bookstore and the publisher need to be coordinated.

The result of the partnership or outsourcing should be measured using appropriate metrics. Items such as return on investment, asset utilization, inventory turnover, inventory holding costs, customer satisfactory level, safety stock level, the number of rush orders, and shortage of required textbooks are all examples of outcome measurements.

4.3.3 Outsourcing benefits and risks

Outsourcing is a process by which two parties make a commitment to a common task or goal. Benefits derived from outsourcing include lower purchase costs, production flexibility, less complicated staff management, reduced procurement overhead, improved contract terms, and a win-win approach to a shared reward.

Since outsourcing has become more popular in recent years, most supply chains are getting correspondingly more complex than they were just a decade ago. Consequently, the more parts, components, services, functions, and processes that a company outsources to its suppliers, the less visibility and control of problems it has. Furthermore, potential problems can be hidden in the supply chain and are not easy to be identified.

Conflicting goals are a risk that a supply chain faces. The risk management strategies that a company intends to implement in order to avoid vulnerability can conflict with the strategies designed to improve supply chain excellence by the other company. For example, a North America healthcare and consumer product manufacturer had ten distribution centers in the US. When it built a massive centralized distribution center in Atlanta to improve its supply chain efficiency, it gradually arranged to have about 80% of its sales funnel through this facility. This strategy was successful until a hurricane struck the facility, ripped off the roof, and cut the power. A contingent risk management plan of stocking two weeks' extra inventory was suggested by a 3PL consultant, but was not well-received.[11] This is because the contingent plan proposed by 3PL was in conflict with the manufacturer's idea of cost saving.

Supplier stability is another risk that virtually all supply chain managers must address. Buyers should have knowledge of what they are buying, and from whom they are buying, and should know the suppliers' financial status, including their profitability, growth, financial strength, management effectiveness, production capabilities, and backup supply plans.

---

[11] Source: Chris Holt (2006). UPS Consulting.

Sourcing from low-cost countries is getting popular. The retailer giant Walmart purchases hundreds and thousands of products from vendors in low-cost countries. There are potential sourcing risks associated with low-cost country sourcing programs. These risks include lead-time management, quality problems, security issues, supply disruption, political environment, and some hidden costs.

4.4 Offshoring and Reshoring

4.4.1 Offshoring

Offshoring is a practice that moves certain business functions or processes to a low-cost foreign country in order to lower production and operational costs or to avoid taxes. Offshoring can be seen in the context of either manufacturing process offshoring or service delivery offshoring. Production offshoring tends to relocate a manufacturing production process to a lower-cost region or country. Organizations usually only offshore non-core components to low-cost regions and countries and keep core competency function such as new product design, research and the development process in their native countries. For example, electronic appliance giants Apple and HP design and develop new products in their North American headquarters and offshore manufacturing processes to low-cost countries such as China. Examples of production offshoring include the manufacture of electronic components in Costa Rica, auto parts in Mexico, cell phone components in China, and apparel and footwear in Bangladesh. Instead of forming a manufacturing supply chain within a single country, the contemporary manufacturing supply chain often consists of partners from around the world. For instance, Apple's iPhone supply chain includes vendors from the United States, Singapore, China, and other countries.

The terms "offshoring" and "outsourcing" are used interchangeably when a firm both outsources and offshores a business function. General Motors in Shanghai, which is a joint venture project between General Motors and Shanghai Automotive Industry Corporation (SAIC), offshores its production to China and also outsources some of its production. The difference between offshoring and outsourcing is that when a company offshores its production process, it may still control and own the process or it may form a joint venture with a local company in the low-cost country. To outsource, on the other hand, is to contract a third party to manage a function or handle a process. For example, when Amazon.com outsources its merchant delivery function to UPS, it does not own the delivery process. UPS is responsible for the delivery service as well as for the design of the service process.

4.4.2 Reshoring

Reshoring, sometimes called back-shoring, happens when the offshored operations are returned to the original country. During the 1990s and early 2000s, there was a trend toward relocating manufacturing to Asia in search of lower costs. Since 2011, some US manufacturing companies that had operated offshore began to shift their manufacturing operations back to the US. Companies such as General Electric, Ford Motors, and Caterpillar are considering moving some manufacturing operations back to the United States.[12] After a total cost analysis including the total cost of production in Asia and the costs of shipping, customs duties, and other fees, ET Water Systems (a California water irrigation producer) found that keeping its production in California was only about 10% more expensive than have it done in China.[13]

Offshoring has both benefits and risks. Some claim that under offshoring their companies lose control and visibility across their extended supply chain, and that product safety and quality are not ensured. Others report the benefits they have reaped from offshoring. In 2013, General Motors posted record sales in China, where GM vehicle sales surpassed the total number of vehicles the company sold in its home market, the United States.[14] GM and its Chinese joint venture partners saw sales surge by 10.6 percent during the first half of 2013, to

---

[12] Brad Plumer, "Is U.S. manufacturing making a comeback — or is it just hype?" Washington Post, May 1, 2013 www.washingtonpost.com/blogs.

[13] "Coming home," The Economist, Jan. 19, 2013. www.economist.com.

[14] Joseph Szczesny, "General Motors' biggest market: China." Date of access: July 3, 2013. www.nbcnews.com/business.

nearly 1.6 million cars, as compared to its US sales of 1.4 million vehicles during the same time period. Offshoring has enabled GM to open up new markets in the world. As of this writing in 2013, GM has 12 joint ventures, two wholly owned foreign enterprises, and more than 55,000 employees in China. Passenger cars and commercial vehicles are sold under the Baojun, Buick, Cadillac, Chevrolet, Jiefang, Opel, and Wuling brands.

Offshoring and reshoring are forms of reconfiguring the global supply chain. Both the offshoring and reshoring movements have to be kept in proportion to serve the home markets as well as the global markets. Cost and benefits analysis should be conducted not just based on total costs, but also on the regulatory issues, social responsibility, environmental considerations, etc.

4.5 Third Party Logistics

Third Party Logistics (3PLs) is the term used to describe the outsourcing of logistics management, which includes providing basic service or value-added service. An example of basic service is renting storage space to a client. An example of value-added service is renting storage space plus managing inventory for a client. In a price-sensitive market, 'return-on-investment' and 'financial performance' are major concerns of a third party logistics provider.

In order to better meet the needs of a global market, more and more companies are focusing on developing their core businesses while outsourcing non-core functions, and logistics is a main operation to be outsourced. Logistics has a great impact on the efficiency and the cost of the entire supply chain. 3PL, as an innovative business form, has been developing rapidly since the 1990s. According to Armstrong & Associates, Inc., 3PL use is rising. The gross revenue of the US 3PL Market in 1996 was 30.8 billion US dollars and was up to about 141 billion US dollars in 2011.[15]

---

[15] Source: Armstrong & Associates, Inc. July 22, 2013, www.3PLogistics.com.

4.5.1 Current state of third party logistics market

A recent report on the current state of 3PL market (2012 3PL Study) conducted by Capgemini in cooperation with the Georgia Institute of Technology reported the results of 3PL services. Two thousand three hundred and forty-two (2,342) industry executives from North America, Europe, Asia-Pacific, Latin America and other regions participated in the study.[16] With the increasing use of third party logistical services, many executives of manufacturing firms are interested in building effective relationships with their third party logistics providers to ensure the best supply chain performance possible. Both 3PL providers and shippers are using these relationships to improve and enhance their businesses and supply chains outcomes, and they largely view their relationships as successful. Shippers reported significant savings from logistics cost reductions (15%), inventory cost reductions (8%) and logistics fixed asset reductions (26%).[15] Shippers are more satisfied than 3PLs (71% to 63%) with the openness, transparency, and good communication in their relationships, and 67% of shipper respondents judge their 3PLs as sufficiently agile and flexible.

Aggregate global revenues for the 3PL sector continue to increase as indicated in Table 4.2. From 2011 to 2012, global 3PL revenue increased by 13.7%. Latin America has the highest growth (43.6%) in 3PL revenue in period 2011-2012 followed by Asia Pacific (21.2%).

On average, shippers spent 12% of their business revenues on logistics, and an average 39% of that figure (12%) is spent on 3PL services.[16] Outsourcing accounts for 54% of shippers' transportation expenses and 39% of warehouse operations costs. Progressive firms are much more likely to outsource their warehousing and transportation functions because they are not skilled at or cannot manage these functions profitably.

Third-party logistics service has evolved from the mass service market segment to the professional service market segment (which is sometimes called 4th-Party Logistics service). The integrated 3PL business model created by UPS Logistics for Cisco Systems is a good

---

[16] John Langley, Jr. (2013). "2012 Third-Party Logistics Study." Capgemini Consulting.

example.[17] UPS Logistics coordinates manufacturing interfaces, inbound and outbound shipments, and customer order fulfillment.

Table 4.2 3PL revenue 2010 – 2011.

Region	2010 Global 3PL Revenues (US$ Billions)	2011 Global 3PL Revenues (US$ Billions)	Percent Change 2010 to 2011
North America	149.1	159.9	+7.2%
Europe	165.1	160.4	-2.8%
Asia-Pacific	157.6	191.1	+21.2%
Latin America	27.5	39.5	+43.6%
Other Regions	42.3	65.2	+54.0%
Total	541.6	616.1	(616.1-541.6)/541.6 = 13.7%

Source: Armstrong & Associates (2012) www.3plogistics.com.

For inbound shipments, UPS provides value-added professional service. When UPS Logistics receives the notification of product shipment from Cisco plants and contract manufacturers all over the world, it picks up the products within 24 hours. Meanwhile, UPS Logistics arranges aircraft to send the shipments to the European logistics center, which is also owned and operated by UPS.

For outbound shipments, UPS Logistics provides more tailored services. When a new shipment is to be transported to a customer, UPS Information Systems generates a solution which is not only based on an optimized algorithm of pricing, time-in-transit and service level, but is also based on a postal code level. The system then provides a RFQ (request for quotation) to identify the most appropriate carrier from an

---

[17] Remko I. van Hoek, "UPS Logistics and to move toward 4PL – or not? Cranfield School of Management, UK.

approved list. Throughout the process, the order status is registered in UPS's information system as well as in Cisco's information system, so Cisco is able to communicate the order fulfillment status to its customers. Additionally, UPS consolidates shipments with common destinations to minimize the number of shipments and to reduce congestion at the loading dock.

The main benefits provided by 3PL include allowing the outsourcing company to concentrate on core competencies, increasing efficiency, reducing logistics cost, reducing inventory cost, reducing logistics fixed assets, and improving order fill rate and order accuracy. Currently, shippers are seeking more innovations in the 3PL market because innovation is an essential driver of growth, differentiation, and profitability in a supply chain. During the past two decades, 3PL providers have demonstrated innovation by introducing process improvements, adding technology, improving execution, and offering new services. Shippers are expecting disruptive innovation, which is an initiative that can disrupt a market or a supply chain by simplifying, automating, generating value, or reducing costs.

4.5.2 Factors that lead to a successful relationship between third party logistics providers and shippers

The growing importance of logistics activities that span the boundaries of supply chain firms has put an emphasis on supply chain relationship management. Managing relationships with supply chain partners requires not only an understanding of the effects of perceived relational benefits on relational outcomes and long-term business relationships, but also requires adequate knowledge of how to properly evaluate relationship benefits and outcomes and how to maintain relationships with outside logistical service providers.

A few key ingredients to successful 3PL-shipper relationships have been identified in "2012 Third-Party Logistics Study" by John Langley, Jr. and Capgemini Consulting:[18]

---

[18] John Langley, Jr. (2013). "2012 Third-Party Logistics Study." Capgemini Consulting.

(a) Openness, transparency, and good communication are viewed by both 3PL and shippers as important factors to share appropriate information with their business partners;

(b) Agility and flexibility are perceived as important attributes in accommodating current and future business needs and challenges;

(c) Gain-sharing comes up frequently when shippers consider the relationship. Many shippers consider gain-sharing to be a useful incentive for themselves and their 3PL providers to use when working toward agreed-upon objectives as it maintains the principles of good collaboration;

(d) Collaborating with other companies, even competitors, to achieve logistics cost reduction and service improvements, is also key method.

There are many other factors that contribute to the successful relationship between shippers and 3PL providers. This section only reports the result from "2012 Third-Party Logistics Study."

4.5.3 Select a 3PL partner in an emerging market

As many companies outsource their manufacturing function or process to emerging markets, selecting 3PLs in the emerging market becomes an important issue to successful fulfillment of the order. Shippers tend to look for two different types of 3PL providers when they outsource to an emerging market: (i) a 3PL that is big enough to have good coverage, good IT infrastructure, good assets, and can help growth and expansion; and (ii) a 3PL who is a niche player, and is good at a specific function.

A global 3PL should be able to coordinate with a local 3PL to operate with or within an emerging market. On the other hand, 3PL partners in the emerging market should have the right resources, should be content experts, should be familiar with the local community network, and should understand local culture and flavor. A 3PL provider may not know it all, but it must have the right network to solve any problems with the assistance of its local 3PL partners in the emerging market.

After the tragedy of September 11th in the United States, the US House and Senate passed the SAFE Port Act in 2006 and President Bush signed the Act into law to ensure national security. The security requirements have changed the procedures that international transportation should follow. Many manufacturers are not familiar with the new compliance rules and often are uncertain about how to abide by the new security regulations. For example, the Customs-Trade Partnership against Terrorism (C-TPAT) program has sought to enhance supply chain security throughout the international supply chain, from point of stuffing through to the first US port of arrival (Customs Trade Partnership against Terrorism, 2006). At the time of shipment, cargo consolidation should be confirmed, pick-up be arranged by the carrier, containers be inspected for integrity, and customs clearance and documentation be taken care of. This is the kind of fraternization which often occurs between the shipper and the 3PL provider. The sense of reduced anxiety, faith in the trustworthiness of the 3PL provider, reduced perceptions of risk, and knowing what to expect are critical value-added benefits to the shipper. Shippers' primary needs from 3PLs in emerging markets are listed below (but their needs are not limited to these items).

Visibility – visibility of shipments to relieve the concerns of added risk and uncertainty of emerging market.

Knowledge of Global Trade Regulation – 3PLs should have the knowledge to advise the shipper on the latest global trade regulations, in order to make sure that the shipper follows the regulation set by the government.

Compliance with Rule and Procedures – In a global supply chain, shippers rely on 3PL's expertise to complete copious documentation regarding importing and exporting, product screening, entering and exiting a country, and other compliance procedures.

Proactive Consulting Services – 3PLs in the emerging market are expected to provide both timely response and constructive ideas to the shipper.

Local Insight and Expertise – 3PLs should have a strong local presence and should know how to overcome local barriers.

Security – 3PLs should be able to solve security-related problems such as GPS systems, engine shut-down systems, and driver's knowledge of security protocols.

Long-Term Commitment – 3PLs should have long term commitment, so the shipper can ensure that the 3PL is not just making short-term profit.

4.6 Dissolve Supply Relationships in the Supply Chain

If the commitment or competence of a supplier no longer meets the requirements of a buyer, the relationship will be dissolved. This happens if quality standards, delivery quantities, or dates are continuously not met; or if the two partners became rivals in the same market (as in the case of Apple and Samsung). In the end stage, the supply chain relationship should be dissolved due to constant interface problems, but it can be very difficult and costly to divorce a once-strategic partner in the supply chain.

Apple is one of Samsung's biggest customers for processors and memory chips. They were ideal partners a decade ago, when the two companies did not compete in the mobile-phone market. But since 2011, Apple and Samsung have sued and countersued each other over the appearance, function, and features of their iPhones. Both companies would like to dissolve the supply chain partnership relationship but have found it very difficult.[19]

Apple has been concerned that its dependence on Samsung's flash memory, which is the microprocessor brain of its iPhone, limits its ability to use different technologies. Apple has cut back on some purchases from Samsung and no longer buys iPhone screens from Samsung. But Apple remains a customer of Samsung because it has invested in working with Samsung to build custom chips for, now, more than a half-decade. There are only a limited number of qualified suppliers that are able to produce components that meet Apple's

---

[19] Yun-Hee Kim, "Apple Finds It Difficult To Divorce Samsung", The Wall Street Journal, June 29, 2013.

requirements. So Samsung is currently the sole supplier of Apple's processor.

Apple is a big-account client of Samsung. In 2012, Apple's component orders from Samsung were about US $10 billion. If Samsung loses Apple as a client, it will suffer a serious financial impact because Apple represents a large portion of Samsung's sales. To completely dissolve the relationship between Apple and Samsung is not easy and takes time.

4.7 Enhancing Value through Supply Relationships and Strategic Sourcing

Strategic partnership and outsourcing not only enhance the value of a supply chain through collaboration but also create a viable virtual business organization. The benefits of strategic outsourcing include core competence enhancement, savings in personnel costs, balance in production capabilities, improvement in flexibility, a quicker time-to-market cycle, lower information system costs, a lower risk of technical obsolescence, process reengineering, fixed cost reduction, and many other benefits. The result is a better position in the supply chain for future growth.

Supply chain competition is becoming increasingly defined by supply chain capability. In particular, the upstream supply chain, which includes the suppliers and supplier network, has been recognized for its supply chain cost-saving potential.

As time passes, business competition becomes increasingly global. The combination of advancing technology and the general breaking down of the trade barriers between global trading regions is moving business toward one dynamic global market. This global orientation makes outsourcing and 3PL even more desirable. For a long time, rising costs simply were passed downstream in the supply chain and were ultimately borne by the end user. Today, end users expect prices to decline each year, even if energy costs, material costs, and other overhead costs rise. Therefore, outsourcing business functions to low-cost countries has become a common practice. Businesses must reduce costs, year after year, or profitability will decline.

4.8 Sourcing Performance Metrics

Sourcing performance is measured in terms of its contribution to the firm's overall success. Traditionally, performance measurements focus on cost.   Now quality, flexibility, and delivery reliability are all important performance indicators.   The following are a number of sourcing performance metrics that can be considered:

- Reducing purchasing cycle time
- Reducing purchasing cost
- Enhancing budgetary control
- Eliminating clerical errors
- Increasing buyer productivity
- Lowering prices through product standardization
- Lowering prices through centralized buying
- Improving information sharing and management
- Improving the payment process

4.9 Summary

In this chapter, we discussed the types of supply chain relationships, strategic partnership relationship, outsourcing, offshoring, reshoring, and third party logistics. Effective supplier management starts with the selection of the most appropriate suppliers, using criteria such as providing high quality parts, aggressive pricing, and reliable delivery. Criteria used to rate suppliers can vary according to the need of the company that is seeking the supplier.

The outsourcing implementation model described in this chapter ensures that the partnership is forged with vision and implemented with appropriate measures. Additionally, a number of the decision models introduced in this chapter provide quantitative tools for evaluating potential suppliers.

Questions for Pondering

1. Why has single sourcing become attractive to companies? Do you see any risks associated with single sourcing?
2. Use the outsourcing implementation model in 4.3.2 to analyze (i) an automobile makers sourcing strategy; and (ii) a business of your choice.
3. Select a commodity that you believe might be strategically important to a company and develop a sourcing strategy.
4. Compare and contrast two types of supply chain collaborations of your choice. Give industry examples to differentiate what drives these differences.
5. Compare and contrast the benefits and risks of 3PL and 4PL logistics.
6. Provide a list of companies that use 3PL logistic services based on your reading in recent articles in newspapers, magazines, and professional journals.
7. Provide a list of companies that use 4PL logistic services based on your reading in recent articles in newspapers, magazines, and professional journals.
8. Develop a survey questionnaire that can be used to evaluate suppliers and define and discuss the characteristics of an effective supplier survey.
9. Explain backward vertical integration. What are the advantages and disadvantages of outsourcing when compared to backward vertical integration?

Problems

1. The East Shore Company is screening three suppliers for subcontracts. Only one supplier will be used. The following estimates have been made for five performance criteria that management believes to be important.

	Rating		
Performance Criteria	Supplier A	Supplier B	Supplier C
Product quality	6	8	3
Schedule flexibility	7	3	9
Unit cost	4	7	5
Responsiveness	10	4	6
Delivery reliability	2	10	5

a. Calculate a total weighted score for each alternative. Use a preference matrix and assume equal weights for each performance criterion. Which supplier is best?

b. Suppose that unit cost is given twice the weight assigned to each of the remaining criteria. (The total weight is still 100). Does this modification affect the ranking of the three potential suppliers?

2. Analyze the decision tree presented below. (Hint: You need to assign the missing probability first.)

    a. What is the expected payoff for alternative 1?

    b. What is the expected payoff for alternative 2?

    c. What is the expected payoff for the best alternative?

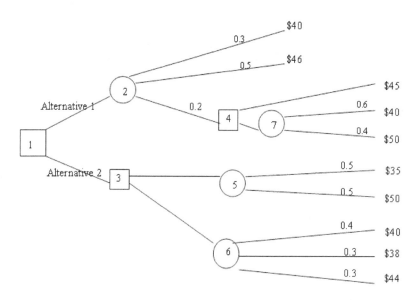

3. (Supplier selection using financial analysis)

Electro, a manufacturer of electronic components, is trying to select a single supplier for the raw materials that go into its main product, the triple-lock, a new component for the cellular phone. Two companies can provide the necessary materials: EXUL and ARC.

EXUL has earned a very solid reputation for its products and charges a higher price due to its reliability of supply and delivery. EXUL dedicates plant capacity to each customer, and therefore, supply is assured. This allows EXUL to charge $1.30 for the raw materials used in each triple-lock.

ARC is a small raw material supplier that has limited capacity. It only charges $1.10 for a unit's worth of raw materials. However, it does not have enough capacity to supply all of its customers all of the time. This means that orders to ARC are not guaranteed. In a year of high demand for raw materials, ARC will have 105,000 units available for Electro. In a year of low demand, all demand will be filled.

If Electro does not get raw materials from its suppliers, it needs to buy them from subcontractors. A subcontractor's price for single lot purchases (such as Electro would need) is $2.00 for the raw material used in a unit.

Electro sold 120,000 triple-locks this year. Next year, the demand has a 75 percent chance of rising 20 percent over this year's demand and a 25 percent chance of falling 10 percent. Electro uses a discount rate of 20 percent. Electro hopes to use only one company as its supplier.

a. What is the demand rate for next year? (Consider both high demand and low demand options.)
b. What is the Net Present Value for each demand option? (Use supplement 4.1 for discount cash flow analysis.)
c. Which supplier should Electro choose?
d. What other information would you like to have in order to make this decision?

References

Alonso, A., Donenberg, D., Gamba, D. and Vely, D. (1996). "Third Party Logistics: Current Issues and World Wide Web Resources," (Kellogg Graduate School of Management, Northwestern University, USA).

APICS Dictionary, 9th edition (1998), (Falls Church, VA).

Ayers, J.B. (2001). Handbook of Supply Chain Management, (The St. Lucie Press, New York).

Chen, I.J. and Paulraj, A. (2004). "Understanding supply chain management: critical research and a theoretical framework." *International Journal of Production Research*. 42(1), pp. 131-163.

Chesbrough, H.W. & Teece, D.J. (1996). "Organizing for innovation: When is virtual virtuous?" *Harvard Business Review*, pp. 6.

Chopra, S. and Meindl, P. (2002). Supply Chain Management, (Prentice Hall, New Jersey).

Fitzgerald, K.R. (2005). "Big savings, but lots of risk." *Supply Chain Management Review*. 9(9), pp. 16-20.

Lambert, D. (2006). "Supply Chain Management: Process, Partnerships, Performance." 2nd edition (SCMI, Sarasota, Florida).

Lemke, F., Goffin, K., Szwejczewski, M., Pfeiffer, R., Lohmuller, B., (2000). "Supplier base management: Experiences from the UK and Germany." *International Journal of Logistics Management*. 11(2), pp. 45-59.

Li, F., Li, L., C Jin, R Wang, H Wang, L Yang (2012). "A 3PL supplier selection model based on fuzzy sets." *Computers & Operations Research*, 39(8), pp. 1879-1884.

Li, L. (2011). "Assessing the relational benefits of logistics services perceived by manufacturers in supply chain." *International Journal of Production Economics*, 132, pp. 58-67.

Neef, D. (2001). "e-Procurement: From Strategy to Implementation." (Prentice Hall, New Jersey).

"Outsourcing in government is growing and getting more sophisticated, finds new research." *eGovernment News*, 20 May 2003.

Supplement 4.1

Discount Cash Flow Analysis

Supply chain design decisions usually remain in place for an extended period of time. Therefore, they should be evaluated as a sequence of cash flows over that period. Discount cash flow analysis evaluates the present value of any stream of future cash flows. It is also referred to as the *rate of return* or the *opportunity cost* of capital.

The present value of a stream of cash flow is what that stream is worth in today's dollars.

$$\text{Discount Factor} = \frac{1}{(1+k)}$$

$$\text{Net Present Value} = C_0 + \sum_{t=1}^{T} (\frac{1}{(1+k)})^t C_t$$

Where:
  k = rate of return
  t = time period
  C_t = cash flow for time period t

Example Problem:

a. The interest rate is 5%. If you invest $100 today, how much do you have in a year?

Solution

$100 * (1+0.05) = $105

b. The interest rate is 5%. If you want to have $105 next year, how much should you invest today?

Solution

Present value $(\dfrac{1}{(1+0.05)})*105 \ = \$100$

Part 3

Demand and Supply Integration in Supply Chain

Chapter 5
Demand Management and Customer Order Forecasting

Chapter 6
Transforming Demand: Planning on Supply Flow

Chapter 7
Managing Material Flow and Inventories in Supply Chain

Chapter 5

Demand Management and Customer Order Forecasting

5.1 Demand Management through Collaborative Forecasting

Demand management is an attempt to influence the timing and quantity of a customer's need of products. Demand management includes forecasting demand, order processing, and order fulfillment. Additionally, when demand is low, the supply chain manager may launch a promotion to stimulate demand. When the demand is higher than the production capacity level, management may increase delivery lead-time and price. Sales promotions may also be applied to increase market share, to introduce new products, and to shift the timing of demand to ease the pressure on production capacity. Demand management can be effective when coordinating efforts exist throughout the supply chain.

The coordinating, planning, and forecasting in a supply chain requires good estimates of customer demand. These estimates typically take the form of forecasts and predictions. For certain types of planning problems, such as inventory control and economical purchasing, forecasting inventory costs and lead-time may be needed as well. This chapter examines how companies manage the relationship between production and customer needs using demand management measures and forecasting procedures.

Collaborative forecasting in a supply chain collects and reconciles the information from diverse sources inside and outside the company in order to come up with a single unified statement of demand for the company and the entire supply chain. In Chapter 1, we mentioned material flow, service flow, information flow, and fund flow, the four flows which move up and down the supply chain. Thus, forecasting uses historical demand information flow to predict material flow and fund flow. Consequently, many companies focus on enabling collaborative planning, forecasting, and a replenishment supply-chain model to balance demand and supply capacity, to manage customer demand with strategic business partners, and to share information and plans with these same partners. Collaborative forecasting works to solve two of the greatest challenges faced by supply chain managers:

(1) Stockout of strategic or leverage products (discussed in Chapter 3) that can lead to lost sales, and
(2) Excessive safety stock and/or wrong inventory that tie up monetary capital.

The first challenge relates to the levels of customer service and revenue management and the second challenge affects the overall cost of the supply chain. In order to prevent excess inventory, forecasts of future demand must be as accurate as possible. Although customers are not able to tell precisely the number of products that they will need in the future, collaborative forecasting can improve productivity and profitability throughout the supply chain.

5.1.1 Forecast characteristics

Customer order forecasting and demand management are vital links in a supply chain. Demand forecasting serves as a prelude to production planning, capacity planning, and inventory management. Although there are different forecasting procedures that one can apply in order to project future demand, a few forecasting characteristics are common to all forecast methods.

First, a forecast will never be accurate because it uses historical data to project future demand. For example, in the past, green tea has not been a popular soft drink in the US market. However, during recent years, due to consumers' healthy diet concerns, the demand for green tea is increasing faster than the demand for other soft drinks.

Second, the forecasting time horizon affects the accuracy level of forecasts. In general, long-term forecasts are less accurate than short-term forecasts. Just as in weather forecasting, it is more accurate to forecast tomorrow's weather than it is to attempt to forecast what the weather will be like a month from today.

Third, the forecast for a family of products is more accurate than the forecast for an individual Stock Keeping Unit (SKU) item. For example, the data for soft drinks can be stable even when the data for Diet Pepsi is unstable.

Fourth, greater distortion of demand information is observed when a firm is farther away from the end user in a supply chain than when a firm is closer to the end user. For example, the demand for Procter & Gamble Pampers diaper is stable at retail stores. However, the distributors' orders to P&G's factory fluctuate much more than the retailers' sales. Furthermore, P&G's orders to its suppliers (such as 3M, a US company located in St. Paul, Minnesota) change even more significantly than the distributor's orders. Consequently, greater distortion of Pampers diaper demand information has been observed at 3M than at the retail stores.

5.1.2 Forecasting in efficient supply chain vs. responsive supply chain

In an efficient supply chain (as opposed to a responsive supply chain, as discussed in Chapter 1), customer demand is fairly stable, forecasting error is low, the product life cycle is long, new product introductions are less frequent, and the product variety is limited. In this case, proactively managed customer demand will be the choice of the supply chain manager. As illustrated in Fig. 5.1, time series forecasting methods are the predominant procedures applied to predict future demand when demand uncertainty is low. The need from the end users is usually satisfied with inventory. For example, the demand for Perdue chicken is stable, with an upward trend over years. Therefore, Perdue Farms forecasts the quantity of eggs it needs for chicks and pushes the product all the way down the supply chain to the end users. When there are unexpected incidents such as bird flu, promotion and coupons are used as proactive demand management approaches to increase sales.

	Efficient Supply Chain	Responsive Supply Chain
High ↑ Volume ↓ **Low**	•Male-to-stock – e.g. Perdue chickens •Push system – starts at egg production •Time series method to forecast the need for the final products	•Assemble-to-order – e.g. Dell computer •Push system – parts & components •Pull system at the starting point of assembly •Time series methods to forecast parts, components •Forecast production capacity cushion •Judgmental and causal methods to forecast trend
	•Make-to-stock – e.g. Textbooks •Push system – starts at book writing •Time series method to forecast on final products	•Make-to-order – e.g. cooling towers •Pull system – starts at build •Forecast on standardized items •Increase collaboration and production system flexibility •Causal model to forecast trend

Low ◄─── Demand Uncertainty ───► High

Fig. 5.1 Forecast methods for efficient and responsive supply chain.

A responsive supply chain, on the other hand, reacts quickly to uncertain demand. In this case, demand predictability is low, forecasting error is high, the product life cycle is short, new product introductions are frequent, and the product variety is high. To meet customer demand, the supply chain will forecast system flexibility and capacity cushions. If both demand variability and sales volume are high, the forecasting may focus on parts and components. The users will pull the production of the final product. For example, since every computer will need microchips, the demand variation of chips is low. Dell Inc. uses a push system to forecast its need for computer chips. At the same time, Dell Inc. predicts the capacity cushion it requires to support direct orders from end users using its pull production system. The need for parts and component inventory is forecast based on historical data, but final assembly is pulled by customer orders. The interface of the push-and-pull system occurs at the stage before assembly starts.

5.1.3 A better method: Collaborative forecasting in the supply chain

Let us consider a supplier-and-inventory scenario. Culex is a manufacturer of cooling towers, and 3G is the supplier of its gearbox. Suppose Culex Industries uses G32 gearboxes in the production of cooling towers. On average, Culex builds 20 cooling tower units each month. Because G32's gearbox is critical to Culex's production, its supplier, 3G, normally keeps 40 G32 gearboxes in stock.

However, in early March, Culex's managers decided that they needed to build 80 cooling units in April in order to meet the high demand before the beginning of summer. Since 3G Distribution always has an ample supply of gearboxes in stock, it did not occur to the Culex's buyer to notify 3G of the increased need for production that would occur in four weeks.

At the beginning of April, Culex started the production of cooling towers. After completing 40 units, they stopped production because there were no more gearboxes. Culex's production manager strongly expressed his unhappiness to the buyer. The buyer, in turn, was frustrated at 3G. As a result, Culex experienced capacity imbalance and extra production costs. 3G gave excuses for not meeting the unusual demand and offered to increase its G32 gearbox inventory from 40 to 80 units. Consequently, 3G had an unhappy customer and carried additional stock that increased 3G's inventory holding costs.

This situation occurred due to the seasonal demand of cooling systems, the promotion plan of the manufacturer, and poor communication between the trading partners. If Culex and 3G had implemented the CPFR system, Culex would have notified 3G of the increased need for the gearboxes as soon as it had created April's production plan and 3G would have ordered more gearboxes for the summer promotion. From the Culex example, we are able to draw the following conclusions of critical needs:

(i) Understanding and communicating the type of data needed for forecast between the trading partners;

(ii) Determining forecast procedure that is most appropriate for the nature of the products;

(iii) Synchronizing forecasts between different trading partners of the supply chain.

In recent years, supply chain coordination has become a popular way to manage demand. Collaborative forecasting comprises estimating customer demand for all of the participating firms, identifying and resolving any differences in demand among participating firms, and developing a feasible sales forecast. For example, in the spring of 2001, Sears and Michelin (a French company) began discussions on collaboration. Later that year, they implemented a collaborative planning, forecasting, and replenishment information system. The mutual goal of the two companies was to 1) improve order fill rate, and 2) reduce inventory at Sears' distribution centers and at Michelin's warehouses respectively. As a result of implementing CPFR systems and better forecasting, Sears' distribution-centers-to-store fill rate increased by 10.7 percent. The combined Michelin and Sears inventory levels were reduced by 25 percent. This practice indicates that advanced information technology, coordination, and collective decision making can offer companies the opportunity to radically transform and improve their supply chain performance. Such a transformation can have dramatic benefits and can create competitive advantages.[1]

5.2 Components of Demand Forecasting

5.2.1 Patterns of demand

5.2.1.1 Spatial demand versus temporal demand

Spatial demand addresses the **place where** the demand occurs. Spatial location of demand is needed to plan warehouse locations, to balance inventory levels across the supply chain network, and to geographically allocate transportation resources.

---

[1] Steermann, H. (2003). "A practical look at CPFR: the Sears - Michelin experience." *Supply Chain Management Review*, July/Aug, pp. 46-53.

Temporal demand addresses the **time when** the demand takes place. Timing is one of the most important outcomes of forecasting. Demand variation associated with time is a result of growth or decline in sales rates, seasonality in the demand pattern, and general fluctuations caused by a multitude of factors.

5.2.1.2 Regular versus lumpy demand

Demand patterns can be decomposed to include average demand, and trend, seasonal, and random components. The major demand patterns are shown in Fig. 5.2. Observing the four patterns clock-wise, we can tell that:

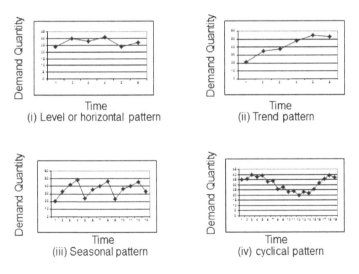

Fig. 5.2 Demand patterns.

(i)   Indicates a level or random demand pattern with no trend or seasonal elements;

(ii) Shows a random demand pattern with an increasing trend but with no seasonal element. In general, its trend can be either up or down and may be linear or non-linear;

(iii) Plots a random demand pattern with seasonal elements. Values in a series move up or down on a periodic basis which can be related to the calendar; and

(iv) Shows a cyclical demand pattern. The value of a series moves through long-term upward and downward swings, which are not related to the calendar year.

5.2.1.3 Independent versus dependent demand

Independent demand is forecast. For example, the number of tables a furniture store will sell is forecast. Dependent demand is derived. For example, the number of legs and tabletops a manufacturer needs to produce is derived from the number of tables that the manufacturer needs to make.

5.2.2 Managing the forecast process

Regardless of what product is forecast and which method is employed, there are some common steps in the forecasting process as illustrated in Fig. 5.3.

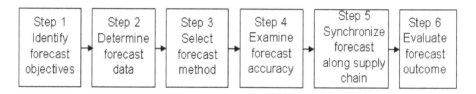

Fig. 5.3 Forecasting process.

Step 1. *Identify forecast objectives.* Forecasting uses historical data to project future demand. Therefore, we need to decide what to forecast. Forecast units may vary at the different levels of an organization and in the supply chain. For example,

- The sales people may forecast sales volume;

- The manufacturing function may forecast SKU units needed for master production schedule;
- The financial function may forecast sales dollars to prepare budget;
- The shipping company may forecast the number of containers it is going to transport.

Step 2. *Determine forecasting variables and data.* Data used in forecasting should be determined first. For example, demand and shipments are two different types of data. If there is a shortage of certain products, a portion of demand will not be satisfied. As a result, a customer may use a substituted product or may simply fill the order from a competitor. Therefore, actual demand can be higher than shipments. Forecast data may include:

- Demand – the overall market demand for a certain product
- Supply – the amount of product available
- Product character – the product features that affect demand
- Market competition – market competition from producers of similar products, promotions, and sales
- Historical data, sales projections, promotion plans, etc.
- Market share data, trade inventory, and market research

Step 3. *Select forecasting method.* In general, forecasting methods can be grouped into two categories: qualitative and quantitative methods.

(i) *Qualitative forecasting method.* This method is known as judgmental forecasting. Forecasting is based on an educated guess or on expert experience. This method may be useful when a firm tries to predict the demand for a new product for which it does not have historical information.

(ii) *Quantitative methods.* Quantitative methods are based on mathematical models. The most often-used methods are the time series and the causal model.

(a) *Time series*. The Time Series is a set of numbers which are observed on a regular, recurring basis. Historical observations are known, while future values must be forecast. Forecasting can be generated based on patterns in the data. For example, grocery stores can forecast the demand for milk based on the pattern of historical data.

(b) *Causal method*. The causal forecasting method assumes that demand data is correlated with some environmental factors. For example, sales volume is associated with product price. As such, promotion sales and coupons can be used to increase sales volume.

A forecasting model which has been tuned to fit a historical data set, may not necessarily forecast future demand accurately. A complicated model can fit the old data well, but it will probably work poorly with new demand.

If the time series or the regression method is chosen, software can be used. There are numerous versions of stand-alone forecast software available.[2]

Step 4. *Examine forecast accuracy*. Accuracy is a measure of how closely a forecast aligns with observations of the series. Bias is the persistent tendency of a forecast to over-predict or under-predict demand. Bias is, therefore, a kind of pattern which suggests that the procedure being used is inappropriate.

Once the forecast has been conducted, the forecast outcome is evaluated by the managers along the supply chain to ensure that the forecast demand is acceptable. If the demand is seasonal, a method that incorporates seasonality should be selected. Meanwhile, a top-down forecasting approach can be used to aggregately forecast a family of product first, and then to specify each SKU item. Another

---

[2] Elikai, F., Badaranathi, R. and Howe, V. (2002). "A review of 52 forecasting software packages." *Journal of Business Forecasting & Systems*, 21(2), pp. 19-27.

method is bottom-up forecasting, which forecasts each SKU product first, and then aggregates a family of products.

Step 5. *Synchronize forecast results.* Different functions in an organization prepare their own forecasts which reflect their focus. Marketing focuses on trends occurring in the marketplace; the finance department emphasizes budgeting; and the sales department forecasts based on sales quotas. While, in theory, all of these forecasts would roll up the same number, this is rarely the case. Therefore, a few forecasts can be prepared: one for production planning, one for marketing and sales, and another for accounting and finance. It is important that forecasts are synchronized collectively, in order to reduce forecast variation and to plan for production flexibility.

Roth Products, a division of Abbott Laboratories, found that the forecasting needs of the entire company could be met with three forecasts: one for marketing, one for production, and one for finance.[3]

Step 6 *Evaluate forecast outcome.* Forecast results should be evaluated periodically to refine the forecast and to determine the best component to forecast in the supply chain.[4] For example, Sport Obermeyer continuously refines its forecast procedure. In addition to forecasting the demand for its finished goods, it forecasts the need for production capacity so that it can reserve its suppliers' capacity for making products on a later date.

5.3 Quantitative Forecasting Methods

There are many forecasting models in common use. These models include the time series, the causal model, simulation, and qualitative methods. The selection of the model depends on the nature of the demand observation and the type of industry. For example, demand for

---

[3] Helms, M.M., Ettkin, L.P., and Chapman, S. (2000). "Supply chain forecasting – Collaborative forecasting supports supply chain management." *Business Process Management Journal*, 6(5), pp. 302.

[4] Fisher, M.L., Hammond, J.H., Obermeyer, W.R., and Raman, A. (1994). "Making supply meet demand in an uncertain world." *Harvard Business Review*. May-June, pp. 83-93.

diapers is constant, so the moving average method can be a choice. On the other hand, allergy medicine, sun block lotion, and Christmas items are seasonal products. Consequently, a seasonal method should be considered.

When there is no historical information (as for new products, fashion products, or high tech products), the judgmental approach and expert experience are appropriate approaches.

Time series methods are often chosen for short-term forecasting with a time horizon of three months to one year. In this book, we will focus on time series techniques.

5.3.1 Moving average

A moving average is the arithmetic average of a certain number of the most recent observations. As each new observation is added, the oldest observation is dropped. The value of the number of periods to be included for the average reflects responsiveness versus stability.

$$F_{t+1} = (\Sigma L_t) / n \qquad\qquad (5.1)$$

Where:

n = number of periods to be included for computing average
L_t = demand observation for period t
F_{t+1} = forest demand for period t+1 (which is next period)

Example problem 5.1: Moving average

The demand for napkins is given in the table below. Use a moving average number of period (n) = 4 to predict the demand for December 2014. (Round the results to integers.)

Solution to example problem 5.1

Using the first four months' data (n = 4) to predict the fifth month's demand by averaging the demand from June through September, the forecast for October is 101. December's forecast is computed by averaging the demands from August through November. So, the demand forecast for December is 98.

2014	Sales	Forecast
June	97	
July	112	
Aug.	98	
Sept.	96	
Oct.	102	101
Nov.	94	102
Dec.		98

In general, the fewer number of periods of historical data used to predict future demand, the better the forecast will reflect recent demand trend. Conversely, the more number of periods of historical data used, the greater weight to past demand the forecast gives.

5.3.2 Weighted moving average

In the moving average problem shown above, each demand observation is weighted equally. For example, for a 4-period problem, each observation is weighted 0.25. Sometimes, analysts want to give certain observations more weight to reflect the real situation. This is called a weighted moving average. The formula for a weighted moving average is as follows:

$$F_{t+1} = \sum_{t=1}^{n} W_t * L_t \qquad (5.2)$$

Where:

W_t = weight for period t; the sum of all the weights is 100%
L_t = demand observation for period t
F_{t+1} = forecast demand for period t+1 (which is next period)

Example problem 5.2: Weighted moving average

John wants to forecast sales of floor detergent for April using a weighted moving average method. The sales information for January through March is given in the table below. (Round the results to integers.)

Month	Sales	Forecast		Weight
January	650			0.2
February	600			0.3
March	700			0.5
April	680			Sum=1.00
May				
June				

Solution to example problem 5.2

The forecast for April is 660 and for May is 675. But we complete June's forecast a little differently. Since we do not have actual sales data from May, we use the forecast value for May to predict the sales for June, which is 679.

Month	Sales	Forecast		Weight
January	650			0.2
February	600			0.3
March	700			0.5
April	680	660		Sum=1.00
May		675		
June		679		

$$F_{t+1} = \sum_{t=1}^{n} W_t * L_t$$

$F_4 = 0.2(650) + 0.3(600) + 0.5(700) = 660$
$F_5 = 0.2(600) + 0.3(700) + 0.5(680) = 675$
$F_6 = 0.2(700) + 0.3(680) + 0.5(675) = 679$

Averaging is not the answer. Simple average demand can conceal underlying trends, seasonality, or irregular demands, each of which requires a different approach to that needed for the control of regular demand products. A product with a volatile history can convert to a 'flat' weekly forecast by simple averaging. In order to make forecasting useful, a company with more than a few hundred product codes should include all of the features of a product. At the same time, it should allow manual intervention to accommodate market intelligence and planned promotions.

5.3.3 Exponential smoothing

Exponential smoothing is a weighted moving average forecast technique that allows weights to be used for forecasting. There are three components to know before making a forecast.

(i)   the actual demand for time period t
(ii) the forecast for time period t
(iii) a smoothing coefficient

The exponential smoothing model is:
$$F_{t+1} = F_t + \alpha (D_t - F_t) \tag{5.3}$$

Where:
   D_t = sales volume for period t
   F_t = forecast for period t
   α = smoothing coefficient ($0 \leq \alpha \leq 1$)

The following are the key issues of the exponential smoothing method:

1.   The value of α is between 0 and 1 ($0 \leq \alpha \leq 1$).
2.   A value of α close to 1 produces a forecast that reacts more quickly to changes in the data.

3. The term $(D_t - F_t)$ is the difference between the actual demand and forecast in period t and is known as forecast error. If we use a large α value, the model is more responsive to the recent discrepancy.
4. What is a good α value? It all depends on the pattern of the data.
   - Large α values emphasize recent levels of demand and result in forecasts more responsive to recent changes in the underlying average.
   - Small α values treat past demand more uniformly and result in more stable forecasts.

Example problem 5.3: Exponential smoothing

The actual sales data are given in the column titled "Sales" in the table below. We assume that the forecast for July is also 56. If alpha (α) is 0.2, calculate the forecast for August through January next year. (Round the results to integers.)

Month	Sales	Forecast
July	56	56
August	67	
September	62	
October	58	
November	65	
December	60	
January		

Solution to problem 5.3

Apply formula (5.3)

$$F_{t+1} = F_t + \alpha (D_t - F_t)$$
$$F_{Aug} = F_{July} + \alpha(D_{July} - F_{July}) = (56) + .2(56-56) = 56$$

Month	Sales	Forecast
July	56	56
August	67	56
September	62	58

October	58	59
November	65	59
December	60	60
January		60

$$F_{Sept} = F_{Aug} + \alpha(D_{Aug} - F_{Aug}) = (56) + .2(67-56) = 58$$

Repeat the above steps to complete the forecast for January. The forecast demand for January is 60.

5.3.4 Double exponential smoothing for trended data

The following model demonstrates a way to manage linear trend. The procedure separates the average demand from the trend in the data and develops an estimate for each component. To complete double exponential smoothing for the trended data forecast, we need to use three formulas.

$$L_t = \alpha D_t + (1 - \alpha)(L_{t-1} + T_{t-1}) \qquad (5.4)$$
$$T_t = \beta(L_t - L_{t-1}) + (1 - \beta) T_{t-1} \qquad (5.5)$$
$$F_{t+1} = L_t + T_t \qquad (5.6)$$

Where:
  L_t = the average demand, also known as level demand
  T_t = the trend value
  α = the weight for average demand $(0 \leq \alpha \leq 1)$
  β = the weight for trend $(0 \leq \beta \leq 1)$
  F_t = the forecast for period t

The following are a couple of issues related to the double exponential smoothing method:
1. Both values of α and β are between 0 and 1.
2. A value of α or β close to 1 is responsive to the changes in the demand data but is unsteady; a value of α or β close to 0 generates a forecast

that is stable and calm. Appropriate α or β values are usually determined through trial and error.

Example problem 5.4: Double exponential smoothing for trended data

The sales data from July to December are given in the table below. We assume the average sales (which is level sales) for July is 300 and the trend value is 50. If alpha (α) is 0.4 and beta (β) is 0.6, calculate the forecast for August through January next year. (Round the results to integers.)

Month	Sales	Level	Trend	Forecast
July	310	300	50	
Aug.	400			
Sept.	380			
Oct.	485			
Nov.	550			
Dec.	535			
Jan.				

Solution to problem 5.4

Since the value for level and trend are given for July, the forecast for August is:

$$F_{t+1} = L_t + T_t$$
$$F_{Aug} = L_{July} + T_{July} = 300+50 = 350$$

Starting from the forecast for September, we need to apply the formulas (5.4) - (5.6):

$$L_t = \alpha D_t + (1 - \alpha)(L_{t-1} + T_{t-1})$$
$$L_{Aug} = \alpha D_{Aug} + (1 - \alpha)(L_{July} + T_{July})$$
$$= 0.4(400) + (1-0.4)(300 + 50) = 370$$

$$T_t = \beta(L_t - L_{t-1}) + (1 - \beta)T_{t-1}$$

$$T_{Aug} = \beta \, (L_{Aug} - L_{July}) + (1 - \beta) \, T_{July}$$
$$= 0.6 \, (370 - 300) + (1-0.6) \, (50) = 62$$

$$F_{t+1} = L_t + T_t$$
$$F_{Sept} = L_{Aug} + T_{Aug} = 370 + 62 = 432$$

Month	Sales	Level	Trend	Forecast
July	310	300	50	
Aug.	400	370	62	350
Sept.	380	411	50	432
Oct.	485	470	55	461
Nov.	550	535	61	526
Dec.	535	572	46	597
Jan.				618

Repeat the above steps to complete the forecast for January. The projected demand for January is 618.

5.3.5 Holt-Winter's method for additive seasonal data

Most products have a seasonal demand pattern. For example, the demand for sun block lotion is higher in summer than it is in other seasons. Holt-Winter's method is one of the methods that we can apply to estimate sales with trend and seasonal components. The procedure of Holt-Winter's additive seasonal method assumes that the different components affect the time series additively. Holt-Winter's additive seasonal model is presented as follows.

$$L_t = \alpha \, (D_t - S_{t-p}) + (1-\alpha)(L_{t-1} + T_{t-1}) \tag{5.7}$$
$$T_t = \beta(L_t - L_{t-1}) + (1-\beta)T_{t-1} \tag{5.8}$$
$$S_t = \gamma \, (D_t - L_t) + (1-\gamma)S_{t-p} \tag{5.9}$$
$$F_{t+n} = L_t + nT_t + S_{t+n-p} \tag{5.10}$$

Where:

L_t = the average demand, also known as level demand

T_t = the trend value

S_t = the seasonal factor

α = the weight for average demand ($0 \le \alpha \le 1$)

β = the weight for trend ($0 \le \beta \le 1$)

γ = the weight for seasonal effect ($0 \le \gamma \le 1$)

F_{t+n} = the forecast for period $t+n$

It takes four steps to complete the forecast using Holt-Winter's method.

(1) Calculate the level demand L_t for time period t by applying formula (5.7).
(2) Calculate the estimated trend value T_t for the time period t by applying formula (5.8).
(3) Calculate the estimated seasonal factor S_t for the time period t by applying formula (5.9).
(4) Compute the forecast F_{t+n} for period $t + n$ by using formula (5.10).

In order to be able to calculate forecast, we need to set up the initial level demand value, trend value, and seasonal factors before we can actually forecast.   We will use the following method to estimate the initial seasonal factors. Equation (5.11) indicates that the initial seasonal factors will be the difference between the actual demand for the time period t and the average demand for the first p periods. For example, if we have observed that quarters have seasonal influence, then we will use 4 as the value of p.

$$S_t = D_t - \sum_{i=1}^{p} \frac{D_i}{p}, \qquad t = 1, 2, ..., p \qquad\qquad (5.11)$$

Example problem 5.5: Seasonal method

The following is the quarterly sales of sun block lotion for 2011, 2012, and 2013. The manager wants to forecast the quarterly sales of sun block lotion for 2014. We use $\alpha = 0.2$, $\beta = 0.1$ and $\gamma = 0.8$.

Quarter	2011	2012	2013
1	114	212	250
2	384	418	458
3	312	388	436
4	222	218	264

Solution to problem 5.5

In order to compute the forecast for 2014 using equations (5.7) – (5.10), we need to estimate the initial seasonal factors for time periods 1– 4 by using equation (5.11). We use $p = 4$ because there are 4 quarters in a year.

$$S_t = D_t - \sum_{i=1}^{p} \frac{D_i}{p}, \qquad t = 1, 2, \ldots, p$$

$S_1 = 114 - (114 + 384 + 312 + 222) / 4 = -144$
$S_2 = 384 - (114 + 384 + 312 + 222) / 4 = 126$
$S_3 = 312 - (114 + 384 + 312 + 222) / 4 = 54$
$S_4 = 222 - (114 + 384 + 312 + 222) / 4 = -36$

To apply equations (5.7) – (5.10) to the forecast for periods 5 to 8, we need to know the level demand for the previous period, which is stated as *t-1* in the formula. To begin the computation of forecast for period 5, we assume that the level demand for the 4th period is the difference between the actual sales and the seasonal factor of the 4th period {222–(–36) = 258}. We set the trend for the 4th period as zero.

Since we have the level demand value and the trend value for period 4, we can compute the forecast for **period 5**.

$F_{t+n} = L_t + nT_t + S_{t+n-p}$
$F_5 = 258 + 0 + (-144) = 114$

Next, we are going to compute the forecast for **period 6** and apply formulae (5.7) – (5.10).

$L_t = \alpha (D_t - S_{t-p}) + (1-\alpha)(L_{t-1} + T_{t-1})$; here t is period 5 and p is 4.
$L_5 = 0.2[212 - (-144)] + (1-0.2)(258+0) = 277.6$

$T_t = \beta(L_t - L_{t-1}) + (1-\beta)T_{t-1}$
$T_5 = 0.1(277.6-258) + (1-0.1)0 = 2$

$S_t = \gamma (D_t - L_t) + (1-\gamma)S_{t-p}$
$S_5 = 0.8(212 - 277.6) + (1-0.8)(-144) = -81.3$

$F_{t+n} = L_t + nT_t + S_{t+n-p}$
$F_{5+1} = 277.6 + 2 + 126 = 405.6$

Year	Qtr.	Period (t)	Actual Sales	Level Demand	Trend	Seasonal Factor	Forecast
2011	1	1	114	--	--	-144.0	--
	2	2	384	--	--	126.0	--
	3	3	312	--	--	54.0	--
	4	4	222	258.0	0.0	-36.0	--
2012	1	5	212	277.6	2.0	-81.3	114.0
	2	6	418	282.0	2.2	134.0	405.6
	3	7	388	294.2	3.2	85.8	338.3
	4	8	218	288.7	2.3	-63.8	261.4
2013	1	9	250	299.1	3.1	-55.5	209.8
	2	10	458	306.6	3.6	147.9	436.2
	3	11	436	318.2	4.4	111.4	396.0
	4	12	264	323.6	4.5	-60.4	258.8
2014	1	13	-	-	-	-	272.5
	2	14	-	-	-	-	480.5
	3	15	-	-	-	-	448.5
	4	16	-	-	-	-	281.1

Now complete the forecast for periods 7 and 12 using the procedure expressed above, by yourself. We can move on to calculate forecasts for year 2014 (periods 13 – 16).

$F_{13} = L_{12} + 1(T_{12}) + S_9 = 323.6 + 1(4.5) - 55.5 = 272.5$
$F_{14} = L_{12} + 2(T_{12}) + S_{10} = 323.6 + 2(4.5) + 147.9 = 480.5$
$F_{15} = L_{12} + 3(T_{12}) + S_{11} = 323.6 + 3(4.5) + 111.4 = 448.5$
$F_{16} = L_{12} + 4(T_{12}) + S_{12} = 323.6 + 4(4.5) - 60.4 = 281.1$

There are other forecast methods that are available to predict trend and seasonal demands. In this section, we discuss a few commonly applied procedures.

5.4 Qualitative Forecasting Method

In supply chain settings, there are not always historical data available for forecasters to use in predicting future demand. When a company launches a new product, the forecaster often combines his expert judgment with the information that he receives from leading market indicators, news reports, and analyses from third parties. There are a variety of approaches that forecasters may apply: they may use their judgment to adjust statistical forecasts, or they may adjust their own initial forecast on the basis of a forecast received from some other sources. For example, a university bookstore manager may make sets of statistical forecasts for a number of textbooks based on historical data. Then, he may adjust his forecasts after he receives information on student enrollment, the number of students in certain majors, their like or dislike of certain instructors, etc. From a supply chain management perspective, the process of conducting initial forecasts, obtaining forecasts from other relevant sources, and then combining judgments with the forecasts seems to be an efficient way of estimating demand levels. It appears that judgmental adjustment can improve accuracy when forecasters have expert knowledge about the market, the customer, and the demand characteristics. In this sense, a judgmental forecast can be a strong complement to the statistical forecasts in the supply chain. Nevertheless, sometimes a judgmental forecast may introduce bias.

There are a number of ways that a judgmental forecast can be integrated into statistical forecasts. For example, individual judgmental forecasts, interactive group forecasts, and combinations of judgmental and statistical forecasts are a few methods that are used in judgmental forecasting.

(i) Individual judgmental forecasts. A forecaster has been in the area for a long time and knows the demand characteristics. Based on his expert experience, he may add or reduce inventory order quantity when he notices the change in the market.

(ii) Interactive group forecasts. There are two approaches by which individual forecasts can be grouped:
   - The first is behavioral aggregation, in which the forecaster, sales person, marketing analyst, and supply chain managers discuss the demand for the product, the product's life-cycle stage, and any potential competitor's penetration, and then come to a consensus on the forecast. This is often considered to be an *interactive group forecast.*
   - The second is a mathematical approach, in which some statistical model is applied to make an average of the individual judgmental forecasts. This approach is also called a *staticized group forecast.*

(iii) Combinations of judgmental and statistical forecasts. Combining forecasts is fairly effective when the forecasts used are not highly correlated. While judgmental and statistical forecasts typically do not have a high correlation, their combination has been shown to be quite useful. Furthermore, it is reasonable to expect improvements in forecast accuracy as the constituents of forecasts improve.

5.5 Reduce Forecast Variability

5.5.1 Sources of variability

There are two sources of demand variability. One is identifiable variability and the other is random variability

Identifiable demand variability, such as the anticipation for higher toy sales during the Christmas season, can be managed and reduced. For example, Toys "R" Us builds anticipation inventory in advance in order to satisfy high demand during the holiday season. At the same time, Toys "R" Us proactively manages demand through promotional sales in October, in order to shift demand to a less-busy season. By doing this, inventory can be reduced and production capacity can be better balanced.

Random demand or supply variability, such as oil production disruption due to a hurricane, cannot be avoided. Therefore, the only method available is to reduce random variability.

To reduce demand and supply variability, we need to understand where the variability comes from. The following are a few examples of sources of variability:

- Demand uncertainty in time, quantity, and location. It is difficult to precisely predict what customers want to buy, when they buy, and what they buy.
- Supply uncertainty in quantity, time, and quality. There is no guarantee that suppliers will deliver the product in the right quantity, at the right time, and in the right quality.
- External factors such as promotions that trigger a high demand level.
- Sales promotions at the end of a season can lead to high demand.
- Market competition, such as new products or substitutable products that can cause demand variation.
- Inconsistent forecast measurement units that can create variability. For example, the production department might forecast in SKU units, the sales department might forecast in number of orders, and the finance department might forecast in dollar value. The outcome of a forecast can be very different.

Demand variability is a common phenomenon and there is no way to eliminate it. Therefore, we should be able to measure the variability, and determine the acceptable variability and the unacceptable variability. Section 5.5.2 discusses variability measures.

5.5.2 Measure variability

Variability from both demand and supply is constant in a supply chain. So, do not cover the variability. Rather, measure it, minimize it or eliminate it.

We discussed a few forecast models in section 5.3. Different forecast models generate different forecast results. So the question is: "which forecast approach is a better one?" Usually, managers tend to select a model that has a smaller forecast error. The following are a number of methods we can apply to measure forecast variability:

- Forecast error (e_t) is the difference between the actual demand for period t (D_t) and the forecast demand for period t (F_t). The term e_t is the forecast bias.

$$e_t = D_t - F_t \tag{5.12}$$

- Mean Absolute Deviation (MAD), a common measure of forecast error is Mean Absolute Deviation (MAD). MAD is easy to compute and interpret. It measures the accuracy of a forecast model.

$$MAD = \frac{\sum_{t=1}^{n} |e_t|}{n} \tag{5.13}$$

- Mean Squared Error (MSE). MSE measures the disposition of forecast errors.

$$MSE = \frac{\sum_{t=1}^{n} e_t^2}{n} \tag{5.14}$$

- Mean Percentage Error (MPE). MPE measures bias and presents a percentage of forecast error.

$$MPE = \frac{\sum_{t=1}^{n} \frac{e_t}{D_t} *100}{n} \qquad (5.15)$$

- Mean Absolute Percentage Error (MAPE). MAPE is a method which measures accuracy and presents errors as a percentage (which is often easier to understand). For example, when you compare the forecast errors of two different items, a high volume item and a low volume item, the high volume item tends to have a bigger error number and the low volume item tends to have a smaller error number. MAPE can be used here because it uses a standardized measure: percentage of error.

$$MAPE = \frac{\sum_{t=1}^{n} \frac{|e_t|}{D_t} *100}{n} \qquad (5.16)$$

5.5.2.1 Measure bias and accuracy

Example problem 5.6: Forecasting error measurement

The following table gives 6-month demand and forecast for Klee, Inc. Determine forecast errors and variability.

Month	Demand	Forecast	Error	|Error|	Error^2	Error%	|Error%|
1	623	620					
2	512	660					
3	624	620					
4	590	660					
5	695	620					
6	723	660					
Total							

Solution to problem 5.6

Take the 1st month as an example.
 Error = 623-620 = 3
 |Error| = |623-620| =3
 Error^2 = 3^2 = 9
 Error% = 3/623 $\cong$ 0.0048 = 0.48%
 |Error%| = |0.48%| = 0.48%

The complete answer is given in the following table.

Month	Demand	Forecast	Error	|Error|	Error^2	Error%	|Error%|
1	623	620	3	3	9	0.48%	0.48%
2	512	660	-148	148	21,904	-28.91%	28.91%
3	624	620	4	4	16	0.64%	0.64%
4	590	660	-70	70	4,900	-11.86%	11.86%
5	695	620	75	75	5,625	10.79%	10.79%
6	723	660	63	63	3,969	8.71%	8.71%
Total			-73	363	36,423	-20.1%	61.4%

Error		Description
CFE	-73	Cumulative Forecast Error (**CFE**) measures bias. The forecast overestimates demand.
MD	(-73)/6= -12	**MD** measures bias; on average, forecast overestimates demand about 12 units.
MAD	363/6= 61	**MAD** measures accuracy; the difference between forecast and demand is 61 units.
MSE	36,423/6 = 6071	**MSE** is difficult to explain. This term is used to determine the root mean squared error in the next row.
RMSE	$\sqrt{36423/6}$ =78	**RMSE** measures accuracy; the difference between forecast and demand is 78 units.
MPE	(-20.1%)/6= -3.4%	**MPE** measures bias; the forecast overestimates demand about 3.4%.
MAPE	61.4%/6= 10.2 %	**MAPE** measures accuracy; the forecast error is about 10.2%.

5.5.2.2 Tracking signal

Tracking signals help to monitor forecast quality and are used to signal to the planner when the forecasting model applied needs to be modified. A tracking signal is the ratio of the sum of forecast errors (the difference between forecast demand and actual demand) and the mean absolute deviation (MAD).

$$\text{Tracking Signal (TS): } TS_t = \frac{\sum_{t=1}^{n}(D_t - F_t)}{MAD} \tag{5.17}$$

In general, when the value of a tracking signal is within the range of ±6 (some people accept the range of ±4), the forecast method is considered acceptable for most exponential smoothing forecasting. Bias can exist when the cumulative actual demand varies from forecasting. The problem is in guessing whether the variance is due to random variation or to bias, which is identifiable. If the error is due to random variation, the error will correct itself. If the error is due to bias, then the forecast should be corrected.

5.5.3 Understand the product life cycle

5.5.3.1 Forecasting for new products

When a new product is introduced and there is no historical data that can be referenced in order to predict the demand level, forecasting is a genuinely inaccurate endeavor. A number of studies have reported the inaccuracy of new product forecast. For example, Tull studied 53 new products from 16 companies and found that the mean forecast error was 58%. What does this 58% mean to a manager? It means that the company is either going to stock twice as much inventory as it can sell or it can only meet half of the actual demand. A study of the forecast performance of North American consumer products indicated that the forecasting error for new items is considerably higher than that of existing products. Weekly demand bias of new products is 21% as compared to 6% for existing products.[5]

Because of low forecast accuracy, a number of attempts have been made to improve the new product forecast and to reduce forecast variability:

(i)   Recognize the importance of the new product forecast;
(ii)   Obtain a new product forecast data source that can help to bring the forecast closer to the market demand;
(iii)   Forecast new product demand with more than one forecast method that includes both quantitative methods (statistical method) and qualitative methods (expert judgment); and
(iv)   Include the factors of consumer purchasing behavior and the volatility of the new market.

Time series methods alone seem to be less adequate when forecasting for new products. We need to consider if a new product is a complete new innovation, an improvement of an existing item, a line extension, or a new category entry. We also need to consider whether the new product is new to the company or is new to market. Table 5.1 shows four types of new products, each is at a different level of newness to the company and the market. For example, when the Coca-Cola Company first introduced Coca-Cola as a soft drink in the 1940s, it was a new innovation to both the company and the market. Coca-Cola Cherry and Coca-Cola Zero are modifications of an existing product. When the Diet Coke was introduced, it expanded an existing product. When Coca-Cola cloned a power drink, it was a new product to Coca-Cola; however, the power drink is not new to the market because Gatorade was already known for its power drink in the market.

The following list gives some possible approaches that can be useful in predicting demand for new products and can be used with statistical forecast methods:

---

[5] Byrne, R.F., (2012). "Forecasting performance for North American consumer products." *Journal of Business Forecasting*, Fall, 31(3), pp. 12.

- Customer research and market research
- Jury of executive opinion
- Sales force opinion
- Delphi method
- Focused group
- Trend line analysis
- Time series
- Linear regression
- Expert systems
- Simulation
- Decision trees
- Neural network

Table 5.1 Types of new products.

Types of New Product	Newness of the Company	Newness to the Market
Modification of an existing product or service	Low	Low
Expansion of an existing product or service	Low	Low
Clone of a competitor's product or service	High	Low
Introduction of a new product or service	High	High

New product forecast is not simply an application of forecast techniques. Forecasting new products should be viewed as a process that involves such issues as relevant input data for forecasting, forecasting technique selection, and forecast accuracy measurement. Efforts to improve new product forecasting accuracy can help to ensure new product success, to improve business performance, and to enhance customer services.

Forecast is usually presented as a single data point. For example, the demand for a new touch screen laptop produced by Exul, Inc. is estimated to be 10,000 units for year 2014. A better approach might be to provide a range, for example, 10,000 ± 1000 units. This range is an important consideration for decision making. What-if scenarios, standard deviations, and confidence intervals can provide a reasonable sense of real demand with randomness and bias.

5.5.3.2 Managing end-of-life-cycle products

For many retailers, distributors, and manufacturers, managing end-of-life products effectively can have a huge impact on supply chain inventory costs and product line profitability. While most companies devote major resources toward new product development and early-stage growth opportunities, some attention should be devoted to products that are past their growth and maturity stages. These products are usually in their decline stage and are leading to termination. When a supply chain observes increasing inventories resulting from product line extension, product improvement, and increased competition, it should consider redesigning its end-of-life processes to more effectively deal with declining sales, rising inventories, and ineffective methods for terminating product lines. In general, poor end-of-life product management results in lost profits. When a product has less than one sales order hit in a year, an inside inventory management team may propose options to deal with the end-of-life products before they are completely obsolete or perished. The following provides a few options to handle end-life-cycle products:

- Run sales or offer discounts on these products;
- Contact outside brokers to get the best price available for useable products that have been made obsolete by new or competitive products;
- Identify alternative markets in different geographic regions to promote the product; and
- Discontinue production of these products.

Better management of end-life-cycle products can improve cash flow and can reduce indirect operational costs and other variable costs associated with managing these products within the firm and in the supply chain.

5.5.4 Reduce demand variability and increase production flexibility

Demand variability is a common phenomenon. Therefore, there is no way to eliminate it. If the demand is higher than the average demand, stock-out is a problem. However, if the demand is lower than the average demand, there will be too much inventory. Excessive inventory is also a problem. Managers spend a considerable amount of time and resources dealing with variability from the projected demand. There are three things a manager can do:

(i) Increase safety stock to hedge demand uncertainty in quantity and timing. For example, retailers do not know precisely when customers will buy Quaker oatmeal and how much they will buy, so they can increase their amount of safety stock to prevent shortage; and

(ii) Increase the flexibility of the production system for assembling the final product as it is needed. For example, Dell Inc. runs a flexible manufacturing system to meet its customer demand.

Either case requires investment: option one requires an investment in inventory and option two requires an investment in production capacity. The third option is to proactively manage demand, such as running a sales promotion in a slow season to reduce demand variability.

In general, it is easy to plan average demand. However, the problem is deviation from the average demand. Managers should first try to reduce and eliminate identifiable variability, then try to reduce unavoidable variability by increasing supply chain flexibility. Reducing the variability and increasing the accuracy of a forecast will give a supply chain a competitive edge in the market place.

5.6 Forecasting for Demand Management

5.6.1 Enhance value through synchronizing demand forecast

In an e-Biz environment, collaborative planning, forecasting, and replenishment are applied in order to synchronize the demand forecast. For a collaborative planning, forecasting, and replenishing (CPFR) system to be successful, it is crucial that all of the trading partners monitor the accuracy of the collaborative forecasts. In other words, they should determine if the customer routinely buys a quantity close to what the system has forecast. The following suggests a few methods that can enhance synchronizing the demand forecast in a supply chain.

(1) *Developing an order-fill forecast based on the length of supply chain cycle time.* First, estimate an initial production quantity. When the demand stabilizes, a more reasonable forecast can be projected based on the sales order data. For example, Sport Obermeyer focuses on keeping raw material and factory production capacity undifferentiated as long as possible. Sport Obermeyer keeps raw materials in stock and books factory production capacity for the peak demand periods well in advance, but does not specify the exact styles to be manufactured until a later date. Sport Obermeyer assumes the risk of supplying the correct raw materials to the factory and the factory agrees to hold production capacity for Sport Obermeyer to be used later.[6] In this way, Sport Obermeyer can reduce the variability of demand for the final product, which is more costly than stocking raw material. However, the manufacturer needs to provide production flexibility.

(2) *Supporting manufacturing strategy with the appropriate forecasting method.* A company's choice of delivering products to its market affects its demand management. The choices can be make-to-stock, make-to-order, assemble-to-order, or engineer-to-order. This decision influences the choice of forecasting methods. If it is a make-to-stock supply chain, the forecast units will be the final products in terms of stock keeping units (SKU). However, if it is a make-to-order supply chain, the forecast will focus on a production capacity cushion and the speed at which the product can be supplied to the customer.

(3) *Fostering supply chain communication.* In a CPFR situation, data and forecast may be communicated to customers and to suppliers. However, a firm needs to determine which data and forecast will be

---

[6] Source: Sport Obermeyer Ltd., HBS Premier Case Collection, Publication Date: Oct 13, 1994.

shared with other supply chain members. For instance, a SKU-level forecast is jointly developed by retailers and next-tier suppliers. Even when an electronic collaborative forecasting system has not been implemented, trading partners may simply ask other members of the supply chain about their future projects and needs on a regular basis.

(4) *Aligning supply chain strategy with uncertainty from both the customer and the supplier.* For the supplier, uncertainty may come from lead-time, from quantity, and from quality. For the customer, the uncertainty may come from the timing and quantity of demand. Uncertainty increases variability. Supply chain managers should work to reduce uncertainty or to develop mechanisms to control uncertainty. They should also understand the data and information needed to generate forecasts and should utilize data warehousing and data mining to improve the accuracy of forecast.

5.6.2 Delayed differentiation and postponement

Delayed differentiation and postponement are relatively new initiatives developed to manage demand uncertainty. Recently, many manufacturers and retailers have begun to apply a postponement or a delayed differentiation strategy to reduce forecast variability and to strike the right inventory level. By holding inventory at the parts and components stage as Dell Computer does, companies are able to offer customized products. However, postponement (which means to postpone the final assembly of a product), calls for a high degree of collaboration in planning and forecasting among the trading partners in the supply chain.

Designing standard components and configurable modules provides a basis for the postponement of producing end items because products can be differentiated quickly and inexpensively, once the actual demand is known. The Oracle/Cap Gemini Ernst & Young survey found that by implementing successful postponement strategy, industry leaders were able to reduce inventory costs by as much as 40 percent.[7] This model

---

[7] Matthews, P. and Syed, N. (2004). "The power of postponement." *Supply Chain Management Review*, 8(3), pp. 28-34.

allows companies to move from the push-oriented supply chain to the pull-oriented supply chain, and finally to the demand-driven supply chain.

5.7 Demand Management Performance Metrics

The performance of the forecasting process should be measured. Forecast performance metrics are used to improve forecast accuracy, to reduce inventory investment, and to improve the level of customer service. The following is a set of measures that can be applied to evaluate forecast performance. Important issues for demand management are:

- Error management (wrong product or specification, wrong amount, wrong shipping date, etc.)
- Number of backorders and units
- Customer service policy issues
- Order responsiveness
- Order lead-time management
- Order scheduling
- Customer priority rules
- Resource allocations
- Product substitution or upgrade
- On-time performance
- Lead-time management
- Safety stock investment
- Production safety capacity

5.8 Summary

Demand management and customer order forecasting are important components of supply chain management. This chapter examined how companies manage the linkage of their production with their customers' needs by using demand management measures and forecasting procedures. We discussed collaborative forecasting, the forecasting process, forecasting models, variability reduction, and performance evaluation. Collaborative forecasting should be considered in conjunction with collaborative planning and replenishment, which will be discussed in Chapters 6 and 7, respectively.

Questions for Pondering

1. Why and to what extent should the supply chain manager be interested in demand management? How do you suppose that interest might be different if the supply chain manager were associated with
   a. a food manufacturer?
   b. an aircraft producer?
   c. a large retail chain?
   d. a hospital?
2. Give illustrations of
   a. spatial versus temporal demand.
   b. lumpy versus regular demand.
   c. derived versus independent demand.
3. Why should a manager be suspicious if the forecaster claims to be able to forecast historical demand without any forecast error?
4. What is the problem if a manager uses the previous year's sales data instead of the previous year's demand to forecast demand for the coming year?
5. Some people have argued that it is more important to have a low bias (mean deviation) than to have a low mean absolute deviation (MAD). Do you agree? Give an example to support your argument.

Problems

1. If the forecast for January is 150 units and the actual demand is 85 units, what is the exponential smoothing forecast for February, assuming that Alpha is 0.3?

2. Estimate the forecasts for August, September, October, November, December, and January of next year using the exponential smoothing method. The smoothing factor, alpha, is 0.3, and the forecast for July is 250.

Month	Actual Demand	Forecast
July	245	
August	260	
September	250	
October	235	
November	255	
December	260	

3. Demand information for the past 6 months is given in the following table.

Month	Actual Demand	Forecast
June	78	
July	46	
August	53	
September	80	
October	68	
November	70	
December		

a. Graph the demand pattern.
b. What is the forecast for October, November, and December, using three-month moving average?
c. Calculate the forecasts by using the exponential smoothing method, alpha=0.3. Assume that the forecast for June is 69.
d. Use error measure methods to compare the results of the two different forecast methods. When computing the error term, consider September to November for both methods. Which forecasting approach will you recommend to the manager? Why?

4. Use the following information to estimate the forecast for each period by using the double exponential smoothing method for trended data. Alpha = 0.3, beta = 0.3, $Level_1$ = 100, $Trend_1$ = 50.

Period	Demand	Level	Trend	Forecast	Error
1	350	100	50		
2	450				
3	468				
4	520				

5. Calculate the seasonal forecast for periods 9-12 based on the following sales information. Alpha = 0.2, beta = 0.1, gamma = 0.4, $Level_4$ = 100, $Trend_4$ = 10.

Year	Qtr.	Period (*t*)	Sales	Level demand	Trend	Seasonal Factor	Forecast
2011	1	1	685				
	2	2	585				
	3	3	765				
	4	4	892	100	10		
2012	1	5	785				
	2	6	625				
	3	7	818				
	4	8	906				
2013	1	9	-				
	2	10	-				
	3	11	-				
	4	12	-				

a. Compute the seasonal factors for periods 1-4.

b. Compute the forecast for periods 9-12.

References

APICS (1998). *Dictionary*, 9th edition, (Falls Church, VA).

Arnold, J.R.T. (1998). Introduction to Materials Management, 3rd edition, (Prentice Hall, New Jersey).

Ballou, R.H. (2004). *Business Logistics Management*, 5th edition, (Prentice Hall, Upper Saddle River, NJ, USA).

Fredendall, L.D. and Hill, E. (2001). *Basics of Supply Chain Management*, (The St. Lucie Press, NY, USA).

Kahn, K.B. (2002). An exploratory investigate of new product forecast practices. *The Journal of Product Innovation Management*. 19, pp. 133-43.

Lambert, D. (2006). "Supply Chain Management: Process, Partnerships, Performance." 2nd edition, (SCMI, Sarasota, Florida).

Lee, H L., Padmanabhan, V., Whang S. (1997). The bullwhip effect in supply chains. *Sloan Management Review*, 38(3), pp. 93-103.

Matthews, P. and Syed, N. (2004). The power of postponement. *Supply Chain Management Review*, 8(3), pp. 28-34.

Ragsdale, C.F. (2008). *Spreadsheet Modeling & Decision Analysis*, 5th ed. (South-Western, Mason, OH, USA).

Schreibfeder, Jon (2005). Achieving Effective Inventory Management, 3rd edition, (Effective Inventory Management, Inc., Coppell, TX, USA).

Syntetos, AA, MZ Babai1, Y Dallery and R Teunter (2009). Periodic control of intermittent demand items: theory and empirical analysis. *Journal of the Operational Research Society*, 60, pp. 611-618.

Supplement 5.1

Synchronizing Production and Inventory Management in the Supply Chain: Introduction to Beer Game

1. Introduction

The goal of supply chain management is to fulfill customer demands and requests through the process of transforming raw materials into finished goods. Consequently, the transformation process is associated with material flow, information flow and fund flow, as we discussed in Chapter 1. The transformation process may include multiple companies and can be modeled in a simple supply chain that contains a retailer, a wholesaler, a distributor, and a manufacturer. Beer Game is a simulation game that allows users to imitate the dynamics of production capacity and inventory management in a supply chain.

In the 1960s, Beer Game was first introduced by the faculty at the Massachusetts Institute of Technology's Sloan School of Management to illustrate the bullwhip effect. This simulation game shows what happens in a hypothetical supply chain and how to coordinate the actions of the different companies in a supply chain.

In his book *The Fifth Discipline*, Peter M. Senge uses a hypothetical scenario to show how the bullwhip effect gathers momentum and what can be done to avoid it.[8] The beer game starts with retailers experiencing a sudden but small increase in customer demand for a certain brand of beer called Lover's Beer. Orders are put together by retailers and passed on to the distributors who deliver the beer. Initially, these orders exceed the distributor's on-hand inventory so they ration out their supplies of Lover's Beer to the retailers and place even larger orders for the beer with the brewery that makes Lover's Beer. The brewery cannot instantly

---

[8] Senge, Peter M. (1990). *The Fifth Discipline* (*The Fifth Discipline: The Art and Practice of the Learning Organization*), (Doubleday/Currency, New York).

increase production of the beer so it rations out the beer it can produce to the distributors and begins building additional production capacity.

The scarcity of the beer prompts panic buying. After a couple of weeks, the demand on the manufacturer is hundreds of cases a day while the demand at the retail level is only four to eight cases. Then, as the brewery increases its production outputs and ships the product in large quantities, the orders that had been steadily increasing due to panic buying suddenly decline. The opposite effect occurs: the retailer has too much inventory than is needed and decides to order zero quantity for several days. This is eventually transmitted back upstream of the supply chain and the manufacturer has to stop production. The shortage then flows downstream, back to the retailer. The whole mess starts all over again and the bullwhip effect occurs. The real change in orders from consumers is only four cases a day.

In this case, all of the members in the supply chain bear the costs of the bullwhip effect. The brewery increases production capacity to satisfy an order stream that is much higher than actual demand. The distributor stocks extra inventory to handle the volatility in order levels. Retailers experience problems with product availability and with extended replenishment lead times. During periods of high demand, there are times when the available capacity and inventory in the supply chain cannot cover the orders being placed. This results in product rationing, longer order replenishment cycles, and lost sales due to lack of inventory.

This scenario occurs in the real world every day. The actual fluctuation in monthly demand in the automotive industry is less than 10%, but second and third tier suppliers often adjust their capacity by as much as 50%. In the apparel industry, seasonal fluctuation compounds the demand variation along the supply chain. The high and low waves of demand continue to occur in the supply chain despite the demand of the end user being relatively flat.

2. Play the Beer Game

The Beer Game is a simulation game that models a supply chain of beer production and distribution. This game can be played with a group of four people. There are four players in the game: the retailer, wholesaler, distributor, and manufacturer. The order begins with the retailer and goes back to the wholesaler, the distributor, and finally to the manufacturer, as illustrated in Fig. 5.4. The sequence of delivering beer is from the factory to the distributor, then to the wholesaler, and finally to the retailer. The main task of the retailer, the wholesaler, and the distributor is the management of inventory, while the main task of the manufacturer is the management of the production capacity.

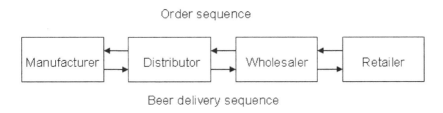

Fig. 5.4 Beer game.

The average daily demand for beer is four kegs. The demand can be as low as two units and as high as six units. The maximum change in order from consumer is four kegs per day.

There is a two-week transportation delay between each pair of the trading partners. For example, beer shipped from the factory in week one will be received by the distributor in week three.

Only two relevant costs are considered in the game: the inventory holding cost (that is $0.50 a week for each keg of beer), and the backorder cost (that is $1.00 a week for each keg of beer). The total cost is computed weekly.

The group can play for up to 30 weeks. After that, a summary of the 30 weeks' performance on holding cost, backorder cost, and total cost is analyzed. Bullwhip effects are included.

Chapter 6

Transforming Demand: Planning on Supply Flow

6.1 Transforming Demand through Production Planning

A company has to manage its production in order to transform customer orders into products and to add value to the product. The question is how it can best and most smoothly transform demand forecast and customer orders into end-user products in the supply chain. The answer exists in an effective manufacturing planning and control system.

A company generally belongs to one supply chain. However, many companies belong to more than one supply chain. Production planning is a mechanism that coordinates not only the activities within operations, but also other functions in the firm such as marketing, sales, human resources, engineering, accounting, and the entire supply chain.

The goal of production planning is to ensure that planned production matches customer demand. Still, demand uncertainty and variation are inevitable. There are two approaches to managing demand fluctuation: one is to increase production capacity flexibility so that production can be scheduled when the demand is there, and the other is to raise or lower inventory to meet that demand. Both solutions require resources. Consequently, production planning should balance the resources (such as workforce, inventory, and overtime) that are required to manufacture products to meet customer demand. Customer demand, which is an output of demand management activity discussed in the previous chapter (Chapter 5), is a crucial input into production planning.

Fig. 6.1 illustrates a hierarchical production planning process in which production planning is based on a product family. This plan provides an overall balance of what the customer needs and what the manufacturer can produce. A master production schedule (MPS) is planned around stock keeping unit (SKU) items, which are the items that are shipped out of the factory (Fig. 6.1). For example, at the production planning stage, garden sprayers are stated in the units of product family, which does not specify the demand for various colors or sizes. The MPS, on the other hand, derives from the number of garden sprayers that are stated in the production plan and are disaggregated to SKU items. The production quantity and time for each SKU item is specified in the master production plan. Rough-cut capacity planning is conducted at the master production schedule level to ensure that the company will have adequate capacity.

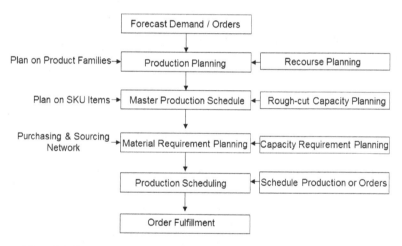

Fig. 6.1 An overview of production planning and scheduling.

Material requirement planning (MRP) translates the master production schedule into the requirements needed for producing the product, such as raw materials, parts, and components. MRP is a software and today, it is a module of an Enterprise Resource Planning (ERP) system that assists managers in both ordering materials and scheduling inventory replenishment. At the MRP stage, capacity requirement planning is performed to ensure that the capacity of key workstations is adequate to support production.

Scheduling is the last manufacturing stage in transforming demand. At this stage, capacity and materials are ready for customer orders to be launched to the shop floor for production. After this stage, orders are ready to be shipped out of the factory.

Since it moves from traditional materials management to supply chain management, demand transformation is more visible in terms of planning, forecasting, and replenishment. The transformation process allocates available capacity and inventory to satisfy customer orders. When a product or component is not available at a certain place, a system-wide check can identify alternative locations and/or can locate a substitutable item. Manufacturing planning and control is crucial to the transformation of customer orders into products and to making a firm successful in the marketplace.

6.2 Aggregate Production Planning

Production planning is also called aggregate planning because the plan aggregates demand on the product family. Production planning is a statement of time-phased production rates, work-force levels, and inventory holdings, based on customer requirements and capacity limitations. It serves as a link between the strategic goals of a company and the plans for individual items and components. Based on forecast demand, a production plan is typically prepared for the next 12 months. Companies usually update their production plan quarterly to recognize changes in demand. They may do this by reviewing the plan monthly and updating it quarterly. Given the objectives set by a company's business plan, production planning will determine the following:

- the quantity of each product family to be produced in each period;
- the desired inventory level for each period;
- the resources (labor, material, and other resources) required to support the production for each period;
- the allowed backorder level for each period;
- the allowed stock-out level for each period;
- the allowed subcontracting quantity.

The objective of production planning is to minimize the costs of change in production level, the cost of holding inventory, and the cost of stock-out and subcontracting. The information needed to make a production plan includes:

- the forecast demand for the planning horizon;
- the beginning inventory and desired ending inventory;
- resources, such as the labor and material needed for production;
- the allowed backorder level;
- the allowed subcontracting quantity.

There are three basic strategies commonly used in production planning. They include a level strategy, a chase strategy, and a mixed level and chase strategy. More discussion on the production planning strategy is provided in Section 6.2.3.

6.2.1 Dimensions of production planning

Production planning has three dimensions: products (or services), labor, and time. The plan aggregates all three:

(i) Product families
- Grouping forecast demand for a product family and similar markets
- Determining relevant units of measurement, such as barrels, tons, cases, dollars, standard hours, etc.

(ii) Labor
- Planning on the level of workforce needed including regular time and overtime, but not specifying the type of skills needed

(iii) Timing
- Updating the production plan monthly or quarterly
- Planning periods are in terms of months or quarters, not in terms of weeks or days.

6.2.2 Production planning alternatives

Production planning uses a variety of alternatives to manage demand uncertainty and capacity constraints. Typically, two approaches are used: the reactive approach and the proactive approach.

The reactive approach includes workforce adjustment through hiring and firing, using overtime and undertime, adjusting vacation schedules, building up anticipation inventory, using subcontractors, and allowing backlogs, backorders, and stock-outs.

The proactive alternative intends to adjust the demand pattern. Commonly used methods include producing complementary products to manage the seasonal nature of the demand and using creative pricing and promotion methods to level demands in the high season and the slow season.

6.2.3 Production planning strategies

Companies typically use three planning strategies for a production plan: level strategy, chase strategy, and mixed strategy.

Level strategy. A level strategy maintains a constant output rate or a stable work force level over the planning horizon by cumulating anticipation inventory or using overtime and backorders to match the demand for the planning horizon. Anticipation inventory, backorders, stock-out, overtime, and undertime are a few options used to match the demand.

Chase strategy. A chase strategy adjusts output rates or workforce levels to match the demand over the planning horizon without using anticipation inventory or undertime. Chase strategy is accomplished through hires and layoffs, overtime, extra shifts, or subcontracting.

Mixed strategy. A mixed strategy covers a range of strategies, such as the level strategy and the chase strategy. The best strategy may be a mix of some anticipated inventory, some work-force level changes, some overtime, and subcontracting.

6.3 Master Production Schedule

6.3.1 The basics of master production schedule

The Master Production Schedule (MPS) is disaggregated from a production plan, which is discussed in Section 6.2. An MPS is not a sales forecast. Rather, it is the detailed production plan for the end items in terms of Stock Keeping Units (SKU) to be produced by the plant. It is constrained by the production plan. For example, if the production plan calls for 400 window blinds to be produced in June, this may mean that 100 window blinds in an ivory color will be produced in week one, 100 in a white color in week two, 100 in a gray color in week three, and 100 in light blue in week four. This process of identifying each end item is called disaggregation. The demand for each SKU end item may be determined at the retail stores when the item is scanned at the checkout. MPS takes into account the forecast, the aggregate plan, the available capacity, and the available material. The MPS must be feasible because the following planning steps regarding material and capacity assume that the MPS is reliable.

At the master production planning stage, rough cut capacity planning is used to check the feasibility of MPS (Fig. 6.1). Rough cut capacity planning is medium-term capacity planning. The length of time ranges from one week to three months and depends on the company and the industry. If there is not enough capacity, then some demand must be pushed ahead or postponed. Alternatively, extra capacity can be added.

The master production schedule is changed and updated more frequently than the production plan. It is a detailed plan and does not extend as far into the future as the production plan. Therefore, it can be viewed as a contract among the different functional areas within a company.

The company will decide when the MPS should be updated. In Fig. 6.2, the MPS is broken into three time periods and is divided by a curved line. The points below the curved line are orders received from customers. The points above the curved line indicate available production capacity and available-to-promise (ATP) inventory.

The first time period is the one most close to the present, while the MPS is frozen (Fig. 6.2). The frozen section indicates that production has started or that the firm is committed to the materials that it purchased from its vendors. No changes are allowed in this time period. Production will produce everything that is stated on the schedule and the rest of the firm will sell what is produced.

The second time period is from weeks 2 through 8 (Fig. 6.2). A certain level of commitment has been made. For example, a request for parts and components has already been sent to the upstream supplier. At this stage, changes will result in costs, but can be negotiated.

In the third time period (Fig. 6.2), changes can be made without penalty. The agreement of a time fence is to achieve coordination both within and outside the firm. It provides insight into a firm's ability to respond to changes.

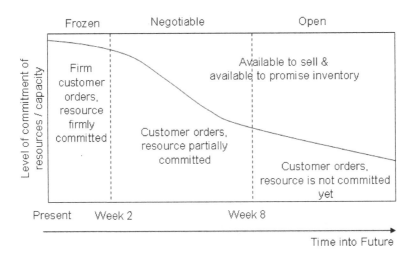

Fig. 6.2 Time fence in master production schedule.

Determining the length of frozen periods, negotiable periods, and open periods is a strategic issue, since it will influence the relationship of the firm to the other members of the supply chain. Where to place the time fence determines the overall flexibility of the firm (and the supply chain) to respond to changes in customer demand. For example, if the company supplies window blinds, fabric production has a four-week time fence. Therefore, it is difficult for the retailer to make changes if the end user wants to change the fabric color three weeks before delivery. However, if the fabric producer has a three-week time fence, then changes can be made closer to the delivery time.

If one partner in the supply chain cannot produce an accurate MPS, then the entire supply chain will be affected. A large amount of variance in MPS will lead to a longer lead-time and large inventories in the supply chain. Therefore, a firm should try its best to plan and schedule production accurately.

Once a firm has a feasible MPS, Material Requirement Planning (MRP) is conducted. To produce the MPS end items, a firm needs to procure or produce intermediate materials. For example, window blinds are assembled from rods, fabric, and string. The material needed is calculated at the material requirement planning stage.

The material requirement plan becomes inputs to the shop-floor scheduling system. The detailed requirements are sent to the suppliers to make sure that required parts, components, or raw materials will be delivered on time, in the right quantity, and with the right quality.

The sales person needs to know what is available, in order to fulfill the customer orders. Available-to-promise (ATP) in the master production plan provides such information. In a make-to-stock production environment, orders are fulfilled from inventory; while in a make-to-order or assemble-to-order production environment, orders are fulfilled from production capacity. The portion of inventory or planned production capacity that has not been consumed by actual customer orders is available to promise to customers.

The following is an example of a master production schedule:

Example problem 6.1: Master production schedule

Window blinds are made in a lot size of 90 units (i.e. MPS quantity). The beginning inventory is 75 units. Forecast demand is 80 units for weeks 1 to 4, 95 units for weeks 5 and 6, and 90 units for weeks 7 and 8. Customer orders received are as follows:

Week 1 – 85   Week 4 – 22
Week 2 – 50   Week 5 – 8
Week 3 – 30   Week 6 – 2

Compute projected on-hand inventory, MPS timing and available to promise (ATP) quantity.

Solution to problem 6.1

The complete solution to problem 6.1 is shown in the table below. First, enter the forecast quantity into the forecast row and the customer orders into the customer orders row.

(1) Projected on-hand inventory at the end of week 1 in January:

On-hand inventory = On-hand inventory at the end of last period + MPS quantity – max (forecast, customer order)   (6.1)

Week 1 in January: Since on-hand inventory at the beginning of week 1 is not enough to cover the order of 85 units (note: choose the bigger number between forecast quantity and customer order quantity), a MPS of 90 units should be scheduled. On-hand inventory by the end of week 1 is computed as:

On-hand inventory$_1$ = 75 + 90 – 85 = 80

Please note that 80 units in Week One is the ending inventory of the week.

	January				February			
Week	1	2	3	4	5	6	7	8
Forecast	80	80	80	80	95	95	90	90
Customer orders (committed)	85	50	30	22	8	2		
Projected on-hand inventory (75)	80	0	10	20	15	10	10	10
MPS	90	0	90	90	90	90	90	90
Available to promise	30		60	68	82	88	90	90

Week 2: Since 80 units of on-hand inventory is available at the beginning of week 2, which is enough to cover the forecast demand of 80 units; no new MPS should be scheduled. On-hand inventory for week 2 is computed as:

On-hand inventory$_2$ = 80 + 0 − 80 = 0

Repeat the same step until all the on-hand inventories are computed.

(2) Available to promise for the 1st period of the planning horizon:
   ATP = On-hand inventory at the end of last period + MPS quantity −
      customer orders due before next MPS   (6.2)

   ATP$_1$ = 75 + 90 − (85 + 50) = 30

(3) Available to promise for periods after the 1st period:
   ATP = MPS quantity − customer orders due before next MPS   (6.3)

   ATP$_3$ = 90 − 30 = 60
   ATP$_4$ = 90 − 22 = 68

Repeat the same step until all of the ATPs have been computed.

6.3.2 Available to promise

In the example problem 6.1, the available-to-promise for the first week is 30 units. This information indicates to the sales department that it can promise as many as 30 units until next MPS quantity is delivered at the beginning of week 3. In week 3, there will be 60 units still uncommitted, and this amount is available to promise new orders.

   If the actual customer order quantity exceeds the ATP quantity, the MPS should be adjusted before more orders can be taken. Alternatively, the customer can be given a later delivery date, which can be the date of the next MPS' arriving date.

6.3.3 Available to sell

Available-to-sell projects the full visibility of the uncommitted supply potential across the entire MPS planning horizon. The idea is to go beyond on-hand uncommitted inventory, which is available to promise. Available-to-sell includes uncommitted inventory, as well as uncommitted capacity that can sell. For example, HP launched an initiative to create an available-to-sell capability. [1] A SKU-level available-to-sell report indicates upstream uncommitted capacity. This provides sales teams with the information that they need in order to steer demand and promotions into the SKU's level, so as to avoid the busy season when the SKU is in tight supply.

6.3.4 Digital solution: Global available-to-promise

To win and maintain the confidence of customers over time, industries strive to provide realistic product delivery dates based on actual and planned material availability, current production capacity, and vendor lead times. In recent years, ERP software companies such as QAD and Made-2-Manage have promoted an e-Business solution, Global available-to-promise (ATP) that automates the search for available production capacity, as well as for inventory, in multiple warehouses, distribution centers, and manufacturing facilities, in order to maximize customer service level.

Global ATP helps the supply chain keep its promises and improves customer satisfaction. This e-business solution enables the supply chain to view the existing inventory, check over production in progress, and identify substitutable products that can be used to fill orders. Additionally, the software allows the supply chain to reallocate its inventory system-wide, based on changing customer needs and market dynamics. By doing this, the supply chain is able to set delivery dates based on available capacity and material constraints, in order to avoid overpromising and underpromising on customer orders.

---

[1] Culbertson, S., Harris, I. & Radosevich, S. (2005). Synchronization – HP style. *Supply Chain Management Review*, March, 9(2), pp. 24-31.

Global available-to-promise uses a rule-based strategy which allows manufacturers to move from a "what if" scenario to "what's the best" decision. Consequently, asset utilization is improved through inventory, and capacity checks are conducted throughout the supply chain in real time to ensure that supply matches demand.

6.4 Collaborative Planning

6.4.1 Overview of collaborative planning

In an openly communicative supply chain, firms may share their production plans with each other, in order to encourage coordinated planning into the future. In this type of environment, it is much more likely that all sources of demand will be accounted for and that there will be fewer surprises that disturb the production plan. Consequently, the production plan is based more on actual demand than on forecasted demand.

A challenging issue facing production planning is demand variation. Retailers, wholesalers, and distributors place orders in batches, periodically, in order to minimize order cost, transportation cost, and administrative effort. However, when orders are grouped into batches, the orders vary according to the size of actual demand from customers. As the orders move up the supply chain, the size of the order gets larger and larger and the demand variance gets bigger and bigger. This is the bullwhip phenomenon as discussed in Chapter 1 and Chapter 5, which can disrupt production planning.

As the supply chain evolves, a process of collaborative planning, forecasting, and replenishment (CPFR) emerges with new supply chain strategy and technology. To react to the variation in demand and supply, companies have begun to link their demand and supply functions using CPFR. For example, in recent years, retailers have established collaborative agreements with their supply chain partners and have an ongoing planning, forecasting, and replenishment process in place with their suppliers. To facilitate the coordination that is needed in supply chains, the Voluntary Interindustry Commerce Standards (VICS)

Association has set up a committee to establish certain procedures for CPFR issues (discussed in Chapter 1). This committee documents best practices for CPFR and creates guidelines for implementing CPFR.

Innovative consumer goods manufacturers and retailers are forging partnerships to advance the implementation of CPFR. For example, Thomson Electronics Company is already doing CPFR with 50 of its retailers and has launched pilot projects with more trading partners. Schering Plough and Johnson & Johnson are taking the lead with Eckerd Drug. Mitsubishi Motors is collaborating with its dealers to reduce customer lead time to two weeks.[2] Each player in the supply chain needs to perform its portion of the collaborative forecasting and planning effort as accurately as possible. The result is a smoother flow of smaller orders that distributors and manufacturers are able to handle more efficiently.

Collaboration in planning production, forecasting demand, and replenishing inventory brings a number of benefits. It helps smooth production flow, balance capacity, reduce inventory, reduce safety stock, and reduce stock-outs. Furthermore, CPFR reduces the bullwhip effect because all of the companies in the supply chain have access to sales data and share sales forecasts. This allows every player in the same supply chain to develop a better production plan, keep ideal inventory levels, and make realistic delivery schedules. Companies that have been able to put CPFR into action have already gained significant competitive edges over their competitors. Walmart, Dell Inc., and Proctor & Gamble, to name just a few, share point-of-sales and inventory data with all of the other companies in their respective supply chains and have yielded better efficiencies and profits for themselves and for the supply chain as a whole.

Nevertheless, collaboration is not easy to implement, and it will take time to become more common in business. Integrating disconnected forecasting and planning across the entire supply chain is challenging. A key issue in improving collaborative efforts is to have supply chain partners get their own organizations in order and have accurate data.

---

[2] Dion, C. The growing pace of CPFR. www.consumergoods.com, Jan/Feb 2000.

6.4.2 Pull and push boundary in production planning

Where to draw the line to determine a supply chain's push-pull boundary depends on the manufacturing production environment. The customer order decoupling point may move from finished goods inventory back to the raw material suppliers. Those who serve their customers from the finished goods inventory usually have a make-to-stock production environment. Those who assemble products from available product choices have an assembly-to-order manufacturing environment. Those who produce tailored goods such as machine tools employ build-to-order or engineer-to-order production systems. Production details vary significantly among make-to-stock, assemble-to-order, and build-to-order production environments. Table 6.1 illustrates some of the features that relate to the pull-push boundary in production planning as well as to the level of flexibility that the supply chain intends to achieve.

Table 6.1 indicates that the make-to-stock production environment focuses on the maintenance of finished goods inventories. The push-pull boundary is located at the finished goods inventory. For the make-to-stock production environment, there are very few customer orders, since demand has been forecast and a push system has been applied. Flexibility is usually low.

The assembly-to-order manufacturing environment handles numerous end-item configurations and is an option for mass-customization. A combination of a push-pull system is implemented. The push-pull boundary exists at the beginning of assembly. Demand management defines customer orders in terms of alternatives and options. In the assembly-to-order production environment, customer orders are booked several periods into the future. Capacity flexibility is reserved to accommodate the promises of the delivery date. A Master Production Schedule is typically set up in the form of Final Assembly Schedule (FAS).

Make-to-order, on the other hand, produces customized products in low volume after the manufacturer receives the orders. In a make-to-order production environment, the challenge is to manage a large backlog of customer orders. A large capacity cushion is needed to satisfy customer needs, since what the customer will order is uncertain. The push-pull boundary locates itself at components and subassembly units. In the make-to-order production environment, the production plan is based on orders received. Instead of fulfilling the orders from inventory, companies with a make-to-order strategy use backlogs to fulfill customer orders. Backlog occurs when customer orders are received but have not yet been shipped.

Table 6.1 Push-pull boundary and manufacturing environment.

	Engineer-to-order	Make-to-order	Assembly-to-order	Make-to-stock
Volume	**One-of-kind**	**Small**	**Medium**	**Large**
Push/Pull boundary	Design & raw materials	Raw material & common components	Components & subassembly units	Finished products
Production planning	Engineering capacity	Determine capacity flexibility & capacity cushion	Determine production & delivery cycle time and dates	Forecast finished goods inventory level
Master Production Schedule	Final production	Final production	Mix forecasts & actual demands	Forecast demands
Capacity flexibility	High	High	Moderate	Low
Key performance metrics	Engineering resource, delivery due date & capacity flexibility level	Delivery due date & capacity flexibility level	Delivery due date	Customer service level

Engineer-to-order produces products with unique parts and drawings required by customers. The engineering resource is important in this production environment. Communication between the manufacturing firm and the customer is crucial in order to make sure that customers' special needs are satisfied and that delivery due dates are met. The push-pull boundary exists at the design stage of the product.

6.4.3 Manufacturing flexibility

Supply chain flexibility creates a system that can adapt to environment changes quickly and can modify the process and the product configuration with little cost and time. Flexibility can be expressed through five areas:[3]

- Volume flexibility. Volume flexibility is the ability to operate economically at different production volumes.
- Mix flexibility. Mix flexibility is the ability to change the variety of products being made in a period.
- Product flexibility. Product flexibility is the ability to design new products or to modify existing ones.
- Process flexibility. Process flexibility is the ability to produce a certain product by using alternative manufacturing routes.
- Delivery flexibility. Delivery flexibility is the ability to deliver orders at the time when a customer wants the product and to the place where the customer wants it.

Flexibility is needed to respond to market and customer requirements with less time and cost, especially when the manufacturing system needs to respond to a wide range of product variability. The challenge is to plan for the right degree of supply chain flexibility, because increased supply chain flexibility means increased cost and investment in excess production capacity. Lot size and cycle time, which vary by products, markets, or the product life cycle phase, should be well analyzed to determine their level of flexibility. A trade-off between stocking inventory and keeping capacity cushion is a strategic issue that reflects a

---

[3] G. J.C. da Silveria (2005). "Effects of simplicity and discipline on operational flexibility: An empirical reexamination of rigid flexibility model." *Journal of Operations Management.* 24 (6), pp. 932-947.

supply chain's overall objective. Since flexibility requires investment, it should match the design nature of both the product and the manufacturing system.

Two manufacturing initiatives that have been popularized in recent years are lean manufacturing and agile manufacturing. Both approaches aim at satisfying customer needs at a competitive cost structure and with increased system flexibility.

The lean system that began in a Toyota production system had the goal of eliminating waste from the production system through cycle time reduction and pull system implementation. When cycle time is reduced, the system can be more flexible to respond to customer needs. A lean manufacturing system is most suitable for a line processing production environment and lends itself to an efficient supply chain, where components are fairly standardized and product variety is low.

An agile manufacturing system is created in response to mass customization. One of the best examples is Dell Computer's assembly system, which can quickly respond to varied demand in product complexity, volume, variety, and delivery schedule. An agile approach is preferred when there is a large amount of product variety, demand is highly unpredictable, new product introduction is fast, and the product's life cycle is short. The agile method suits a responsive supply chain.

In order to make the system more flexible in the process of demand transformation, supply chain collaboration in capacity planning is desirable. For example, Sport Obermeyer continuously refines its forecast procedure to better predict customer needs. In addition to forecasting its finished goods demand, it forecasts the need for production capacity, so that it can reserve its supplier's capacity for making products at a later date. Reserving a capacity cushion gives Sport Obermeyer flexibility to meet its customers' needs in terms of size, color, and style, and to avoid mismatches in supply and demand.

6.4.4 Synchronization supply flow — HP example

When it is implemented correctly, CPFR is an effective tool that can generate significant value. When Hewlett-Packard's Imaging and Printing business division realized that it regularly produced too many of the wrong products and not enough of the right ones, it decided to synchronize its supply chain by working back from its customers to its raw material suppliers.

In 1999, HP Imaging and Printing's business division employed a top-down forecasting method for long-range production planning and a bottom-up CPFR process for detailed information about a retailer's sales plan, promotions, and the operational policies needed for production.[4] After receiving a 12-week order forecast every week from its account teams, HP Imaging and Printing's business division set up a spreadsheet database to keep track of changes in orders. Then, changes in demand were aggregated and analyzed. Short-term forecasts were compiled weekly, based on the account level demand information. The primary output of the collaborative demand analysis was a short-term SKU-level order, which is an important input for master production schedule.

The next step was to match supply with demand through integrating the results from the previous week. Using a demand forecast that was updated weekly, all of the previous week's requests were satisfied first before the new demand was allocated. Retailers were informed what they would receive in the next 12 weeks, in response to their weekly forecast. Three fundamental changes were made through CPFR:

(1) The factory moved to weekly production measures and weekly execution of the delivery plan (instead of monthly). With a weekly plan, the channel members had more up-to-date information about the synchronized demand plan and the CPFR process.
(2) The HP factory trimmed the number of weeks frozen in the master production plan from five to two weeks, making the system more flexible. At the same time, a biweekly cycle for deciding product mix and volumes within the specified guidelines was implemented.
(3) The upstream supplier's responsiveness increased. Their Asian suppliers reserved more capacity cushion for the HP factory. This led to less inventory in HP's factory, as compared to the inventory level they had before synchronization was implemented.

---

[4] Culbertson, S., Harris, I. & Radosevich, S. (2005). Synchronization – HP style. *Supply Chain Management Review*, March, 9(2), pp. 24-31.

At the same time, the HP Imaging and Printing business division launched a team to create an available-to-sell capability. The idea was to go beyond on-hand uncommitted inventory. This gave account teams the information they needed to steer demand and promotions into the SKU level, so as to avoid busy season when the SKU is in tight supply.

With solid production plans, the synchronization initiative achieved a number of encouraging results as listed below:

- As compared to the baseline year 1999, inventory investment across the supply chain was reduced by 20 percent.
- At the outset, the division could only meet 70% of a four-week forecast, but the number climbed to 97% and has stayed there.
- SKU level forecast and data quality improved, as well.

6.5 Demand Transformation

6.5.1 Enhancing value through demand and supply flow management

A supply chain is a sequence of activities that add value at each stage of production. For example, a supply chain of bread starts with forecasting customer demand, wheat production, flour production, scheduling production, inventory management, transportation, and distribution, and the process extends all the way to the final customers. In this process, production adds a considerable amount of value as the product moves through the supply chain.

Value-add in demand transformation is enhanced by the appropriate choice of manufacturing system. The right manufacturing system increases flexibility and agility, reduces bullwhip effects and bottlenecks, and improves the order fulfillment rate. Manufacturing systems, such as make-to-order and make-to-stock, have their own capability constraints, which are critical in achieving the order fulfillment objectives. Capacity constraints expressed in bottleneck may happen in equipment or labor. Therefore, constraints need to be identified and communicated well in advance with the supply chain partners to ensure a smooth demand transformation process.

Well-connected value-add points in the supply chain are important to a smooth production flow. That is to say, there are many value-add points in a supply chain. Given that each company that is a member of the chain and contributes its own value-add point, a seamlessly connected chain is desirable for optimum demand transformation flow. This can be done through identifying the push-pull boundary that a company desires to set. Where should a company start the value-add point? Should the value-add point be at the parts production stage, at the sub-assembly stage, or at the final assembly stage? This question can be answered according to the role that the company plays in the supply chain, the nature of the product, and the manufacturing system. When the pull-push decoupling points of various partners of a supply chain are determined, production flows better in the supply chain, and customer orders are transformed properly.

6.5.2 Demand transformation performance metrics

Traditionally, the metrics for production management focus on efficiency and cost reduction. This performance criterion leads to the large volume production of standardized products.

In recent years, mass customization has become a common practice. The demand transformation process focuses on better manufacturing flow management, consistent availability of products that meet customer needs, and a higher sales and profit margin. The following is a set of measures that can be applied to evaluate demand transformation performance:

- Reduction of production cost. Production cost can be reduced as a result of reduced labor and material costs, better capacity management (through better forecasting customer needs), and more effective scheduling of customer orders.
- Reduction of non-manufacturing expense. Non-manufacturing expense can be reduced through appropriate manufacturing system choice and the number of expedited shipments and rush orders.
- Reduction of inventory investment. Better flow management reduces inventory investment, improves inventory turns, accommodates

demand with the right product, and reduces inventory obsolescence. As a result, asset utilization improves.

• Improved customer service level. A good customer service level can be achieved through a better order fill rate, on-time shipments, and a shortened cycle time.

6.6 Summary

Demand transformation realizes what customers need through converting raw materials to finished goods. The process of demand transformation is a value-add process and is a critical component of supply chain management. This chapter examined how companies select a manufacturing system that best fits the product nature and the demand pattern. We have discussed aggregate planning, master production scheduling, push-pull boundary determination, and the application of flexible and agile manufacturing. Pertinent performance metrics were suggested as well. Collaborative planning and forecasting should be considered in conjunction with the collaborative replenishment of inventory in the supply chain, which will be discussed in Chapter 7.

Questions for Pondering

1. In recent years, some leading companies (such as HP) focus more on master production schedules than on aggregate planning. What makes available-to-promise, available-to-sell, and capability-to-promise gain more attention than aggregate planning in supply chain management?

2. The linear decision model for aggregate production planning developed by Holt, Modigliani, Muth, and Simon in the 1950s has been considered a classic piece of aggregate planning. Later, many modified versions of aggregate planning were developed to guide production planning. Is aggregate planning no longer useful in supply chain management? Support your argument with reasons and examples.

3. Explain how to apply various aggregate planning strategies to various manufacturing environments with different levels of demand uncertainty.

4. Why would a retailer want to offer a price promotion before the holiday season, which is the peak demand period? How can the supply chain best plan for this type of promotion?

5. A week before Father's Day, Sunday June 9, 2013, Best Buy advertised Dell computers. What kind of demand pattern would lead Dell to imitate its competitor's supply chain strategy? How could this make-to-stock strategy affect Dell's production plan and master production schedule?

Problems

1. (MPS) The Best Pump, Inc. forecast requirements for a medium size pump for the next six weeks: 25, 55, 20, 30, 60, and 45. The marketing department has received four orders for weeks 1, 2, 3 and 4 in the quantity of 30, 40, 20, and 35, respectively. Currently, there are 35 units in inventory. MPS quantity is 55 units and lead time is 1 week.

   a. Develop the MPS record for the pump.

   b. A utility company placed an order of 26 units. What is the appropriate shipping date for the order?

2. The following table gives the information regarding a desk clock for the MPS. The MPS quantity is 50 units, beginning inventory is 35 units, and lead-time is one week. Forecast and customer orders are as follows:

Item: desk clock								
	Week							
	1	2	3	4	5	6	7	8
Forecast	57	28	38	47	32	33	22	28
Customer orders booked	32	33	25	27	18	10	8	8
Projected on-hand inventory								
MPS quantity								
ATP								

a. Complete the MPS for desk clock.

b. Five new customer orders have just arrived in sequence (as shown in the table below). Assume that the sequence of order cannot be changed (i.e. first come, first served) and that orders have to be delivered on the required date. Which orders can be fulfilled?

New Orders	Quantity	Desired Delivery Date
1	48	4
2	43	5
3	30	1
4	20	7
5	20	6

References

APICS dictionary 9th edition (1998). (APICS, Fall Church, VA).

Arnold, J.R.T. (1998). Introduction to Materials Management, 3rd edition, (Prentice Hall, New Jersey).

Dion, C. (2000). The Growing Pace of CPFR, Jan/Feb, www.consumergoods.com.

Hugos, M. (2003). Essentials of supply Chain Management, (John Wiley & Son, Inc., New York, NY).

Ritzman, L.P. and Krajewski, L.J. (2003). Foundations of Operations Management, (Prentice Hall, New Jersey).

Vollmann, T.E., Berry, B., Whybark, D.C. and Jacobs, F.R. (2005). Manufacturing Planning and Control for Supply Chain Management, 5th edition, (McGraw-Hill, New York, NY).

Chapter 7

Managing Material Flow and Inventory in the Supply Chain

7.1 The Importance of Managing Material Flow and Inventory

In any country, its inventory is its artery; inventory represents the material wealth of a nation. For a company and its supply chain, its inventory is its assets. Consequently, inventory management is extremely important. For example, when Hurricane Katrina hit New Orleans in the US in the summer of 2005, The Food Bank supplied 2.4 million pounds of food from its inventory to people who were housed in emergency shelters. It helped people in communities affected by the disaster survive the difficult time.[1]

Inventory, which is the material flow that runs through the supply chain, is everywhere. When we buy a gallon of milk for a week's supply, we create inventory at home. Our intuition tells us that inventory makes our life convenient. Inventory is very important to a manufacturing company that produces commodities. For example, a bakery stocks its supply of flour and sugar for further production.

Since the industrial revolution, manufacturers have favored large-scale production, which creates quantities greater than consumption requirements and generates inventory. As such, many different inventory management models have been developed. Table 7.1 provides a brief summary of a few seminal models that have influenced both inventory theories and practices.

---

[1] Caruso, David B. (2005). "Some food banks say Katrina drained aid." Associated Press, November 23.

Written records of inventory management can be traced back to the creation of the **Economic Order Quantity (EOQ) model,** a formula that primarily controls an independent demand inventory system. The origin of the EOQ model was recorded in a 1913 article by Ford Whitman Harris in *Factory: the Magazine of Management* and in a *Harvard Business Review* article by R.H. Wilson in 1934.[2]

The EOQ model illustrates the total cost of holding inventory. The decision rule of the EOQ model dictates the best order quantity that will minimize the total cost associated with the quantity. Balancing annual order costs against annual carrying costs is the basis for arriving at the economic order quantity.

Table 7.1 History of material management.

Topic	Contributor	Time
EOQ	Ford Whitman Harris	1913
	R.H. Wilson	1934
MRP	IBM developed BOM software;	Late
	George Plossl & John Orlicky discussed concepts	1960s
JIT	Toyota production system	Early 1970s
MRPII	Evolved from MRP	1980s
CPFR	The Voluntary Interindustry Commerce Standards (VICS)	1990s

Nevertheless the EOQ model does not provide lead-time visibility, a critical factor, to dependent demand inventory management. When a product has many components and its product structure has many layers, the lead-time associated with each level should be integrated into the model. In the 1960s, IBM was the first company to introduce a Bill of

---

[2] Roach, B. (2005). "Origin of the economic order quantity formula: transcription or transformation?" *Management Decision*, 43(9), pp. 1262-1268.

Material (BOM) software that tackled dependent demand inventory management issues. In the late 1960s, **Material Requirements Planning (MRP)** was introduced by George Plossl and John Orlicky. The significance of MRP is to identify what product the customer requires. It compares the required quantity to the on-hand inventory level and determines the quantity and timing of the required items that need to be produced. Later, MRP evolved to **Manufacturing Resource Planning (MRPII)** which included financial and other resources needed for production.

Meanwhile, the **Just-In-Time (JIT)** production method was popularized during the 1970s, which has an emphasis on lean production and supplier relationships. The philosophy of JIT is to eliminate waste by cutting excess inventory and to remove non-value-added activities. JIT was first adopted by Toyota manufacturing plants under the direction of Taiichi Ohno. The main concern at that time was to meet consumer demand. After the successful introduction of a JIT system by Toyota, many companies followed, suit, and around the mid-1970s and early 1980s, JIT was used broadly by companies worldwide.

The idea of **Collaborative Planning, Forecasting, and Replenishment (CPFR)** advances the concept of inventory control in supply chain management. The enabler of CPFR is information technology. For example, Walmart has engaged in CPFR with about 600 trading partners.[3] Its collaboration is evident in so many areas of business, such as vendor-managed inventory, sharing information with vendors without charge, and the cross-docking inventory distribution method. Walmart's inventory management is revolutionary and is a model of best practices. Consequently, inventory is of strategic importance to supply chain management.

---

[3] Cutler, Dave (2003). "CPFR: Time for the breakthrough," *Supply Chain Management Review*, May/June, pp. 54-60.

7.2 Inventory Concepts

7.2.1 Definition of inventory

Inventory is the stock of any item or resource used in an organization. *An inventory system* is a set of policies and procedures that determines what inventory levels should be maintained, when stock should be replenished, and how large orders should be.

Manufacturing inventory types include:

- Raw Materials
- Work-in-Process inventory (which includes component parts)
- Finished products inventory

Inventory held at distribution centers and retailers' warehouses is usually finished goods inventory.

7.2.2 Purpose of holding inventory in supply chain

Inventory is created when supply exceeds demand. The purpose of holding inventory is to achieve economies of scale, to protect suppliers from stock-out due to uneven and uncertain demand, and to shelter demand variation during lead-time. The following discusses cycle inventory, safety stock, seasonal inventory, and in-transit inventory.

Cycle Inventory. Cycle Inventory is the inventory that accrues in the supply chain as the result of the purchase or production of larger lots than are currently demanded by customers. Cycle inventory exists because each stage of the supply chain attempts to exploit economies of scale and thus reduce total costs.

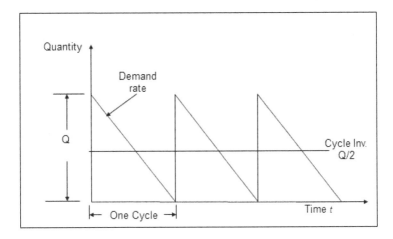

Fig. 7.1 Cycle inventory.

Fig. 7.1 illustrates the cycle inventory level. This is a two-dimensional inventory problem. The horizontal direction shows time. From the beginning of a cycle to the end of the cycle indicates the time between orders. The vertical direction shows the quantity of inventory on hand. We assume that there is no safety stock. When inventory reaches zero, an order is placed and received simultaneously.

The two questions regarding the two-dimensional problem are: "When to place the order?" and "How much to order?" The two costs associated with the two questions are the ordering cost and the inventory holding cost. The total cost is the sum of the ordering cost and the inventory holding cost.

Safety Inventory. Safety inventory is created to protect against fluctuations and uncertainty in demand, supply, and lead-time. There are two major sources of uncertainty: quantity and timing.

The quantity of demand from the customer side fluctuates from period to period. Sometimes, the demand exceeds the forecast sales, while at other times, the demand is lower than the expected sales. Safety stock, in this case, is required to cover excess demand during the order lead-time.

From the supplier side, replenishments from suppliers may have quality problems that result in fewer usable units than were originally ordered. Additionally, suppliers may not be able to deliver orders on time. Safety stock is used to hedge quality and late delivery problems.

Seasonal Inventory. When demand is seasonal, seasonal inventory is created to absorb uneven rates of demand. Seasonal inventory is also called anticipation inventory.

In-transit Inventory. In-transit inventory is a function of demand during lead-time. In-transit inventory provides a safeguard during supply delivery time. In-transit inventory can be called pipeline inventory.

7.2.3 Inventory for independent demand and dependent demand

Independent demand comes from many sources external to the firm and is not a part of other products. In other words, it is unrelated to the demand for other products.

Dependent demand, on the other hand, is derived demand based on production levels; the need for one item is directly related to the need for some other items. For example, a furniture producer forecasts demand for dining tables, which is an independent demand. However, the number of table legs that the manufacturer needs to produce is derived from the number of tables it is going to produce. Therefore, table legs are dependent demand.

7.2.4 The cost of holding inventory

Inventory is used to improve customer service level. However, money invested in inventory is an opportunity cost to the company and its supply chain. Therefore, the supply chain manager needs to balance the advantages and disadvantages of holding both low and high inventory. There are two major costs associated with inventory. One is holding cost and the other is ordering or set-up costs.

The primary reason for keeping inventory low is the cost associated with holding inventory. Money invested in inventory cannot be used for other investment. Inventory holding cost includes the costs for storage, facilities, handling, insurance, pilferage, breakage, obsolescence, depreciation, taxes, and the opportunity cost of capital.

The primary reason for keeping inventory high is the cost of replenishing inventory and the risk of the future unavailability of the item. Ordering cost and set-up cost are the two major costs. Ordering cost includes the managerial and clerical costs associated with preparing the purchase. Setup cost, which is often used in a manufacturing setting, includes equipment setups, filling out required papers, and material handling activities.

To calculate annual inventory cost, three pieces of data are required.

(i) Inventory holding cost, which is the percent of item cost. The annual cost of carrying inventory is a percentage of inventory value, including financing, devaluation, storage, insurance, theft, and scrap.

(ii) Ordering cost, which includes clerical work, administrative handling, shipping and transportation costs. Purchasing cost maybe included depending on a specific situation.

(iii) Customer service level, which is expressed in the amount of safety stock held. For example, it will include the number of locations that are required to meet the most stringent customer service requirements. This data is available from the marketing and sales department.

7.2.5 The cost of inaccurate inventory information

Many companies try to manage their inventory more effectively because inventory is treated as an asset. It is not unusual to learn that a member of the customer service department is constantly going to the warehouse to check the warehouse inventory against the inventory listed by the computer system. Warehouse clerks spend hours searching for items that have been misplaced, damaged, or stolen. Purchasers constantly fill backorders for items that have been received but cannot be located. Inaccurate inventory can cost a company or a supply chain thousands or even millions of dollars and can affect profit margins, inventory turns, the order fill rate, and customer service levels. Additionally, inaccurate inventory disrupts purchasing and warehouse operations.

Let's consider a hypothetical situation. Assume your company earns a 5% net profit before taxes. You lose $150 in net profit every month due to inaccurate inventory. How much in new sales revenue should your company generate to make up for this loss of $150 a month?

New sales in dollars * % of net profit before taxes = loss   (7.1)
New sales in dollars * 5% = $150
$3000 * 5% = $150

If we divide $150 by 5% we get $3,000. That means that your company has to generate $3,000 in new sales per month to make up for the loss of $150 in net profit due to inaccurate inventory. Now, pick a number in Column One of Table 7.2 and determine how much it costs your company if your inventory is not accurate.

Table 7.2 Effect of inaccurate inventory.

Value of loss in net profit due to inaccurate inventory per month	Net Profit Loss Before Tax			
	1%	2%	5%	10%
	New sales needed to make up the loss per month			
$10	$1,000	$500	$200	$100
$100	$10,000	$5,000	$2,000	$1,000
$1,000	$100,000	$50,000	$20,000	$10,000
$10,000	$1,000,000	$500,000	$200,000	$100,000

Let's take the row of marked "value of loss in net profit of $10" as an example.

Loss = New sales in dollars * % of net profit before taxes
$10 = $1,000 * 1%
$10 = $ 500 * 2%
$10 = $ 200 * 5%
$10 = $ 100 * 10%

If the company's net profit before taxes is 1%, the company needs to generate $1,000 new sales to cover the loss of $10 due to inaccurate inventory. Similarly, if the company's net profit before taxes is 10%, the company needs to generate $100 new sales to cover the loss of $10 due to inaccurate inventory. Inaccurate inventory prediction will affect the company's bottom line and financial performance.

7.2.6 Inventory measures

Inventory measures evaluate how effectively a supply chain uses its resources to satisfy customer demand. Inventory measures start with the physical counting of units, weight, or volume. Three measures of inventory are commonly used: the average aggregate inventory value, inventory turnovers, and weeks of inventory supply.

Average aggregate inventory. Average aggregate inventory includes the raw materials, the work-in-process inventory, and the finished goods inventory a company holds for the year. It is usually expressed in dollars.

Inventory turnover. Inventory turnover measures the speed at which inventory can be sold in a year. A higher turnover rate usually generates higher profits and is more desirable. The formula used to compute inventory turnover (INVT) is as follows:

$$INVT = \frac{\text{Annual cost of sales}}{\text{Average aggregate inventory value}} \quad (7.2)$$

Weeks of Supply. Weeks of Supply means the number of weeks' supply that a company holds as on-hand inventory that can be used to fulfill orders. From an inventory cost perspective, the fewer the weeks of supply, the less the inventory cost. Weeks of inventory supply (WKS) is determined as follows:

$$WKS = \frac{\text{Average aggregate inventory value}}{\text{weekly sales at cost}} \quad (7.3)$$

Example problem 7.1: Inventory measures

A recent accounting statement of EXUL, Inc. showed that its average aggregate inventory value (which includes raw material, work-in-process inventory, and finished goods) is $10,000,000. This year's cost of goods sold is $20 million. The company operates 50 weeks a year.

a) How many weeks of supply are being held?
b) What is the number of inventory turnovers?
c) If the industry's average weeks of supply is 12 weeks and its number of inventory turns is 5, what do you think about EXUL's asset utilization performance?

Solution to example problem 7.1

a) Weeks of supply:

$$\text{WKS} = \frac{\text{Average aggregate inventory value}}{\text{weekly sales at cost}}$$

$$= \frac{\$10,000,000}{\$20,000,000/50} = 25 \text{ weeks}$$

b) Inventory turns:

$$\text{INVT} = \frac{\text{Annual cost of sales}}{\text{Average aggregate inventory value}}$$

$$= \frac{\$20,000,000}{\$10,000,000} = 2 \text{ turns}$$

c) EXUL's asset performance is not as good as the industry's average. The industry's inventory turnover rate is 5 times a year, while EXUL only has two turns. Additionally, EXUL holds a lot more inventory than the average weeks of supply of the industry. Since inventory is an asset to a company, EXUL needs to reduce its weeks of inventory supply so as to reduce inventory cost and increase inventory turns. This will improve its profit.

7.3 Managing Inventory Cost — EOQ-based Inventory Models

7.3.1 Economic order quantity

Economic Order Quantity (EOQ) minimizes total annual ordering cost and inventory holding cost through ordering an optimal lot size and achieving economies of scale. A few of the assumptions needed to implement EOQ model are:

1. Demand is fixed, known, and constant
2. Holding and ordering costs are the only relevant inventory costs
3. Holding and ordering costs are fixed, known, and constant
4. Inventory lots are received all at once
5. There are no price discounts and joint order of multiple items
6. Lead time and safety stock are not considered

As stated above, the only costs relevant to this model are the holding and ordering costs. Based on this information, a total cost equation for a given order quantity is provided as follows.

$$\text{Total Cost} = \left(\frac{D}{Q}\right)S + \left(\frac{Q}{2}\right)H \tag{7.4}$$

Where:
   Q = Order Quantity
   h = holding cost percentage
   C = cost per unit purchased
   $H = hC$, annual holding cost per unit
   S = Cost to place an order or set up cost in manufacturing
   D = Annual demand

Ordering costs or setup costs are fixed costs that are incurred each time an order is placed. Ordering costs include the managerial and clerical costs associated with ordering, as well as shipping and receiving costs. Total annual ordering costs decrease with increased order lot size.

Generally speaking, inventory holding costs are a function of capital cost, insurance, taxes, damage, and obsolescence, etc. Total holding cost increases as lot size and average cycle inventory increases.

The EOQ is found by determining the minimum cost point. The minimum cost point can be found by taking the first derivative of the total cost curve, with respect to quantity. Alternatively, making the holding cost equal the ordering cost will help to solve for the optimal quantity.

$$\frac{Q}{2}H = \frac{D}{Q}S$$

Economic order quantity (EOQ) = $\sqrt{\dfrac{2DS}{H}}$ (7.5)

Where:
Q = Order Quantity
h = holding cost percentage
C = cost per unit purchased
H = hC, annual holding cost per unit
S = Cost to place an order or set up cost in manufacturing
D = Annual demand

When using the above equation, it is important to make sure that the time units for demand and holding cost are the same. For example, if demand is expressed as annual demand, then holding cost per unit will be annual cost. The EOQ model indicates that the manager must make a fundamental trade-off between holding costs and ordering costs when selecting an order quantity. For example, when Toyota implemented the JIT system, it significantly reduced setup time, which resulted in a reduction in setup cost. A lower setup cost makes JIT's small lot size possible. Small lot sizes reduce inventory holding costs.

The Optimal Time between Orders. The optimal time between orders (TBO) or the optimal order frequency is given per year according to the following equation.

Time between Orders (TBO) = $\dfrac{EOQ}{D}$ (7.6)

Where:

D = Annual demand

TBO can be expressed in weeks or in months, as you prefer. For example, if you want TBO in weeks, multiply TBO by the number of working weeks in a year. Example problem 7.2 gives detailed instructions.

Example problem 7.2: EOQ and TBO

Quik Motors uses 50,000 gear assemblies each year and purchases them at $2.40 per unit. It costs $50 to process and receive each order and it costs $0.90 to hold one unit in inventory for a whole year.

a) What is the Economic Order Quantity?
b) How frequently will orders be placed if EOQ is used?

Solution to example problem 7.2

a) $EOQ = \sqrt{\dfrac{2DS}{H}} = \sqrt{\dfrac{2(50,000)(50)}{0.90}} = 2,357$

b) If EOQ is used, orders should be placed about every two and half weeks. Time between orders can be expressed in months and year as shown below.

$TBO_{week} = \dfrac{EOQ}{D} * (52 \text{ weeks a year}) = \dfrac{2,357}{50,000} (52) = 2.45 \text{ weeks}$

$TBO_{month} = \dfrac{EOQ}{D} * (12 \text{ month a year}) = \dfrac{2,357}{50,000} (12) = 0.57 \text{ month}$

$TBO_{year} = \dfrac{EOQ}{D} * (1 \text{ year}) = \dfrac{2,357}{50,000} (1) = 0.047 \text{ year}$

7.3.2 Inventory replenishment — Reorder point system

A reorder point system, which is also known as a Continuous Review System, is an inventory policy that tracks inventory position. Whenever inventory level reaches the reorder point, an order is placed to replenish inventory. The reorder point has two components: (i) average demand during lead-time and (ii) safety stock. The reorder point is calculated as follows.

$$R = d'L + z\sigma\sqrt{L} \qquad\qquad (7.7)$$

Where:
 R = reorder point
 L = replenish lead time
 d' = average demand
 z = z-score
 σ = standard deviation of demand per period

Example problem 7.3: Reorder point system

A distributor of TV sets is trying to set inventory policies at the warehouse for one of the TV models. Suppose that the lead time is two weeks. The distributor would like to ensure that the service level is 97%. The average weekly demand is 200 units, and there are 52 weeks in a year. The standard deviation of weekly demand is 50 units. It costs $60 to process and receive each order and it costs $1.20 to hold one unit in inventory for a whole year.

a. What is the safety stock?
b. What is the reorder point?
c. What is the order quantity?
d. How many weeks of demand (i.e. average weekly demand) can on-hand inventory at the reorder point supply?

Solution to example problem 7.3

a. For a service level of 97%, the z-score is 1.88 from the Normal Table (Table 7.5).

Safety stock = $z\sigma \sqrt{L}$ = 1.88 * 50 * $\sqrt{2}$ = 133 units

b. Reorder point = d' L + $z\sigma \sqrt{L}$ = 200(2) + 1.88 (50) $\sqrt{2}$ = 533 units

c. Order quantity: EOQ = $\sqrt{\dfrac{2DS}{H}}$ = $\sqrt{\dfrac{2(200*52)(60)}{1.20}}$ = 1,020 units

d. Weeks of demand can be supplied at the reorder point:
   533 / 200 = 2.67 weeks (average weekly demand)

Note:

- A stock-out can only occur during lead time. A stock-out occurs when demand during lead time exceeds the Reorder Point, which is the quantity available from stock during lead time.
- During a stock shortage, demand is either backordered or lost.

7.3.3 Inventory replenishment — Periodic review system

The periodic review system reviews inventory position in a fixed time interval. This inventory system simplifies delivery schedule because it follows a routine replenishing cycle. A periodic review system also has two components: (i) average demand during lead time plus fixed time interval, and (ii) safety stock. The formula is as follows:

Target Order Level (TOL) =

   average demand during lead time and order interval + safety stock

$$TOL = d' (L + OI) + z\sigma \sqrt{L + OI} \qquad (7.8)$$

Where:
   d' = average demand
   L = lead time
   OI = order interval or time between orders
   σ = standard deviation of demand per period
   z = z-score

Example problem 7.4: Periodic review system

Weekly demand for GameKid at a Game-R-Us store is normally distributed with an average weekly demand of 1,500 units and a weekly standard deviation of 200. Replenishment lead time is two weeks. The store manager wants to have a 95% cycle service level and has decided to review inventory every four weeks.

a. Using the periodic review policy, evaluate safety inventory and target order level.

b. Currently there are 1,275 units on hand. How much should the store manager order now?

Solution to example problem 7.4

a. Find the z-score for the probability of 95% from the Normal Table (Table 7.5). A 95% cycle service level has a z score of 1.645.

Safety inventory: $z\sigma \sqrt{L+OI} = 1.645\ (200)\ \sqrt{2+4} = 806$ units

$TOL = d'\ (L + OI) + z\sigma\ \sqrt{L+OI} = 1{,}500\ (2{+}4) + 806 = 9{,}806$ units

b. Number of units that should be ordered: 9,806 - 1,275 = 8,531 units

7.4 Improving Customer Service Level — Managing Safety Stock

7.4.1 Safety stock

In general, there are two reasons to keep safety stock. The first reason is to protect against demand variation. The second reason is to protect against time and quantity variation from the supply side. Suppliers may deliver orders later than the promised due dates or there may be defects in the delivered items. In these cases, the usable quantity is reduced and safety stock can be used to protect against a shortage. The amount of safety stock is the difference between the average demand during lead time and the inventory on-hand.

Safety stock is related to forecasting the error in demand. In Chapter 5, we discussed deviations between forecast demand and actual demand. This kind of deviation is inevitable and can be offset by safety stock.

7.4.2 Cycle service level

The cycle service level, a term that is widely used in supply chain management, is the probability that all demand will be satisfied from available stock during any given replenishment cycle. Stock-out is a situation that exists when demand exceeds the quantity on hand during lead-time. Cycle service level can be ensured by using safety stock. Cycle service level and safety stock are expressed as follows:

$$\text{Cycle Service Level (CSL)} = 1.0 - p \text{ (stock-out)} \qquad (7.9)$$

$$\text{Safety stock} = z * \sigma * \sqrt{\frac{L}{FP}} \qquad (7.10)$$

Where:
   z: z-score
   L: lead-time
   σ: standard deviation of demand
   FP: forecast periods

Note:

If forecast periods (FP) and lead-time are expressed in the same time unit (e.g., in weeks), then safety stock can be written as: $z*\sigma*\sqrt{L}$.

Example problem 7.5: Safety stock

How much safety stock is needed if the desired cycle service level is 98%, the lead-time is 3 weeks, the time period used for the forecast is expressed in weeks, and the standard deviation of weekly demand is 35 units?

Solution to example problem 7.5

Using the Normal Table (Table 7.5, p.237), we determine that a cycle service level of 98% has a z-score of 2.05. The forecast period is expressed in weeks.

$$\text{Safety stock} = z * \sigma * \sqrt{\frac{L}{FP}} = 2.05 * 35 * \sqrt{3/1} = 124 \text{ units}$$

7.4.3 Fill rate

Fill rate is the probability that any given randomly selected demand will be instantaneously satisfied from available inventory. Fill rate is computed using the following formula:

$$\text{Fill Rate (FR)} = 1 - \frac{E(US)}{Q} \qquad (7.11)$$

Where:

Q = order quantity or lot size

E (US) = expected units short per replenishment cycle

When demand is normally distributed, we can use Table 7.6 (p.238), the Table of Unit Normal Loss Integrals. This table converts a z-score into standard deviation's worth of expected units short. The fill rate achieved by a given amount of safety stock can be found as:

$$\text{Fill Rate (FR)} = 1 - \frac{N[z]s}{Q} \qquad (7.12)$$

Where:

E (US) = N [z] s

N [z] is z-score conversed

s = standard deviation of demand.

The value of N [z] can be found in The Table of Unit Normal Loss Integrals (Table 7.6). The safety stock needed to achieve a given fill rate can be found by calculating the necessary N [z] value:

$$N [z] = \frac{(1.0 - FR)Q}{s} \tag{7.13}$$

In this case, the z factor is needed to achieve the desired fill rate.

Example problem 7.6: Compare cycle service level and fill rate

GameKid Co. uses an order quantity of 1,000 units. The standard deviation of weekly demand is 100 units. The replenish lead time is one week. Compare the fill rate and the cycle service level.

Solution to example problem 7.6

Let's take z =1 as an example. When z = 1, we find that the cycle service level is 0.841 from Table 7.5, the Normal Table. The stock-out probability is 0.159 (1- 0.841).

Table 7.3 Cycle service level vs. fill rate.

	Cycle Service Level		Fill Rate		
z	Cycle Service Level	Probability of Stock-out	N [z]	Expected Units Short: N [z]*s	Fill Rate
0.50	0.6915	0.3085	0.1978	19.78	0.98022
1.00	0.841	0.159	0.0833	8.33	0.99167
1.50	0.933	0.067	0.0293	2.93	0.99707
1.65	0.951	0.050	0.0206	2.06	0.99794
1.96	0.975	0.025	0.0094	0.94	0.99906
2.00	0.977	0.023	0.0085	0.85	0.99915
2.33	0.990	0.010	0.0034	0.34	0.99966
3.00	0.999	0.001	0.0004	0.034	0.99996

Similarly, when z = 1, N[z] = 0.0833 from Table 7.6, the Table of Unit Normal Loss Integrals.

Standard deviation, s = 100, N[z]*s = 0.0833*100 = 8.33

Order quantity is 1,000, Fill rate = $1 - \dfrac{N[z]s}{Q} = 1 - \dfrac{8.33}{1,000} = 0.9917$

When z-score = 1, the cycle service level is 84% and the fill rate is about 99%; and the actual expected units short is about 8. For the same z factor, the fill rate is much higher than the cycle service level.

Speaking about a 69% cycle service level (when the z-score is 0.5) may make supply chain managers panic because they envision a 30% stock-out rate. Actually, 69% cycle service levels typically lead to a 98% fill rate. In general, an increase in safety stock will improve both the fill rate and the cycle service level.

7.5 Innovative Approaches to Managing Inventory

Inventory is a core component of the supply chain and has a direct impact on business performance. Today, supply chain management is transforming inventory management both in theory and practice. Vendor Managed Inventory (VIM), Everyday Low Price (EDLP), the pull system, and CPFR (to name a few) are impacting the way inventory is managed.

7.5.1 Countermeasure to bullwhip effects

The bullwhip effect is an ineffective situation that happens due to lack of information sharing and/or communication in the supply chain. The bullwhip effect uses excessive safety stock and triggers exponential movements down the supply chain. Manufacturers, wholesalers and retailers all hold extra safety stock. Incongruent information across the supply chain leads to backlog and to the building of excessive inventory in order to prevent stock-outs.

As we mentioned in Chapter 1, Chapter 5, and Chapter 6, the bullwhip effect is essentially the artificial distortion of consumer demand figures as they are transmitted back to the suppliers from the retailer. Many leading companies have developed countermeasures to address bullwhip effects. The following are a few countermeasures that can be considered to reduce bullwhip effects:

- Countermeasure 1: Reduce demand uncertainty. Provide centralized demand information on actual customer demand and focus on stock keeping unit (SKU) demand information.
- Countermeasure 2: Reduce demand variability. Possible approaches for managing customer demand variability include Everyday Low Price (EDLP), which can lead to a stable demand pattern. On the supplier side, Vendor Managed Inventory (VIM) can reduce order variability to the upstream of the supply chain.
- Countermeasure 3: Shorten lead-time. Shortening lead-time through communicating and sharing information with trading partners can lead to reduced supply lead-time.
- Countermeasure 4: Improve information accuracy. Forge strategic partnerships within the supply chain to share demand, inventory, and production information in order to reduce inventory. Provide trading partners with point-of-sale data. CPFR can be used as a vehicle for this measure.
- Countermeasure 5: Reduce order size. Reduce order cost by implementing an Electronic Data Interchange (EDI) and an inventory control information system. Use a third-party logistic service to counter full truckload economies. Order small lot sizes frequently in order to reduce inventory.

A successfully integrated supply chain is important to decrease a company's overall inventory supply costs. Information is important in achieving an equilibrium between responsiveness and efficiency in a supply chain. Bullwhip effects can be reduced if information is accurate, relevant, and timely.

7.5.2 Push-pull strategy in inventory management

In the e-Business environment, production and inventory are driven by either a push or a pull system. To push inventory down the supply chain without knowing customer needs often creates the phenomenon of sending the wrong products to the wrong location. Meanwhile, the market is starving for the right merchandise, and consequently, retailers lose money. If a product takes three weeks to replenish, the demand variability is much larger than if the same product that takes three days to replenish. In other words, the retailer could carry much less inventory if lead-time were three days instead of three weeks. As such, the pull inventory approach becomes very attractive to supply chain managers.

For a long time, John Deere, a US agricultural machinery manufacturer, used a "basic rule of thumb" to maintain 30 percent of annual sales in inventory for each dealer. But this rule of thumb did not take into account seasonal variability and the specific requirements of individual dealers. To overcome this deficiency, the commercial and consumer equipment division of John Deere decided to move from a push inventory management approach to a pull inventory management system. Since the project began in 2002, John Deere has invested in a $3-million supply-chain optimization software called SmartOps, which enables John Deere to move from a traditional push inventory management approach to a pull model. The return on investment has been dramatic. John Deere has reduced its inventory-to-sales ratio by half and the value of its inventory by $1 billion.[4]

SmartOps loaded the data from three John Deere plants and 25 dealers into its Multistage Inventory Planning and Optimization (MIPO) module. Products included everything from ride-on lawn mowers to golf course maintenance equipment, aerators, and utility tractors. By designing a model that forecasts what products should be at which locations each week, the MIPO system makes the pull inventory system possible at John Deere. Customer service levels have been improved while safety stock investment is reduced.

---

[4] Schwartz, E. (2005). "John Deere's Supply-Chain Victory." *InfoWorld* May 13, http://www.crmbuyer.com/story/43103.html.

The key purpose of converting a push system to a pull system is to better manage the amount of inventory that a supply chain carries in order to cover variability in both supply and demand.

7.5.3 Vendor managed inventory

Vendor Managed Inventory (VMI) is a coordinated approach to managing inventory in supply chain. The manufacturer is responsible for the inventory level of the wholesaler or retailer. The manufacturer receives electronic data using Electronic Data Interchange (EDI), or via the Internet, that tells him the distributor's sales and stock levels. At the same time, the manufacturer has access to the wholesaler's or retailer's inventory data and can view every item that the distributor has in inventory. Using VMI, the manufacturer is the one responsible for creating and maintaining the inventory plan, not the distributor or retailer. The purpose of VMI is to optimize inventory management in the supply chain.

Both manufacturing and service firms have applied VMI. Baxter, a hospital supply company, has developed a new type of partnership with its hospital customers. A set of clear and predetermined criteria is used to select target accounts.[5] The hospital specifies its stock requirements for each ward. An on-site Baxter employee counts the stock in each ward each day or every few days. The vendor's employees enter this information into a hand-held device and transmit it to Baxter's warehouse, where a replenishment order is derived at the warehouse. The order is placed into ward-specific containers and is delivered the following day or in a few days, directly to the ward. Finally, Baxter sends the invoice to the hospital.

The vendor managed inventory system creates a powerful new channel that has changed the ground rules for all other hospital supply companies. The stockless system was very attractive to larger accounts because hospitals prefer to outsource a non-core function. Nevertheless,

---

[5] Copacino, William C. and Byrnes, Jonathan L. S. (2002). "How to become a supply chain master." *Supply Chain Yearbook*, pp. 37-42.

the stockless system required significant delegation of account control to operations managers and multidisciplinary account teams.

7.5.4 Inventory reduction: Lean inventory system

Generally speaking, a lean inventory system has been applied across a variety of industries, such as automotive, computer, and distribution. For example, Dell Inc. has discovered the profitability of a lean inventory system by implementing a direct selling model with no pre-assembled finished goods inventory.

Toyota is another example. Before the introduction of its lean system, there were a lot of manufacturing defects at Toyota, such as large lot production, long setup time, excessive inventory, and late deliveries. Consequently, lean manufacturing management was developed as a mechanism to control these problems. Instead of producing large lots of one type of products, Toyota conducted research on setup time reduction and began to produce more diversified goods to gain efficiencies from frequent deliveries of small quantities to meet immediate demands. As a result of implementing the lean system, cycle inventory has been reduced, and so has inventory, at all levels of the organization.

An Electronic Data Interchange (EDI) is a useful tool for implementing lean operations within a company and across a supply chain. Using EDI, customers can pull off inventory by a remote center control point. It is the integration of computer systems and information sharing that makes the demand and inventory data flow within the supply network. Additionally, when implementing a lean inventory system, the trading partners in a supply chain have to develop trust and good relationships with each other because lean practice requires a stable, fast, and flexible supply of materials.

Differentiating various stock keeping units (SKU) by demand pattern is one of lean inventory management's strategies used to control costs and inventory. Traditionally, the supply chain treats every SKU the same way. Retailers place large orders of all SKUs and manufacturers produce large quantities of SKUs. Today, manufacturers produce more styles and sizes than ever before. Some are slow-selling items and some are fast movers. The risk faced by the supply chain is that it has to absorb a huge financial loss if slow-selling items are out of favor. Recently, large retail chains such as Walmart and Home Depot have initiated lean retailing strategy by requesting their manufacturers to deliver small lots to retailing stores on an ongoing basis.[6] Different SKU items should be treated with different sourcing methods. Large usage volume, low variance, and fast moving SKUs can be replenished on an ongoing basis and offshore vendors can be used to reduce costs. Long-term contracts can be negotiated with cost, delivery, and service terms. On the other hand, small usage items with large variance, or slow moving SKUs, should be taken care of by local vendors to reduce sourcing lead time. By fine-tuning inventory according to SKU-levels, supply chains can increase profits and reduce inventory risks.

7.5.5 Issues related to information technology

Most computer systems provide a lot of information. But management and employees who depend on the analyses and reports generated by computer software sometimes make critical business decisions without knowing what factors were used for calculation and how these numbers were generated.

Let us consider an example. A soft drink distributor noticed a drop in the sales of a particular soft drink called Sweeter than Sugar, but the inventory software produced reports that suggested that more inventory was needed for the product. The usage history is illustrated in Table 7.4.

From Table 7.4, we can tell that the usage for the soft drink decreased since January 2013. Yet the inventory system generated a demand for September 2013 of 138 cases. Inventory analysts described that the demand forecast was based on an average of what had been sold in the past. As such, the average demand for the product had been calculated over the entire time it had been in inventory. The item had been stocked for 16 months at the distribution center. During that time, the company had sold 2,215 cases of the product, or about 138 cases per month.

---

[6] Abernathy, Frederick H., Dunlop, John T., Hammond, Janice H. and Well, David (2000). "Control your inventory in a world of lean retailing." *Harvard Business Review*, Nov.-Dec., pp. 169-176.

Consequently, the predicted usage for September 2013 was 138 cases. The inventory manager explained that the inventory information system analyzed the need according to the way it was programmed.

Table 7.4 Soft drink usage for the past 16 months.

Year 2012	Usage	Year 2013	Usage
May	214	January	98
June	256	February	88
July	276	March	76
August	252	April	82
September	178	May	78
October	162	June	80
November	118	July	75
December	106	August	76

Let us consider another example. A distributor experienced a decrease in demand for an item. However, the inventory information system was projecting a 7% increase in demand for the item. The increase trend was calculated by comparing the sales recorded during the past three months this year to the sales recorded during the same three months of last year. Recent sales data indicated that the product had suffered a 5% decrease in the number of units sold in the past 5 months. Further investigation showed that the inventory information system was designed to calculate trend factors based on the cost of goods sold, not on the number of units sold. This year, there had been a 12% increase in the cost of goods sold over the previous year. Therefore, the computer system automatically projected an increase in demand. As a result, the distribution center had faced an overstock of wrong product.

Supply chain professionals have to realize that information systems are only as good as their designers and programmers. Human intelligence is critical to managing demand and inventory.

7.6 Enhancing Value through Inventory Management in Supply Chain

Peter Drucker describes the myth of inventory management by saying that we know little more about distribution today than Napoleon's contemporaries knew about the interior of Africa. This is why economic downturns affect inventory so much. During the contraction period of 1981-1982, GNP in the US fell by $105 billion, while inventory investment was reduced by $95 billion.[7] This means that the reduction in inventory accounts for almost 90 percent of the reduction in GNP. This phenomenon indicates the importance of inventory management to a nation's wealth.

The single most important control point of a supply chain is its markets or customers served. A supply chain can be synchronized by focusing on this control point and arranging all of the other resources around this point. Synchronizing the links of a supply chain through CPFR is a solution to treat the supply chain as one entity driven by the actual market demand. Orders are consolidated from all retailers and production is planned accordingly. Safety stock is determined by the size of variation from customer demand and production capacity; flexibility is reserved to protect large demand surges.

A supply chain's success is dependent not only on sales, but also on its ability to ensure that the right item is in stock at the right place, when a customer needs it. Better inventory control puts the supply chain in a uniquely advantageous position in the marketplace as evidenced by the best practices of Walmart. Now that we have played the Beer Game, we realize that the key to keeping costs down and improving customer service levels is to have a joint business plan for the entire supply chain, to develop a feasible sales forecast for all of the participating firms, and to develop an efficient production and delivery schedule.

---

[7] Heng, M.S.H., Wang Y.C.W. & He, X. (2005). Supply chain management and business cycles. *Supply Chain Management: An International Journal.* 10(3), pp. 157-161.

7.7 Inventory Management Performance Metrics

Regarding inventory management performance metrics, most logistics managers rate accounts receivables, return-on-assets, and cash-to-cash cycle times as the most important inventory metrics.[8] This is a good summary of how an industry evaluates inventory performance. More detailed metrics follow:

- Reduce inventory handling cost
- Implement new order fulfillment models
- Provide reliable delivery dates
- Eliminate unnecessary shipping and handling costs
- Improve order fill rate
- Improve customer service level/cycle service level
- Reduce in-transit time
- Reduce manufacturing cost
- Increase management efficiency and effectiveness

The goal is to maintain a good customer service level at a reasonable cost.

7.8 Summary

In this chapter, we have discussed the history of material management, as well as managing cycle inventory, safety stock, and customer service. The EOQ model described in this chapter can be extended to analyze various inventory management issues. The reorder point system and the periodic review system are based on EOQ model.

Many new initiatives have emerged in recent years that reflect new inventory management initiatives. Vendor managed inventory, the pull-push strategy, the lean inventory system, and the countermeasures to bullwhip effects all significantly contribute to a supply chain's overall

---

[8] Jones, Rene (2005). "Inventory control is perhaps the most powerful tool you have for containing your warehousing costs." November 26, www.trginternational.com.

business strategy. Inventory is the physical item that flows in the supply chain.

Questions for Pondering

1. We have only seen modest growth of CPFR to date despite the fact that it has been embraced by retail giants such as Walmart and Target. Why are industries hesitant to embrace such a promising practice?
2. Under what conditions should a supplier offer quantity discounts? What are the appropriate pricing schedules that a supplier should offer?
3. Does inventory reduction really reduce inventory in the entire supply chain, or do some giant trading partners push inventory back to their suppliers?

Problems

1. The annual demand for screwdrivers at Tool Mart is 2250 units. Tool Mart incurs a fixed order placement, transportation, and receiving cost of $40 each time an order is placed. Each screwdriver costs Tool Mart $10, and the retailer has a holding cost of 20 percent of the cost of the screwdriver.

   a. Evaluate the number of screwdrivers that the store manager should order in each replenishment lot.
   b. If the store manager would like to reduce the optimal lot size to 200, how much of the order cost per lot should be reduced?

2. Best Pharmacy Store uses the reorder point system to replenish inventory. It operates 52 weeks a year. One of the drugs it sells has the following characteristics:

Annual demand: 260 cases
Ordering cost: $35 / per order
Unit cost: $100 per case
On-hand inventory: 25 cases
Holding cost: 20 % of the unit cost
Lead-time: 3 weeks
Cycle service level: 95%
Standard deviation of weekly demand: 3 cases

a. Calculate the EOQ for this drug.
b. Calculate the safety stock.
c. What is the reorder point?
d. A withdrawal of 5 cases just occurred. Is it time to reorder? If so, how much should be ordered?
e. What is the cost implication if the store replaces the current inventory policy (order quantity = 50 units, and reorder point = 28 units) with the reorder point policy you have just developed in parts a, b and c?

3. A grocery store sells a special brand of cheese that has the following characteristics:

Annual demand = 3,640 units
Order quantity = 280 units
Unit purchasing cost = $25.65
Inventory holding cost = 25% of unit cost
Standard deviation of weekly demand 30 units
The store operates 52 weeks a year

a. What reorder point will yield a service level of 85%, 90%, 95%, and 99%?
b. What will be the fill rate if cycle service levels are 85%, 90%, 95%, and 99% respectively?
c. Consider the trade-off between inventory costs and customer satisfaction.

4. A recent accounting statement of the Quik Machine Company showed the raw material, work-in-process inventory, and finished goods inventory to be $1,020,000. This year's cost of sales is $3 million. The company operates 52 weeks per year.

   a. How many weeks of supply are being held?
   b. What is the inventory turns?
   c. Comment on Quik Machine's inventory management performance.

Table 7.5. Normal distribution table.

z	0.00	0.01	0.02	0.03	0.04	0.05	0.06	0.07	0.08	0.09
0.0	0.5000	0.5040	0.5080	0.5120	0.5160	0.5199	0.5239	0.5279	0.5319	0.5359
0.1	0.5398	0.5438	0.5478	0.5517	0.5557	0.5596	0.5636	0.5675	0.5714	0.5753
0.2	0.5793	0.5832	0.5871	0.5910	0.5948	0.5987	0.6026	0.6064	0.6103	0.6141
0.3	0.6179	0.6217	0.6255	0.6293	0.6331	0.6368	0.6406	0.6443	0.6480	0.6517
0.4	0.6554	0.6591	0.6628	0.6664	0.6700	0.6736	0.6772	0.6808	0.6844	0.6879
0.5	0.6915	0.6950	0.6985	0.7019	0.7054	0.7088	0.7123	0.7157	0.7190	0.7224
0.6	0.7257	0.7291	0.7324	0.7357	0.7389	0.7422	0.7454	0.7486	0.7517	0.7549
0.7	0.7580	0.7611	0.7642	0.7673	0.7704	0.7734	0.7764	0.7794	0.7823	0.7852
0.8	0.7881	0.7910	0.7939	0.7967	0.7995	0.8023	0.8051	0.8078	0.8106	0.8133
0.9	0.8159	0.8186	0.8212	0.8238	0.8264	0.8289	0.8315	0.8340	0.8365	0.8389
1.0	0.8413	0.8438	0.8461	0.8485	0.8508	0.8531	0.8554	0.8577	0.8599	0.8621
1.1	0.8643	0.8665	0.8686	0.8708	0.8729	0.8749	0.8770	0.8790	0.8810	0.8830
1.2	0.8849	0.8869	0.8888	0.8907	0.8925	0.8944	0.8962	0.8980	0.8997	0.9015
1.3	0.9032	0.9049	0.9066	0.9082	0.9099	0.9115	0.9131	0.9147	0.9162	0.9177
1.4	0.9192	0.9207	0.9222	0.9236	0.9251	0.9265	0.9279	0.9292	0.9306	0.9319
1.5	0.9332	0.9345	0.9357	0.9370	0.9382	0.9394	0.9406	0.9418	0.9429	0.9441
1.6	0.9452	0.9463	0.9474	0.9484	0.9495	0.9505	0.9515	0.9525	0.9535	0.9545
1.7	0.9554	0.9564	0.9573	0.9582	0.9591	0.9599	0.9608	0.9616	0.9625	0.9633
1.8	0.9641	0.9649	0.9656	0.9664	0.9671	0.9678	0.9686	0.9693	0.9699	0.9706
1.9	0.9713	0.9719	0.9726	0.9732	0.9738	0.9744	0.9750	0.9756	0.9761	0.9767
2.0	0.9772	0.9778	0.9783	0.9788	0.9793	0.9798	0.9803	0.9808	0.9812	0.9817
2.1	0.9821	0.9826	0.9830	0.9834	0.9838	0.9842	0.9846	0.9850	0.9854	0.9857
2.2	0.9861	0.9864	0.9868	0.9871	0.9875	0.9878	0.9881	0.9884	0.9887	0.9890
2.3	0.9893	0.9896	0.9898	0.9901	0.9904	0.9906	0.9909	0.9911	0.9913	0.9916
2.4	0.9918	0.9920	0.9922	0.9925	0.9927	0.9929	0.9931	0.9932	0.9934	0.9936
2.5	0.9938	0.9940	0.9941	0.9943	0.9945	0.9946	0.9948	0.9949	0.9951	0.9952
2.6	0.9953	0.9955	0.9956	0.9957	0.9959	0.9960	0.9961	0.9962	0.9963	0.9964
2.7	0.9965	0.9966	0.9967	0.9968	0.9969	0.9970	0.9971	0.9972	0.9973	0.9974
2.8	0.9974	0.9975	0.9976	0.9977	0.9977	0.9978	0.9979	0.9979	0.9980	0.9981
2.9	0.9981	0.9982	0.9982	0.9983	0.9984	0.9984	0.9985	0.9985	0.9986	0.9986
3.0	0.9987	0.9987	0.9987	0.9988	0.9988	0.9989	0.9989	0.9989	0.9990	0.9990
3.1	0.9990	0.9991	0.9991	0.9991	0.9992	0.9992	0.9992	0.9992	0.9993	0.9993
3.2	0.9993	0.9993	0.9994	0.9994	0.9994	0.9994	0.9994	0.9995	0.9995	0.9995
3.3	0.9995	0.9995	0.9995	0.9996	0.9996	0.9996	0.9996	0.9996	0.9996	0.9997

Table 7.6. Unit normal loss integrals.

{z Factor / N[z] Conversion}[9]

z	.00	.01	.02	.03	.04	.05	.06	.07	.08	.09
0.0	.3989	.3940	.3890	.3841	.3793	.3744	.3697	.3649	.3602	.3556
0.1	.3509	.3464	.3418	.3373	.3328	.3284	.3240	.3197	.3154	.3111
0.2	.3069	.3027	.2986	.2944	.2904	.2863	.2824	.2784	.2745	.2706
0.3	.2668	.2630	.2592	.2555	.2518	.2481	.2445	.2409	.2374	.2339
0.4	.2304	.2270	.2236	.2203	.2169	.2137	.2104	.2072	.2040	.2009
0.5	.1978	.1947	.1917	.1887	.1857	.1828	.1799	.1771	.1742	.1714
0.6	.1687	.1659	.1633	.1606	.1580	.1554	.1528	.1503	.1478	.1453
0.7	.1429	.1405	.1381	.1358	.1334	.1312	.1289	.1267	.1245	.1223
0.8	.1202	.1181	.1160	.1140	.1120	.1100	.1080	.1061	.1042	.1023
0.9	.1004	.0986	.0968	.0950	.0933	.0916	.0899	.0882	.0865	.0849
1.0	.0833	.0817	.0802	.0787	.0772	.0757	.0742	.0728	.0714	.0700
1.1	.0686	.0673	.0660	.0647	.0634	.0621	.0609	.0596	.0584	.0573
1.2	.0561	.0550	.0538	.0527	.0517	.0506	.0495	.0485	.0475	.0465
1.3	.0455	.0446	.0436	.0427	.0418	.0409	.0400	.0392	.0383	.0375
1.4	.0367	.0359	.0351	.0343	.0336	.0328	.0321	.0314	.0307	.0300
1.5	.0293	.0287	.0280	.0274	.0267	.0261	.0255	.0249	.0244	.0238
1.6	.0232	.0227	.0222	.0217	.0211	.0206	.0202	.0197	.0192	.0187
1.7	.0183	.0179	.0174	.0170	.0166	.0162	.0158	.0154	.0150	.0146
1.8	.0143	.0139	.0136	.0132	.0129	.0126	.0123	.0120	.0116	.0113
1.9	.0111	.0108	.0105	.0102	.0100	.0097	.0094	.0092	.0090	.0087
2.0	.0085	.0083	.0081	.0078	.0076	.0074	.0072	.0070	.0068	.0067
2.1	.0065	.0063	.0061	.0060	.0058	.0056	.0055	.0053	.0052	.0050
2.2	.0049	.0048	.0046	.0045	.0044	.0042	.0041	.0040	.0039	.0038
2.3	.0037	.0036	.0035	.0034	.0033	.0032	.0031	.0030	.0029	.0028
2.4	.0027	.0026	.0026	.0025	.0024	.0023	.0023	.0022	.0021	.0021
2.5	.0020	.0019	.0019	.0018	.0018	.0017	.0017	.0016	.0016	.0015
3.0	.0004	.0004	.0004	.0003	.0003	.0003	.0003	.0003	.0003	.0003

[9] The value in this table can be approximated from $N[z] = e^{[-0.92-1.19(z)-0.37z^2]}$ when z is positive.

References

Amaral, J. (2005). "How 'rough-cut' analysis smoothes HP's supply chain." *Supply Chain Management Review*, 9(6), 38-45.

Chopra, S. and Meindle, P. (2013). Supply Chain Management, Prentice Hall: New Jersey.

Fredendall, Lawrence D. and Hill, E. (2001). Basics of Supply Chain Management. The St. Lucie Press: New York.

Krajewski, L.J. & Ritzman, L.P. (2002). Operations Management, 6th edition, Prentice Hall: New Jersey.

Master, J. (1994). Logistic Management, Course Packet, Ohio State University, Columbus, Ohio.

Schreibfeder, Jon (2006). "Do You Know Where Your Information Comes From?" Effective Inventory Management, Inc. Date of access: March 2007. http://www.effectiveinventory.com

Simchi-Levi, D., P. Kaminsky, et al. (2003). Designing and Managing the Supply Chain. 2nd edition, New York, McGraw-Hill

Zipkin, P. (2000). Foundation of Inventory Management. McGraw-Hill: Boston.

Date of access: March 2007. http://www.vendormanagedinventory.com

Supplement 7.1

Quantity Discount

One of the assumptions of the EOQ model is that material costs remain constant regardless of the quantity purchased. Now, we want to explore the impact of the quantity discount by relaxing the no-quantity-discount assumption of the EOQ model.

Two commonly used lot size-based discount schemes are:

(1) All unit quantity discount
(2) Marginal unit quantity discount

(1) *All-unit quantity discounts*

A quantity discount is a common practice in a supply chain. For example, a manufacturer may offer $10 per unit for an order between 1-49 units, $9.80 per unit for an order between 50-99 units, and $9.60 per unit for an order of 100 units or more.

The EOQ model is applied to determine the order quantity with respect to each price break quantity. The EOQ at a particular price break level may be feasible, but it may not have the lowest total cost as compared to the total cost at other price levels. In this case, the lowest total cost option is chosen. The solution procedure is as follows:

Step 1: Compute the EOQ for each price break, starting with the lowest price, until a feasible EOQ is found. The feasible EOQ is the one that is within the price break quantity.

Step 2: If the first feasible EOQ is for the lowest price break, then the lot size is the optimal lot size. Otherwise, compute the total cost for the first feasible lot size and the total cost of each lot size with a lower price break. Then settle on the lot size that minimizes the overall cost.

The total costs are a function of the material acquisition costs, the holding costs, and the ordering cost. Each of these costs varies with lot size Q.

The total cost computation for quantity discount is shown in Equation 7.14.

$$\text{Total cost} = \left(\frac{Q}{2}\right)H + \left(\frac{D}{Q}\right)S + PD \qquad (7.14)$$

Where:

Q = Order Quantity

H = hC, annual holding cost per unit; h is holding cost percentage & C is cost per unit purchased

S = Cost to place an order or set up cost in manufacturing / per order

D = Annual demand

P = Purchasing cost per unit

Example problem: All-unit quantity discount

Toy Mall is an online retailer of toys. GameKid represents a significant percentage of its sales. Demand for GameKid is 2,000 per month. Toy Mall incurs a fixed order placement, transportation, and receiving costs of $300 each time an order for GameKid is placed with the manufacturer. Toy Mall incurs a holding cost of 20 percent of the purchasing price. The price charged by the manufacturer varies according to the following all-unit discount-pricing schedule. Evaluate the number of GameKid units that the Toy Mall manager should order in each lot.

Order Quantity	Unit Price
0 up to 1,000	$ 30.00
1,000 up to 2,000	$ 29.00
2,000 or more	$ 28.00

The solution to this problem is presented in an Excel spreadsheet format on the next two pages. The company should take the $28 unit price approach because this option generates the lowest total cost.

Solution to example problem: All-unit quantity discount in Excel format

	A	B	C	D
1	All Units Quantity Discount			
2				
3	Demand = 2,000/month		2,000	
4	Operating 12 mon / year		12	
5	Annual demand (D)		24000	
6	Ordering cost (S)		$300	
7	Holding cost (h)		0.2	
8				
9	Order Quantity	Unit Price (C_i)		
10	0	$30		
11	1,000	$29		
12	2,000	$28		
13				
14	Index	i=2	i=1	i=0
15	C_i	$28	$29	$30
16	Price Break Q	2,000	1,000	0
17	EOQ[C_i]	1,604	1,576	1,549
18	Q_{ci}	2,000	1,576	1,549
19	DC_i	672,000	696,000	720,000
20	$S*(D/Q_{ci})$	3,600	4,569	4,648
21	$hC_i(Q_{ci}/2)$	5,600	4,569	4,648
22	$TC[Q_{ci}]$	681,200	705,139	729,295

Excel Codes for All Units Quantity Discount:

	A	B	C	D
1	All Units Quantity Discount			
2				
3	Demand = 2,000/month	2000		
4	Operating 12 mon / year	12		
5	Annual demand (D)	=C3*C4		
6	Ordering cost (S)	300		
7	Holding cost (h)	0.2		
8				
9	Order Quantity	Unit Price (C_i)		
10	0	30		
11	1000	29		
12	2000	28		
13				
14	Index	i=2	i=1	i=0
15	C_i	28	29	30
16	Price Break Q	=A12	=A11	=A10
17	EOQ[C_i]	=SQRT((2*$C$5*$C$6/($C$7*B12)))	=SQRT((2*$C$5*$C$6/($C$7*B11)))	=SQRT((2*$C$5*$C$6)/($C$7*B10))
18	Q_{di}	=MAX(B16:B17)	=MAX(C16:C17)	=MAX(D16:D17)
19	DC_i	=$C$5*B15	=$C$5*C15	=$C$5*D15
20	S*(D/Q_{di})	=$C$6*($C$5/B18)	=$C$6*($C$5/C18)	=$C$6*($C$5/D18)
21	hC_i(Q_{di}/2)	=($C$7*B15)*(B18/2)	=($C$7*C15)*(C18/2)	=($C$7*D15)*(D18/2)
22	TC[Q_{di}]	=SUM(B19:B21)	=SUM(C19:C21)	=SUM(D19:D21)

(2) *Marginal unit quantity discount*

A marginal unit quantity discount is another price discount method in a supply chain. For example, a manufacturer may offer $10 per unit for an order between 1-49 units; $9.80 per unit for the range of 50-99units; or $9.60 per unit starting from unit 100 or more.

The objective is to maximize profit, which, in this case, is equivalent to minimizing the total cost. The solution procedure evaluates the optimal lot size for each marginal price and then settles on the lot size that minimizes the overall cost.

The solution procedure is as follows:

Step 1: Compute the marginal cost at each price break.

Step 2: Compute the EOQ for each price break, including the marginal cost computed in Step 1 as part of the ordering cost. Start with the lowest price until a feasible EOQ is found. The feasible EOQ is the one that is within the price break quantity.

Step 3: Compute the average unit price using the EOQ for each feasible price break, including the marginal cost.

$$\text{Average unit price} = \frac{C_i(EOQ_{ci}) + MC_i}{EOQ_{ci}} \qquad (7.15)$$

Where:

C_i = price break cost

MC_i = marginal cost associates with price break

Step 4: Compute the total cost for the feasible lot size within the price break using formula (7.15), and then settle on the lot size that minimizes the overall cost.

Example problem: Marginal unit discount

Toy Mall is an online retailer of toys. GameKid represents a significant percentage of its sales. Demand for GameKid is 3,000 per month. Toy Mall incurs a fixed order placement, transportation, and receiving cost of $350 each time an order for GameKid is placed with the manufacturer. Toy Mall incurs a holding cost of 20 percent. The price charged by the manufacturer varies according to the following marginal unit's discount-pricing schedule.

Evaluate the number of GameKid units that the Toy Mall manager should order in each lot.

Order Quantity	Marginal Unit Price
0 up to 1,000	$ 65.00
1,000 up to 2,000	$ 60.00
2,000 and more	$ 55.00

The solution to this problem is presented in Excel spreadsheet format on the next two pages. The company should take the $55 unit price approach because this option generates the lowest total cost.

Solution to marginal unit discount in Excel format:

	A	B	C	D
1	Marginal Unit Discount Algorithem			
2				
3	Demand = 3,000/mon		3000	
4	Operating 12 mon / year		12	
5	Annual demand (D)		36000	
6	Ordering cost, S		350	
7	Holding cost, h		0.2	
8				
9	Order Quantity	Unit Price		
10	0	$65		
11	1,000	$60		
12	2,000	$55		
13				
14	Index	i=2	i=1	i=0
15	Purchase cost (C_i)	$55	$60	$65
16	Price break quantity (Q_i)	2,000	1,000	0
17	Fixed cost penalty (F_i)	$15,000	$5,000	$0
18	EOQ$[C_i]$	10,024	5,666	1,392
19	Order quantity (Q_{ci})	10,024	0	0
20	Average unit cost (Mci)	56.50		
21	Annual purchase cost (MCi * D)	2,033,873		
22	Annual order cost $[S*(D/Q_{ci})]$	1,257		
23	Annual holding cost $[(hMC_i)* (Q_{ci}/2)]$	56,630		
24	Total cost $[Q_{ci}]$	2,091,760		

Notes:

Row 17: The fixed cost penalty due to the incremental nature of the discount. $F_0 = 0$.

Row 18: The EOQ computed at C_i with Fi included as an ordering cost.

Row 19: If row 18 is within the interval of the discount, Row 19 = Row 18. Otherwise, Row 19 = 0, and stop.

Row 20: The average unit cost given the order size is
$$MC_i = [(C_i * Q_i) + F_i] / Q_i.$$

Solution to marginal unit discount in Excel codes:

	A	B	C	D
1	Marginal Unit Discount Algorithm			
2				
3	Demand = 3,000/mon	3000		
4	Operating 12 mon./year	12		
5	Annual demand (D)	=C3*C4		
6	Ordering cost, S	350		
7	Holding cost, h	0.2		
8				
9	Order Quantity	Unit Price (C_i)		
10	0	65		
11	1000	60		
12	2000	55		
13				
14	Index	i=2	i=1	i=0
15	Purchase cost (C_i)	=B12	=B11	=B10
16	Price break quantity (Q_i)	=A12	=A11	=A10
17	Fixed cost penalty (F_i)	=C17+(C15-B15)*B16	=B16+(D15-C15)*C16	0
18	EOQ(C_i)	=SQRT((2*$C$5*($C$6+B17))/($C$7*B15))	=SQRT((2*$C$5*($C$6+C17))/($C$7*B11))	=SQRT((2*$C$5*($C$6+D17))/($C$7*B10))
19	Order quantity (Q_{i})	=IF(B18=B16,B18)	=IF(C16<C18<B16,C18,0)	=IF(D16<D18<C16,D18,0)
20	Average unit cost (MC_i)	=(B15*B19+B17)/B19		
21	Annual purchase cost $(MC_i * D)$	=B20*C5		
22	Annual order cost $[S*(D/Q_{01})]$	=C6*(C5/B19)		
23	Annual holding cost $[(hMC_i)*(Q_{01}/2)]$	=($C$7*B20)*(B19/2)		
24	Total cost $[Q_{01}]$	=SUM(B21:B23)		

Part 4

Logistics Network Design and Transportation

Chapter 8
Logistics Network Design and Distribution

Chapter 9
Transportation Service and Distribution System

Chapter 8

Logistics Network Design and Distribution

8.1 Logistics in Supply Chain Management

The logistics network consists of the suppliers, the manufacturer, the distributor, the retailer, and the users, as depicted in Fig. 8.1. The purpose of an integrated logistics network in a supply chain is to fulfill customer orders by providing place utility to deliver products and services to end users. Logistics is now being considered more than merely an opportunity to minimize cost; it has developed into a core component of fulfilling customer orders in supply chain management.

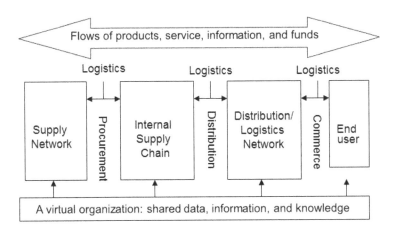

Fig. 8.1 Logistics network.

Place utility is achieved by managing a number of the key functions of a supply chain. These functions include the following:

- Demand management
- Inventory management
- Logistics network design
- Transportation
- Warehousing
- Order processing and fulfillment
- Information management
- Effective customer service

To configure a logistics network in a supply chain, data, analytical techniques, computer software, and information systems are needed. The process that is applied to configure a logistics network determines the material and service flows.

Two important areas of logistics network design in an e-Business environment are the global logistics network and the reverse logistics network. The following two sections discuss these two issues.

8.1.1 Facility configuration of global supply chain

A supply chain is a network of suppliers, manufacturing plants, distribution centers, and retail stores that transform raw materials, parts, and components into finished products, and then distribute these products to customers. As the global competition gets more and more fierce, many companies are reengineering their supply chains by expanding their supply network worldwide to seek the most cost-effective suppliers or to be closer to the markets that they serve.

For example, McDonald's uses suppliers all over the world for their core product, the hamburger. A Big Mac sold in Saudi Arabia uses lettuce from Holland, cheese from New Zealand, beef from Spain, onions and pickles from the United States, sugar and oil from Brazil, buns from Saudi Arabia, and packaging from Germany.[1] Fig. 8.2 presents an example of the McDonald's global supply chain network, where raw material is procured from vendors worldwide, transported to distribution

---

[1] Based on the information provided by "What is operations management," Operations Management Video Series (2005). McGraw-Hill Company, Inc.

centers, and then assembled into the final product served to McDonald's customers. Such a logistics network is complicated and sophisticated in terms of quality control, delivery timing, quantity scheduling, and cost analysis.

1. Saudi Arab	5. United States
2. Holland	6. Brazil
3. New Zealand	7. Germany
4. Spain	

Fig. 8.2 The McDonald's Saudi Arabia supply network.

Suppliers within the McDonald's system play a critical role in its success. McDonald's serves over 45 million customers and is open every day of the year. As such, it is important for the company to locate reliable and quality suppliers. In the US, McDonald's strategically locates its 40 distribution centers so that more than 12,000 restaurants in the country have convenient access to these distribution centers.[2]

---

[2] Source: Date of access: June 2006. http://www.mcdonalds.com.
http://www.aboutmcdonalds.com/mcd/investors/annual_reports.html.

As industries structure and restructure their product lines and market shares, they rebalance their logistics networks to reflect the changes in production and market needs. For example, over the past 20 years, the US auto industry has reconfigured its facility network. In 2006, both Ford and General Motors announced plans to close down some of their production facilities in the US. Throughout 2008, Ford closed down its St. Louis (Missouri) assembly plant, its Atlanta assembly plant, its Wixom (Michigan) assembly plant, its Batavia (Ohio) Transmission plant, the Windsor Casting plant (Ontario, Canada), and the Norfolk (Virginia) assembly plant. These restructuring plans further shaped the logistics network for the auto industry. Recently, American brand cars such as the Ford Fusion are made in Mexico, while Japanese brand cars such as Toyota Camry and Honda Civic are made in the US. When Toyota established its product plant in Kentucky, it also established a network of supply facilities around its assembly factory.

In June 2005, Toyota announced that it would build a new plant in Woodstock, Ontario to produce RAV4 sport utility vehicle to serve the North American market. With the establishment of this new assembly factory, Toyota announced an expansion of Canadian Autoparts Toyota, Inc. in Delta, British Columbia.[3] In his discussion of the new investment via videotape broadcast, Katsuaki Watanabe, the president of Toyota Motor Corporation, noted that twenty years ago, Toyota management made two expansion decisions:

(i) to make a sweeping commitment to manufacturing in North America and
(ii) to make Canada a core part of that commitment. This expansion has strengthened Toyota's ties with its suppliers across North America and has reconfigured its auto supply facilities and supply networks in North America.

---

[3] "Toyota to expand in Canada; first new site for auto assembly plant in Canada in almost 20 years." Date of access: June 2006.
http://origin.www.toyota.com/about/news/manufacturing/2006/02/10-1-tmmna.html.

8.1.2 Reverse logistics network

Recovery, remanufacturing, reuse and recycling of used products and materials have become issues of growing importance. Though reuse or remanufacturing is not a new phenomenon, developing a reverse logistics network is a challenging topic which currently faces supply chain professionals. Some commonly accepted reasons for product recovery include legislative pressures on the environment, commercial benefits, and economic viability.

Implementation of product recovery requires the establishment of a backward logistics network for the arising flows of used and recovered products. Physical locations, facilities, and transportation links need to be chosen to transfer used products from their former users to a producer and then on to future markets. In a reverse logistics context, however, a standard set of models has not yet been established. The question that arises here is whether or not traditional forward approaches can adequately be extended to a backward logistics network in order to recover products.

Fleischmann et al. briefly discussed a few case studies about recovery networks in a variety of industries including carpet recycling, electronics remanufacturing, reusable packages, sand recycling from demolition waste, and the recycling of by-products from steel production.[4] For example, the design of a large-scale European recycling network for carpet waste is supported with a joint effort from both chemical companies and the European carpet industry. Through the network, used carpet is collected, sorted, and reprocessed for material recovery. In this case, large volume is identified as a critical factor for product recovery.

The electronics industry is one of the most prominent sectors in product recovery. Printer producers such as HP and Xerox have created a backward logistics structure for reverse channel functions such as collection, inspection, and remanufacturing. For example, a few years ago, some Uniden cordless phones with a retail price of $34.98 each

---

[4] Fleischmann, Moritz, Beullens, Patrick, Bloemhof-Ruwaard, Jacqueline M, Van Wassenhove, Luk N. (2001). "The impact of product recovery on logistics network design," *Production and Operations Management*, 10(2), pp. 156-173.

were sold to a salvage company for refurbishing. These phones were then sold for $48 in Mexico retail stores.

A sand recycling network is initiated by a consortium of construction waste processing companies in the Netherlands. Since sand is polluted from the demolition process, it needs to be cleaned before it can be reused for road construction. Thus, the design of a logistics network should include cleaning facilities and storage locations.

The recovery process is a closed loop structure. Fig. 8.3 depicts an example of a printer recovery process. The supply network provides application-specific integrated circuits (ASIC), cartridges and PC boards. The manufacturer assembles the printer and distribution centers all over the world deliver the products to various customer zones. After the product is used or worn out, it is sent back through the reversed pipeline for remanufacturing. The typical phases included in the transition from the disposer to the reuse market include collection, sorting, inspection, reprocessing, redistribution, and finally back to the disposal phase. This role of recovery networks as an intermediate between the disposal and reuse markets gives rise to strong coordination between supply and demand. These unique characteristics should be taken into consideration when designing a product recovery logistics network.

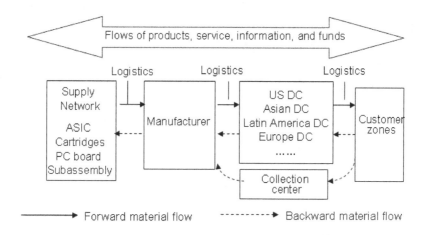

Fig. 8.3 Product recovery logistics network.

8.1.3 Reverse logistics network for used battery recycling

The consumption of industrial or nonindustrial batteries has been increasing year after year. If the used batteries are not properly disposed, the hazardous material they contain can lead to environmental pollution and affect human health. According to the battery industry statistics, for every 1 billion batteries produced, 16 thousand tons of metal zinc, 23 thousand tons of manganese dioxide, 210 tons of other metals, 4,300 tons of carbon rod, and 7,900 tons of ammonium chloride will need to be used.[5] Most of these components are valuable metal substances that can be recycled.

Reverse logistics of the used batteries not only protects the environment, but also promotes the important economic value of the used batteries. Fig. 8.4 gives an example of a used battery reverse logistics network, which involves more participants, a broader region, and higher randomness than a forward logistics network.

First, used batteries are collected and classified. The commonly used processing methods for used batteries include physically breaking down, followed by chemical decomposition such as smelting, direct acid-leaching and crystallizing, roasting acid-leaching and electrolyzing. After the physical break-down and chemical decomposition, the outer plastic wrapping and part of the zinc cover can be reused. Finally, various kinds of liquid and solid waste substances generated during the reverse logistics process will be disposed in an environmental responsible way.

In the entire reverse logistics process, information sharing, transaction coordination, decision support, and the allocation of resources are inseparable from the support of the information systems. Although, the material flow receives the most important attention, integrating the information flow with the reverse flow of materials is significantly important in order to realize the environmental and economic value of the used batteries.[6]

---

[5] Bai, Y., Bai, Q., Wu, P. (2002). "Recycling of used batteries." *Chem Eng*, 9, pp. 34-35.

[6] Shi, X., Li, L., Yang, L., Li, Z., Choi, J.Y. (2012). Information flow in reverse logistics: an industrial information integration study, *Information Technology and Management*, 13(4), pp. 217-232.

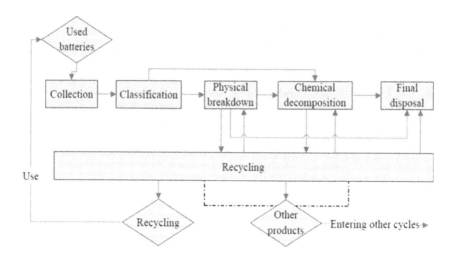

Fig. 8.4 Reverse logistics network of used batteries.

Source: Shi, X., Li, L., Yang, L., Li, Z., Choi, J.Y. (2012). Information flow in reverse logistics: an industrial information integration study, *Information Technology and Mgt.*, 13(4), pp. 217-232; with permission of authors.

8.2 Data for Logistics Network Planning

8.2.1 Data sources

Data internal and external to the firm can be used to plan a logistics network. Examples of major sources include business operating data files stored in an information system, accounts reports, logistic research, published information of the industry, previous experience, and predictions. Additionally, the government also issues some statistics about logistics and transportation. For example, the US Department of Transportation publishes regulatory impact analysis, performance and accountability reports. More data and statistics about logistic issues are released by the Bureau of Transportation.

8.2.2 Data checklist

Designing a logistics network requires a lot of business data. A list of data required is suggested below. Some data is organization or industry specific, other data can be generalized from published data sources.

- Customer demand: products, order time, order size, order frequency, etc.
- Order processing: transit time, order transmittal times, order delivery information, order fill rate, etc.
- Customer service requirements: lead time, customer service level, fill rate, etc.
- Product: product families, product line, stock keeping unit (SKU), product weight, product size, product maintenance condition (such as temperature required), etc.
- Locations: location of customers, retailers, service providers, suppliers, manufacturers, wholesalers, call centers, and distribution centers, etc.
- Transportation: transportation rate or cost by mode, road condition, traffic hours, one way street information, inbound and outbound volume, etc.
- Facility costs: capital cost, facility rate or costs, utility, labor, insurance, operating cost, inventory holding cost, etc.
- Material handling costs: loading and unloading labor costs, dock facility cost, etc.

8.3 Techniques for Logistics Network Configuration

After gathering relevant data and information, the process for searching the best network design starts. This process is complicated and usually is assisted by mathematical modeling and computer simulation. Commonly applied techniques used in the industry include:

- Optimization models
- Computer simulation
- Heuristics models

• Expert systems and decision support systems

8.3.1 Optimization model

Optimization models include linear programming, nonlinear programming, integer programming, dynamic programming models, calculus models, enumeration and sequencing models. These models provide the best solutions mathematically. The limitation of applying optimization models in network design is that they deal with static models such as annual demand or average demand and do not take into consideration demand and supply changes over time.

8.3.2 Computer simulation

Simulation models take into account the dynamics of a logistics network for a specific design and its performance. Simulating a logistics network involves replicating various constraints and cost structures, visualizing the proposed network system, simulating what-if questions regarding the logistics network, exploring operational issues, and integrating available resources. This replication is usually stochastic in nature and is done by the means of mathematical relationship. When the design of a logistics network requires a substantial amount of details and optimization solutions are impossible, simulation is a reasonable option.

8.3.3 Heuristics model

Heuristic models integrate simulation approach and optimization method to find a feasible solution for a complex logistics network design problem. This approach is applied to solve some of the most difficult logistics network problems when too many factors need to be compromised to satisfy the requirements of optimization models. Heuristics does not guarantee an optimal solution but can generate feasible and satisfactory network configuration solutions.

8.3.4 Expert systems and decision support systems

The designers of a logistics network may have accumulated a lot of experience as to how the problem should be solved. These experts can process incomplete data, fuzzy and partial information, as well as unstructured problems. Such experience and knowledge often transcends sophisticated mathematical models and can be used to generate solutions better than using simulation, optimization method, or heuristics models alone.

A decision support system and/or an expert system integrate data, information, and techniques with the aid of computer programs to generate network configuration solutions. Managers use the information to make logistics network configuration decisions.

8.4 Facility Location and Configuration

We now move to the issue of a strategic plan for the logistics network configuration. Before doing this we need to make sure that relevant data are collected and a customer service level is determined.

Alfred Weber suggests that the weight of material can affect the logistics network design. For example, steel making is a weight loss process. Therefore, the facility that processes the raw material should be located close to the source of raw material so as to reduce transportation costs. Soft drink production, on the other hand, is a weight gaining process. Therefore, soft drink production should be placed close to the market so as to save transportation costs.

8.4.1 Single facility location

8.4.1.1 The center of gravity method

One of the most popular methods used to locate a single facility is the center of gravity method. This method only considers transportation cost in the design process. The transportation cost increases linearly as the quantity gets larger. The objective is to find a centralized location that will minimize the total transportation cost. The minimization formula is expressed as follows.

(1) Collect data on the coordinate points of supply and the demand points, the quantity to be moved, and the linear transportation rate per weight unit per mile.

(2) Get an estimate of x', y', and d_i using the following formulas:

$$x' = \frac{\sum_{i=1}^{n} \dfrac{Q_i c_i x_i}{d_i}}{\sum_{i=1}^{n} \dfrac{Q_i c_i}{d_i}} \qquad (8.1)$$

$$y' = \frac{\sum_{i=1}^{n} \dfrac{Q_i c_i y_i}{d_i}}{\sum_{i=1}^{n} \dfrac{Q_i c_i}{d_i}} \qquad (8.2)$$

$$d_i = \sqrt{(x_i - x')^2 + (y_i - y')^2} \qquad (8.3)$$

Where:

x' and y' = estimated coordinates for the located facility

x_i and y_i = coordinates of supply source and markets

d_i = distance from the facility to market i

c_i = freight rate per unit/mile from the facility to market i

Q_i = freight volume to be shipped from the facility to market i

TC = total transportation cost from the distribution center to all the markets

(3) Compute the total cost:

$$\text{Min TC} = \sum_{i=1}^{n} Q_i c_i d_i \qquad (8.4)$$

(4) Substitute the current location estimates with the newly computed estimates, $x_i = x'$, $y_i = y'$, TC = TC'. Repeat steps 2 and 4 until the

newly computed location (x', y') is almost the same as the current (x_i, y_i). Now stop.

Example problem 8.1: The center of gravity method

The window blinds produced by Zerk, Inc. serve three markets. Recently, the company wants to build a new warehouse in a location that will minimize its total transportation cost. Coordinate points, freight volume, and transportation rates are given in Table 8.1.

Table 8.1 The center of gravity method.

Row		Coordinates			
	Site	x_i	y_i	Freight volume	Freight rate cost
1					
2	Plant	8	10	1000	0.25
3	Market A	12	9.5	250	0.5
4	Market B	11	7.5	350	0.5
5	Market C	6	5	400	0.5

Solution to example problem 8.1 the center of gravity method

An Excel spreadsheet is employed to solve this problem. The detailed result is given in Table 8.2 and the Excel spreadsheet codes are provided in Table 8.3.

Use coordinates (0, 0) as the initial warehouse location to start the problem. Let's take row 2 (plant) of Table 8.2 as an example. We start with the estimation of $x^0 = 0$ and $y^0 = 0$ (in Column B, Row 8 and Column D, Row 8 respectively). Column F shows the distance between facilities, as the result of applying formula 8.3. Column G operationalizes the numerator of formula 8.1, Column H operationalizes the numerator of formula 8.2, and Column I gives the denominator of formula 8.1 and 8.2:[7]

---

[7] Note: Spreadsheets keep many decimals. When computing the problem by hand and keeping a couple of decimals, the numbers may be a little different due to rounding.

Table 8.2 Iteration 1.

	A	B	C	D	E	F	G	H	I
1	Site	x_i	y_i	Q_i	c_i	d_i	$Q_i c_i x_i / d_i$	$Q_i c_i y_i / d_i$	$Q_i c_i / d_i$
2	Plant	8	10	1000	0.25	12.81	156.13	195.16	19.52
3	Market A	12	9.5	250	0.5	15.31	97.98	77.56	8.16
4	Market B	11	7.5	350	0.5	13.31	144.63	98.61	13.15
5	Market C	6	5	400	0.5	7.81	153.65	128.04	25.61
6	Total						552.38	499.37	66.44
7									
8	Starting	$x^0=$	0.00	$y^0=$	0.00				
9	Revised	$x'=$	8.31	$y'=$	7.52				

(Column F, Row 2)

$$d_i = \sqrt{(x_i - x')^2 + (y_i - y')^2} = \sqrt{(8-0)^2 + (10-0)^2} = 12.81$$

(Column G, Row 2)	$Q_i c_i x_i / d_i = 1000 * 0.25 * 8 / 12.81 = 156.13$
(Column H, Row 2)	$Q_i c_i y_i / d_i = 1000 * 0.25 * 10 / 12.81 = 195.16$
(Column I, Row 2)	$Q_i c_i / d_i = 1000 * 0.25 / 12.81 = 19.52$
(Column G, Row 6)	Sum column G, rows 2 - 5
(Column H, Row 6)	Sum column H, rows 2 - 5
(Column I, Row 6)	Sum column I, rows 2 - 5
(Column C, Row 9)	Compute new x': 552.38 / 66.44 = 8.31
(Column E, Row 9)	Compute new y': 499.37 / 66.44 = 7.52

This procedure can easily be done using an Excel spreadsheet. Excel codes are provided in Table 8.3. You can accomplish the task simply by applying the copy and paste features of Excel.

We repeat the computation ten times by substituting the current (x_i, y_i) with the most recently computed estimates $(x_i = x', \ y_i = y')$, until the newly computed location (x', y') is almost the same as the current (x_i, y_i). Table 8.4 shows that iterations 9 and 10 obtain the same coordinates (9.01, 8.60) and the same total cost. We should stop here. The new warehouse will be located at coordinates (9.01, 8.60). Since we are not able to find the solution directly, we iterate the procedure until we find a stable solution.

Table 8.3 Excel codes for the problem solved in Table 8.2.

	A	B	C	D	E	F	G	H	I
1	Site	x_i	y_i	Q_i	c_i	d_i	$Q_i c_i x_i /d_i$	$Q_i c_i y_i /d_i$	$Q_i c_i /d_i$
2	Plant	8	10	1000	0.25	=ROUND(SQRT((B2-$C$8)^2+(C2-$E$8)^2),2)	=(D2*E2*B2)/F2	=(D2*E2*C2)/F2	=(D2*E2)/F2
3	Market A	12	9.5	250	0.5	=ROUND(SQRT((B3-$C$8)^2+(C3-$E$8)^2),2)	=(D3*E3*B3)/F3	=(D3*E3*C3)/F3	=(D3*E3)/F3
4	Market B	11	7.5	350	0.5	=ROUND(SQRT((B4-$C$8)^2+(C4-$E$8)^2),2)	=(D4*E4*B4)/F4	=(D4*E4*C4)/F4	=(D4*E4)/F4
5	Market C	6	5	400	0.5	=ROUND(SQRT((B5-$C$8)^2+(C5-$E$8)^2),2)	=(D5*E5*B5)/F5	=(D5*E5*C5)/F5	=(D5*E5)/F5
6	Total						=SUM(G2:G5)	=SUM(H2:H5)	=SUM(I2:I5)
7									
8	Starting	$x^0=$ 0		$y^0=$ 0					
9	Revised	$x'=$ =G6/I6		$y'=$ =H6/I6					

Caution should be taken because the solution generated here may not be feasible for a real physical location. For instance, the coordinates may be located in the middle of a lake or in a residential non-commercial area. However, the result provides managers with the information of the lowest total transportation cost option. As such, a reasonable location that is close to the coordinates (9.01, 8.60) can be identified as the appropriate place to locate the distribution center.

Table 8.4 Summary of ten iterations.

Iteration	x'	y'	Total Cost
1	8.31	7.52	9007.50
2	8.78	8.15	2303.50
3	9.05	8.49	2164.25
4	9.05	8.54	2159.25
5	9.04	8.56	2158.25
6	9.03	8.58	2160.00
7	9.02	8.59	2158.00
8	9.01	8.60	2158.50
9	9.01	8.60	2157.75
10	9.01	8.60	2157.75

8.4.1.2 The median method

The median method yields an optimal solution when the relevant metric is rectilinear distance. It uses median instead of mean for the coordinates of x_i and y_i. The procedure is as follows:

(1) Move across the grid horizontally from left to right, and accumulate the weight at each location reached until 50% or more of the total weight has been accumulated. This method is called median approach. The value of x that puts you at or over 50% is x_m.

(2) Move across the grid vertically from top to bottom, and accumulate the weight at each location reached until 50% or more of the total weight has been accumulated. The value of y that puts you at or over 50% is y_m.

Where:

   x_i and y_i = coordinates of markets

   x_m and y_m = identified median coordinates

Example problem 8.2: Median method

The x and y coordinates of five sites are given in Table 8.5, as is the demand quantity for each site. Determine a central warehouse location that minimizes the total transportation cost by using the median method.

Table 8.5 Median method.

Markets	x_i	y_i	Demand Volume (w_i)
A	2	3	35
B	4	9	65
C	5	7	65
D	6	5	80
E	9	8	55
Total			300

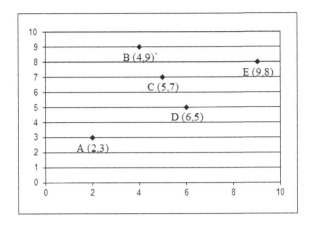

Solution to example problem 8.2 median method

Let's apply steps (1) and (2).

(1) Move across the grid horizontally from left to right. The demand of Market A is 35, the demand of Market B is 65, and the demand of Market C is 65. The accumulative weight of the three markets (A, B, and C) is 165, which is more than 50% of the total weight (i.e. 300). The value of x_m is 5, which is the value of x of Market C.

(2) Move across the grid vertically from top to bottom. The demand of Market B is 65, the demand of Market E is 55, and the demand of Market C is 65. The accumulative weight of the three markets (B, E, and C) is 185, which is more than 50% of the total weight. The value of y_m is 7, which is the value of y of Market C.

Table 8.6 Median method total cost.

Markets	x_i	y_i	Demand (w_i)	$|x_i - x_m| + |y_i - y_m|$	d_i	$w_i * d_i$
A	2	3	35	$|2 - 5| + |3 - 7| =$	7	245
B	4	9	65	$|4 - 5| + |9 - 7| =$	3	195
C	5	7	65	$|5 - 5| + |7 - 7| =$	0	0
D	6	5	80	$|6 - 5| + |5 - 7| =$	3	240
E	9	8	55	$|9 - 5| + |8 - 7| =$	5	275
				Total Cost		955

Using $x_m = 5$, and $y_m = 7$, compute the rectilinear distance and the total cost. The detailed computation is given in Table 8.6.

In the median method, one of the markets can be the optimal location. Sometimes the optimal location falls anywhere on a line segment or anywhere within a rectangle. When applying the rectilinear distance method, the orientation of the grid is an essential part of the input data. Therefore, changing the grid orientation changes the problem itself.

When choosing between a Euclidean model (such as the center of gravity method) and a rectilinear model (such as median method), the decision made should be consistent with the distance measurement that is under consideration. The rectilinear model will almost always produce a higher ton/mile total than a Euclidean model. This is because a diagonal straight line is shorter than the distance of a right angle.

8.4.1.3 Preference matrix method for determining distribution center

The preference matrix method that we discussed in section 4.2.2.1 can be applied to solve a single facility location problem. This method can integrate qualitative data into the consideration. First, identify and categorize the important location factors as dominant or secondary. Then, analyze the data collected and make a selection of the best location according to the total weighted score.

Example problem 8.3: Preference matrix method

The management of a national retail chain is considering three potential locations for a new warehouse. They have assigned the scores shown below to the relevant factors on a 0 to 10 basis (10 is best). Using the preference matrix, which location would be preferred?

Solution to example problem 8.3 preference matrix method

New York: $(10 \times 6) + (20 \times 7) + (15 \times 4) + (35 \times 8) + (20 \times 2)$ $= 580$
Norfolk: $(10 \times 8) + (20 \times 5) + (15 \times 7) + (35 \times 10) + (20 \times 3)$ $= 695$
Savannah: $(10 \times 3) + (20 \times 9) + (15 \times 5) + (35 \times 8) + (20 \times 5)$ $= 665$

The total weighted score of 695 is the highest score; therefore, Norfolk, VA will be selected as the location of the new warehouse.

| Location Factor | Weight | New York, NY | | Norfolk, VA | | Savannah, GA | |
		Score	Weighted Score	Score	Weighted Score	Score	Weighted Score
Labor skill	10	6	60	8	80	3	30
Proximity to markets	20	7	140	5	100	9	180
Proximity to suppliers	15	4	60	7	105	5	75
Proximity to the port	35	8	280	10	350	8	280
Local government tax incentive	20	2	40	3	60	5	100
	100		580		695		665

8.4.2 Configure multiple facilities

Companies often need to configure two or more facilities in a logistics network simultaneously. The possible configurations can be enormous, so this type of problem is more complicated. The goal is to determine the number of facilities needed, the size of each facility, and the location of each facility in a logistics network. A number of techniques have been developed to solve multi-location problems, including linear programming, mixed integer programming, dynamic programming, and simulation, among others.

More recently, geographical information system (GIS) has been applied to solve multi-location logistics problems. GIS is a system of computer software, hardware, and data that a firm's personnel can use to present and/or analyze information relevant to a location decision. It can also integrate different systems to create a visual representation of a firm's location choices. A GIS system can be a really useful decision-making tool because many of the decisions made by business today have a geographical aspect. For example, GIS can help to identify locations that relate well to a firm's target market based on customer demographics. Additionally, coupled with sales forecasting models and geodemographic systems, GIS can give a firm a formidable array of location decision-making tools.

Major costs of designing a multiple facility supply chain network include:

- Fixed facility costs
- Inventory costs
- Transportation costs
- Production costs
- Other costs such as overhead, coordination costs

The Linear Programming method can be used to allocate demand in a logistics network. The Mixed Integer Programming method can be employed when both fixed and variable costs are considered. Both the Linear Programming and the Mixed Integer Programming methods are introduced below.

8.4.2.1 Allocating customers to existing distribution centers considering variable costs only

Example problem 8.4: Allocating markets to existing warehouses considering variable cost only

Games-R-Us Inc. has three warehouses that serve four markets. Managers of the three warehouses need to decide how to allocate the demand to their facility. Fixed cost associated with each plant is not included in the total cost analysis. Only transportation cost (variable cost) is considered. As the cost and demand change, the managers will revise the facility configuration. Table 8.7 provides demand and warehouse capacity data. Transportation cost information is given in the middle of the table. For example, to transport 1 ton product from Warehouse 1 to Virginia Beach will cost 8 dollars and to transport 1 ton product from Warehouse 2 to Norfolk costs $12. Demand from Norfolk is 25 ton and the total supply capacity of warehouse 1 is 50 ton.

The manager wants to know which warehouse will serve which markets, and the total cost of the configuration.

The linear programming method is used for allocating demand to warehouses. All the demands should be met. The available supply of the warehouse cannot be exceeded. Demand from one customer zone can be supplied from one or more warehouses.

Table 8.7 Example problem 8.4 data.

	Virginia Beach	Norfolk	Chesapeake	Suffolk	Capacity
Warehouse 1	8	6	10	9	50
Warehouse 2	9	12	13	7	75
Warehouse 3	12	9	13	6.5	100
Demand (in ton)	45	25	28	30	

Objective Function

$$\text{Min } \sum_{i=1}^{n} \sum_{j=1}^{m} vc_{ij} x_{ij} \tag{8.5}$$

Subject to

$$\sum_{i=1}^{n} x_{ij} = D_j \tag{8.6}$$

$$\sum_{j=1}^{m} x_{ij} \leq Q_i \tag{8.7}$$

$$x_{ij} \geq 0 \tag{8.8}$$

Where:

Decision variable:

x_{ij} = quantity shipped from warehouse i to customer zone j

Parameters:

vc_{ij} = variable cost of one unit shipped from warehouse i to customer zone j per mile

D_j = annual demand from customer zone j, j = 1 to n.

Q_i = annual supply capacity of warehouse i, i = 1 to m.

The objective is to minimize the total transportation cost. Equation (8.6) ensures that all demands are satisfied. Equation (8.7) is a capacity constraint that ensures that the total supply of a warehouse to customer zones will not exceed the warehouse capacity. Equation (8.8) is a non-negativity constraint. *Excel Solver* is applied to solve the problem.

Table 8.8 shows that the total cost is $1,039. Warehouse 1 will serve demand from Norfolk, Chesapeake, and Suffolk. Warehouse 2 will serve demand from Virginia Beach and Warehouse 3 will serve the partial demand from Norfolk and all the demand from Suffolk. There will be 30 units still available in warehouse 2 and 67 units available in warehouse 3 for promising new orders after all the demands are satisfied. Solver codes and the Solver screen are given in Table 8.9.

Table 8.8 Solution to example problem 8.4 using Excel Solver.

	A	B	C	D	E	F
1	Example 8.3 Allocating markets to existing warehouse					
2						
3		Virginia Beach	Norfolk	Chesapeake	Suffolk	Capacity
4	Warehouse 1	8	6	10	9	50
5	Warehouse 2	9	12	13	7	75
6	Warehouse 3	12	9	13	6.5	100
7	Demand	45	25	28	30	
8						
9						
10	*Decision Var*	Virginia Beach	Norfolk	Chesapeake	Suffolk	
11	Warehouse 1	0	22	28	0	
12	Warehouse 2	45	0	0	0	
13	Warehouse 3	0	3	0	30	
14						
15	*Objective Fn*					
16	Cost =	1039				
17						
18						
19	*Constraints*	*Unused Capacity*	Virginia Beach	Norfolk	Chesapeake	Suffolk
20	Warehouse 1	0				
21	Warehouse 2	30				
22	Warehouse 3	67				
23	*Demand*		0	0	0	0

Table 8.9 Example problem 8.4 Excel Solver codes & Solver screen.

	Formula	Cell	Excel Codes
Objective function	$\sum_{i=1}^{n} \sum_{j=1}^{m} vc_{ij} x_{ij}$	B16	= SUMPRODUCT(B4:E6,B11:E13)
Demand constraint	$\sum_{i=1}^{n} x_{ij} = D_j$	C23	= B7 – SUM(B11:B13)
		D23	= C7 – SUM(C11: C13)
		E23	= D7 – SUM(D11: D13)
		F23	= E7 – SUM(E11: E13)
Capacity constraint	$\sum_{j=1}^{m} x_{ij} \leq Q_i$	B20	= F4 - SUM(B11:E11)
		B21	= F5 - SUM(B12:E12)
		B22	= F6 - SUM(B13:E13)

Fig. 8.5 Example problem 8.4 Excel Solver screen.

8.4.2.2 Developing a logistics system considering both fixed and variable costs

Example problem 8.5: Developing a logistics network considering both fix and variable costs

The CEO of Games-R-Us Inc. wants to know if they can save some fixed cost by closing one of the three warehouses they have now. In this case, one market may be served by more than one warehouse. The demand, warehouse capacity, transportation costs, and fixed costs are given in Table 8.10. Which warehouse should be closed and which left open? What is the total cost of the configuration?

. For the capacitated warehouse location model with multiple sourcing, when fixed cost is considered, the problem is solved using Mixed Integer Programming. If the warehouse is open, it is 1; otherwise, it is 0.

Table 8.10 Example problem 8.5 data.

	Fixed cost	Virginia Beach	Norfolk	Chesapeake	Suffolk	Capacity
Warehouse 1	2250	8	6	10	9	50
Warehouse 2	3250	9	12	13	7	75
Warehouse 3	4200	12	9	13	6.5	100
Demand		45	25	28	30	

Objective Function

$$\text{Min } \sum_{i=1}^{n} \sum_{j=1}^{m} vc_{ij} x_{ij} + \sum_{i=1}^{n} fc_i y_i \qquad (8.9)$$

Subject to

$$\sum_{i=1}^{n} x_{ij} = D_j \qquad (8.10)$$

$$\sum_{j=1}^{m} x_{ij} \leq Q_i y_i \qquad (8.11)$$

$$x_{ij} \geq 0 \qquad (8.12)$$

$$\sum_{i=1}^{n} y_i \leq N \; ; \; y_i \in \{0, 1\} \qquad (8.13)$$

Where
Decision variable:

x_{ij} = quantity shipped from warehouse i to customer zone j

y_i = 1 if the warehouse is open, 0 otherwise.

Parameters:

vc_{ij} = variable cost of one unit shipped from warehouse i to customer zone j per mile

fc_i = fixed cost of warehouse i

D_j = annual demand from customer zone j.

Q_i = annual capacity of warehouse i.

N = the number of warehouse sites available.

Equation (8.10) ensures that all demands will be satisfied. Equation (8.11) is a warehouse capacity constraint; it ensures that the total supply to customer zones will not exceed the warehouse capacity. Equation (8.12) is a non-negativity constraint. Equation (8.13) ensures that the total number of open warehouses will not exceed the current available number of warehouses.

Table 8.11 Solution to example problem 8.5 using Excel Solver.

	A	B	C	D	E	F	G
1	Example 8.4 Logistic network with both fix and variable costs						
2							
3		Fixed	Virginia Beach	Norfolk	Chesapeake	Suffolk	Capacity
4	Warehouse 1	2250	8	6	10	9	50
5	Warehouse 2	3250	9	12	13	7	75
6	Warehouse 3	4200	12	9	13	6.5	100
7	Demand		45	25	28	30	
8							
9	**Decision Var**	Open/Close	Virginia Beach	Norfolk	Chesapeake	Suffolk	
10	Warehouse 1	1	45	5	0	0	
11	Warehouse 2	0	0	0	0	0	
12	Warehouse 3	1	0	20	28	30	
13							
14	**Objective Fn**						
15	Cost =	7,579					
16							
17	**Constraints**	**Unused Capacity**	Virginia Beach	Norfolk	Chesapeake	Suffolk	
18	Warehouse 1	0					
19	Warehouse 2	0					
20	Warehouse 3	22					
21	**Demand**		0.00	0.00	0.00	0.00	

Table 8.12 Example problem 8.5 Excel Solver codes & screen.

	Formula	Cell	Excel Codes
Objective function	$\sum_{i=1}^{n} \sum_{j=1}^{m} vc_{ij} x_{ij}$ $+ \sum_{i=1}^{n} fc_i y_i$	B15	= SUMPRODUCT(C4:F6,C10:F12) + SUMPRODUCT(B4:B6, B10:B12)
Demand constraint	$\sum_{i=1}^{n} x_{ij} = D_j$	C21	=C7 – SUM(C10:C12)
		D21	=D7 – SUM(D10: D12)
		E21	=E7 – SUM(E10: E12)
		F21	=F7 – SUM(F10: F12)
Capacity constraint	$\sum_{j=1}^{m} x_{ij} \le Q_i y_i$	B18	=G4*B10 - SUM(C10:F10)
		B19	= G5*B11 - SUM(C11:F11)
		B20	= G6*B12 - SUM(C12:F12)

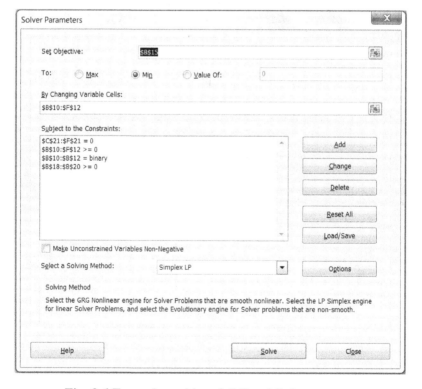

Fig. 8.6 Example problem 8.5 Excel Solver screen.

Table 8.11 reports the results after the problem has been solved using Excel Solver. Warehouses 1 and 3 will stay open and Warehouse 2 will be closed. The total cost of this configuration is $7,579. The Virginia Beach market will be served by Warehouse 1. The Norfolk market will be supplied by Warehouses 1 and 3. Both Chesapeake and Suffolk markets will be served by Warehouse 3. There will be 22 units still available for promising new orders after all the demands are satisfied. Solver codes are given in Table 8.12.

8.5 Warehouse

8.5.1 Nature and importance of warehouses

The warehouse is part of a supply chain's logistics network. It is used for the storage of inventory at all phases of a supply chain. Raw material, semi-finished components, and finished goods can all be stocked in the warehouse.

Most companies use a warehouse as an intermediate point between the manufacturing plant and the customer. Some companies such as the Sears mail order catalog use a warehouse as the point of origin or as sales headquarters.

Direct fulfillment of orders from the warehouse becomes a new business model in the e-Business environment. e-Retailers such as Amazon.com take orders through their Web sites and fulfill orders directly from their warehouses. Amazon opened eight distribution centers in 2001, in addition to the five that it opened in 1999, so that it could handle shipping its goods on its own.[8] In general, the functions of a warehouse include:

- Take advantage of production economies
- Take advantage of transportation economies
- Take advantage of purchasing discount
- Realize firms' customer service commitment

---

[8] "Amazon Distribution Network," Date of access: July 2013 www.mwpvl.com.

- Manage seasonal demand
- Provide place utility

Obviously, a warehouse is an integral component of a supply chain. However, warehousing is expensive and usually accounts for 2 to 5 percent of sales cost.[9] Therefore, trimming down warehousing costs can have important implications for a supply chain's performance, especially on its return-on-assets ratio.

8.5.2 Warehouses in the supply chain

8.5.2.1 Public and private warehouses

There are a couple of different warehouse options in a supply chain, the most common being the public warehouse and the private warehouse. Usually, a rented facility is a public warehouse and an owned or leased facility is considered a private warehouse. Companies generally consider customer service and total cost when choosing between public and private warehousing. Some advantages of using a public warehouse include:

(1) Not needing a capital investment in building, land, material handling, etc.;
(2) Being able to increase or decrease space for seasonal demand without a huge investment in facility;
(3) Having the flexibility to change the warehouse's location according to changes in the marketplace or customer density;
(4) Having better estimates about storage and handling costs, utility costs, and labor costs;
(5) Being able to take advantage of economies of scale when demand volume is low;
(6) Having a tax advantage when a firm does not own property in the state, and avoiding various state taxes; and

---

[9] Frazelle, E. (2002). *World-class Warehousing and Material Handling*, (McGraw Hill, New York).

(7) Insulating labor disputes when a union is involved in a labor dispute with one of the customers. US courts have ruled that a labor union does not have the right to strike against a public warehouse when the union is involved in a labor dispute with one of the customers of that public warehouse.

The disadvantages of using a public warehouse include:

(1) Lack of control of products stocked in the warehouse;
(2) A potential communication problem with the public warehouse;
(3) Lack of specialized services; and
(4) A public warehouse may not have extra space available when the company needs it.

A private warehouse also has some advantages and disadvantages. The advantages of using a private warehouse include:

(1) Having direct control (and a higher degree of control) of the product;
(2) Having flexibility to design and operate the warehouse according to its own needs;
(3) This solution being less costly over the long term, if the company is able to achieve sufficient utilization of the warehouse;
(4) The firm being able to utilize its present human resources; and
(5) Realizing tax benefits, such as depreciation, when a firm owns a warehouse.

The disadvantages of using a private warehouse include:

(1) The lack of flexibility due to fixed space, utility costs, labor costs, and other overhead costs; and
(2) Requiring an initial capital investment to build or buy a warehouse. Additional costs include purchasing material handling equipment, and recruiting and training employees.

8.5.2.2 Types of warehouses

Various products may require special warehousing arrangements. For example, Perdue Farms produces chicken products and requires refrigerated warehouses. In general, there are six types of warehouses:

- General merchandise warehouses for manufactured goods (such as toys, bathroom tissues, etc.);
- Refrigerated or cold storage warehouses for frozen foods;
- Bonded warehouses for storing goods authorized by customs officials until removal, without the payment of duties. Since this kind of warehouse holds bonded shipments, pending customs inspection, it must be secured. Dutiable goods need to be segregated from nondutiable goods;
- Household goods and furniture warehouses;
- Special commodity warehouses, such as hazardous material; and
- Bulk storage warehouse such as Sam's Club and Costco.

8.6 New Logistic Models

In order to best balance inventory management cost, warehousing cost, and a high customer service level, a number of logistic models, such as cross docking and merge-in-transit, have materialized in recent years.

8.6.1 Cross-docking

A cross-docking depot is a transshipment facility for receiving, storage, order picking, packaging, loading, and shipping. The cross-docking approach accepts products at the receiving dock, where they are moved directly to the shipping dock. In this case, products are not put into the storage area, so material handling and storage expenses can be reduced. Outbound trailers serve as extensions of the distribution center. When cross-docking is chosen, more space is allocated to the dock and less space is allocated to the storage area.

Walmart uses the concept of cross-docking to reduce its overall inventory costs. Products from different suppliers are exchanged at the depot between trucks so that each truck going to a retail store holds products from different suppliers. Walmart also allows its retail stores to exchange surplus and shortage items. The logistics network and transportation play an important role in improving the matching of supply and demand at Walmart, aiding in the company's effort to increase customer satisfaction while keeping costs low.

The cross-docking method can be applied at various stages in a supply chain. For example,

- A manufacturer can utilize cross-docking for receiving and consolidating inbound parts and components to support its production.
- A transportation service provider (such as a trucking company) can utilize cross-docking for consolidating shipments from different shippers in less-than-truck-load (LTL) quantities to gain economies of scale.
- A distribution center can apply cross-docking for consolidating inbound products from multiple manufacturers into multiple-SKU pallets, and then sorting them onto outbound trucks.

The benefits of cross-docking include reduced storage space, reduced loading and unloading labor costs, reduced storage overhead costs, and improved lead-time performance. However, when cross-docking is applied, the loading and unloading sequence, scheduling at the dock, and incoming and outgoing vehicle scheduling become important to consider in order to reduce truck waiting time at the dock.

8.6.2 Merge-in-transit

Merge-in-transit is a logistic service that enables final product assembly and transport to occur simultaneously. A carrier fetches separate shipments from two or more places and then delivers the shipments to a location near the final destination, where a merge operation is performed. Merge-in-transit ensures that all of the packages are delivered together to the end user. This method is well-received both in e-retailing and by the on-line shopping business. Dell is one of the companies that applies merge-in-transit.

Let's consider a company that sells personal computers. Each computer is composed of three main parts: a CPU box, a monitor, and speakers. The monitor is produced by a supplier in China and stored in a warehouse in Chesapeake, Virginia. The CPU box is assembled in Dallas, Texas, and the speakers are made in Cary, North Carolina. Under the traditional supply chain model, the speakers, the monitor, and the CPU box would be transported to a centralized warehouse. When an order is placed, the three major components along with other accessories would be assembled, put into a box, and shipped together to fill the order.

Using the merge-in-transit model, the supply chain process is reengineered. When an order is received, a logistics service provider fetches the CPU box from Dallas, Texas, the speakers from Cary, North Carolina, and the monitor from Chesapeake, Virginia, and transports them to the merge center that is closest to the customer. When all of the components arrive at the merge center, the logistics service provider delivers them to the customer.

Some of the benefits of the merge-in-transit model include:

- Increased product configuration flexibility
- Lead-time reduction
- Virtual warehousing operation
- Reduction of inventory carrying cost
- Reduction of obsolete items.

Information technology is an enabler of creating and implementing new logistic models. When the merge-in-transit model is used, client orders are sent to the carrier by the vendor. The data is transmitted to a central database server for inventory compilation and control. The server then sends the data to the proper client location, allowing the client to view incoming items, prepare packages, and schedule delivery.

8.7 Enhancing Value through Logistics Management in the Supply Chain

The logistics network is an integral part of a supply chain. It plays a vital role in providing a desired level of customer service at the lowest total cost possible. A well-designed, sophisticated logistics network makes a quick response supply chain possible. A quick response supply chain leads to reduced cycle time, better demand forecast due to short lead-time, and increased supply chain profits.

As shown in Figure 8.1, logistics and distribution centers are the links among suppliers, manufacturers, distributors, retailers, and customers. Traditional vertical integration of various production stages within a company is gradually losing its appeal. For example, IBM was a fully integrated PC producer in the 1980s. It produced microprocessors, wrote operating system codes, manufactured PCs, and even ran its own retail stores. Today, Dell computer purchases almost all of the parts and components that it needs for production, keeping the final assembly in-house. This transition indicates that supply chain management is managing a logistics network which integrates a set of tasks: 1) to produce the final product, and 2) to provide place and product utilities to the customer.

The reverse logistics network adds value to the supply chain. For example, Sears shuttles customer-returned products from over 2,900 stores to three collection centers in the US. After remanufacturing or refurbishing, the company sells these recovered products for a profit. Over the past two decades, the logistics network has evolved from a relatively minor facet of a company to one of the most crucial functions in a supply chain.

8.8 Summary

In this chapter, we have discussed the effects of global competition on logistics network configuration and the reversed logistics network for the recovery of products. An array of methods is introduced for designing and configuring a logistics network. Since the advancement of computer technology has made this computation much faster and easier, a real-world problem that includes a few hundred customer zones, more than a dozen warehouses, and several hundred product groups can be solved in a reasonable amount of time.

Questions for Pondering

1. In 2006, the Ford Motor Company announced its plan to close down 14 facilities in the US between then and 2008. How did this decision affect Ford's logistics network configuration?
2. What benefits does cross-docking offer? If cross-docking is a solution to inventory reduction and fast inventory turn-over, why do we still need warehouses for stocking goods?
3. Amazon.com and Dell have changed the way that retailers conduct business. What role does a warehouse play in Amazon's e-Business model?
4. How would you determine the performance metrics for a logistics network configuration? What key factors would you take into consideration when evaluating a logistics network?

Problems

1. Develop a list of factors that you think would be important in determining the location of:
   - A fast food restaurant
   - A hospital
   - A shopping mall
   - A bottle water manufacturer
   - An auto component manufacturer

2. The following table gives the location of five demand points served by a central warehouse with coordinates of x=0 and y=0. The coordinates and annual freight volumes of the five markets are:

Market	x	y	Weight	Freight Rate
A	1	1	50 ton	$1 / per ton mile
B	2	3	40 ton	$1 / per ton mile
C	4	2	10 ton	$1 / per ton mile
D	3	5	70 ton	$1 / per ton mile
E	5	4	30 ton	$1 / per ton mile

Determine the facility location that will provide minimum total ton-miles from the warehouse to the five customer locations.

a. Use the center of gravity method to find a location for the warehouse.
b. Use the median method to find a solution.
c. Are there any factors that are not included in the model that you feel are important for a facility network problem? Explain how your manager could use the results from your analysis.

3. A company supplies goods to three customer zones through two warehouses. Demand from Customer 1 is 40 units, from Customer 2 is 50 units and from Customer 3 is 35 units. The capacity of Warehouse 1 is 80 and the capacity of Warehouse 2 has 130. The cost of shipping one unit of product to a customer is given in the table below:

	To		
From	Customer 1	Customer 2	Customer 3
Warehouse 1	25	15	35
Warehouse 2	50	40	10

Please determine which customer is going to be served by which warehouse. Formulate the problem to minimize total transportation costs, and solve the problem using Excel Solver.

4. In Problem 3, if the annual fixed cost for Warehouse 1 is $5,000 and for Warehouse 2 is $9,000, what will be the logistic configuration if the company is going to redesign its logistics network?

References

Ballou, R.H. (2004). Business Logistics/Supply Chain Management, 5th edition, (Person Prentice Hall, Upper Saddle River, New Jersey).

Chopra, S. and Meindl, P. (2013). Supply Chain Management, (Prentice Hall, Upper Saddle River, New Jersey).

Krajewski, L. Ritzman, L. and Malhotra, M. (2010). Operations Management: Process and Supply Chains, 9th edition, (Prentice Hall, Upper Saddle River, New Jersey).

Simchi-Levi, D., Kaminsky, P., and Simchi-Levi, E. (2003). Designing and Managing the Supply Chain, 2nd edition, (McGraw-Hill Irwin: New York).

Prince, Theodore (2000). E-Commerce: Its Impact on Transportation, Logistics, and Supply Chain Management, April 15. *ASCET*, Volume 2.

Stock, J. R. and Lambert, D.M (1987). Strategic Logistic Management, 2nd edition, (Richard Irwin, Homewood, Illinois).

Chapter 9

Transportation Service and Distribution Systems

9.1 Transportation

Transportation moves products to geographically distanced markets in order to provide people all over the world with access to a wide variety of goods from various countries. For example, US companies export agricultural products, lumber, medical equipment, chemicals, pharmaceuticals, manufactured goods, and many other products to overseas markets. Furthermore, American consumers enjoy beer from Holland, automobiles from Germany, leather shoes and bags from Italy, electronic appliances from Japan, garments from China, rugs and furniture from India, and coffee from Colombia. In this sense, transportation offers time and place utility to consumers.

According to the U.S. Chamber of Commerce, the spending in the logistics and transportation industry in the US was about $1.3 trillion in 2011, and averaged 8.5 percent of annual gross domestic product (GDP).[1] The trade flow benefits people throughout the U.S. and around the world. Transportation is an inexpensive way to connect the world's economies. According to the World Shipping Council, the annual cost of transporting America's liner imports is only slightly more than $130 per household, which is a small proportion of household expenses.

More recently, transportation and logistics companies have applied business-to-business (B2B) practices and have utilized e-commerce

---

[1] Source: date of access: Aug. 2013. http://selectusa.commerce.gov/industry-snapshots/logistics-and-transportation-industry-united-states.

solutions to fulfill customer supply chain expectations. Therefore, the transportation function is an opportunity for supply chain managers to minimize cost, to improve customer service, and to improve profitability.

9.1.1 Transportation service provider: Carriers

Carriers are those who provide transportation services to move goods from one point to another. For example, FedEx and UPS are carriers. A carrier such as an airline, railroad, or trucking company needs to provide quality customer service at a competitive cost. When making investment decisions, a carrier needs to consider a range of costs, such as vehicle-related costs, fixed operating costs, trip-related costs, and overhead costs.

Vehicle-related costs includes the size and type of vehicles purchased or leased for moving goods. Trip-related costs are the costs incurred when the vehicle is dispatched for service. These costs usually include fuel and labor expenses, quantity-related costs such as those associated with loading and unloading, terminal fees, airport gate fees, parking fees, and others.

Overhead costs include administrative expenses, marketing expenses, the planning and design of transportation network, scheduling, and investment in information technology.

9.1.2 Customers: Shippers

Shippers are those who require transportation services. For example, when Amazon requires FedEx and UPS to deliver books to its customers, Amazon is a shipper.

A shipper aims to provide responsive service while minimizing the total cost of fulfilling a customer's order. When making transportation decisions, a shipper needs to consider transportation costs, inventory costs, and order processing costs, as well as customer service level.

The transportation cost is the cost of purchasing transportation service from a carrier. The cost of holding inventory incurred by the shipper's supply chain network can include interest, storage and handling, taxes, insurance, and shrinkage. Service level cost is the cost of not being able to meet the specified customer service objectives. Among these costs are shortage costs, backorder costs, and compensation vouchers.

9.2 Overview of Carrier Operations

A variety of transportation tools are available to assist in moving things. Motor carriers, railroads, water, airlines, and pipeline are the five major transportation modes. Additionally, several intermodal services such as rail-motor, water-rail, motor-water, and motor-air are available to offer a combination of more than one transportation tool. We give a brief discussion of each mode in this section.

9.2.1 Motor carrier

Motor carriage is the most popular transportation mode in the U.S. As the interstate system of highway developed from the 1950s, motor carriage gradually replaced rail carriage as the dominant form of freight transportation.

A motor carrier is classified either as a for-hire-carrier or as a private carrier. For-hire-carriers provide service to the public and charge a fee for that service. Private carriers provide service to the organization without a charge. The organization usually owns or leases the vehicle.

A for-hire-motor carrier can be classified in a number of ways, including local vs. intercity, common vs. contract, and regulated vs. exempt. Additionally, it can be a truckload (TL) or a less-than-truck-load (LTL) service provider. Fig. 9.1 gives a classification of for-hire motor carriers.[2]

---

[2] John Coyle, Robert Novack, Brian Gibson, and Edward Bardi (2011). *Transportation*, 7th edition, (South-Western Cengage Learning, Mason, OH, USA).

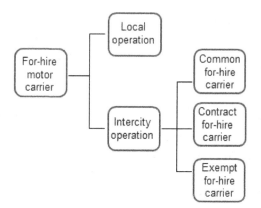

Fig. 9.1 For-hire motor carrier classifications.

A for-hire-carrier can either be a local or an intercity service provider. If a carrier focuses on local service, it will pick up and deliver the freight within the city; if it is an intercity carrier, it will operate between specified commercial zones or cities.

For-hire-exempt-carriers have the privilege of being exempt from economic regulation. Their exempt status can be obtained by the type of commodity, such as (1) the agricultural items that it transports, or (2) the type of operation it uses to move goods, such as being a supplementary service to water transportation.

A common carrier, by law, provides services to the public for a fee. The US post office and UPS are examples of common carriers.

Contract carriers, on the other hand, serve specific shippers with whom the carrier has a contract and do not provide service to the public. A contract carrier usually adapts its equipment or technology to meet the special requirements of the shipper. For example, FWCC, Inc. is a contract carrier that provides transportation services to contracted customers. Its service includes long haul, truckload transportation of van, and temperature controlled freight.

The truckload carriers provide service to shippers who meet the TL volume requirement and pay the TL transportation rate. The TL carrier picks up the shipment at the point of origin and delivers the same truckload to the destination. The less-than-truckload carrier provides services to shippers whose shipment volume is less than the truckload. The LTL carrier consolidates the small shipments for the intercity movement and then disaggregates the truckload at the destination city. Therefore, LTL rates are usually higher than TL rates. For example, Amazon.com hires UPS to deliver less-than-truckload packages to its customers.

The cost structure of a motor carrier is determined by fixed and variable costs. The fixed cost is low because the highway cost is supported by the public, the size of the fleet is easy to adjust, and there are no requirements for terminals in TL operations. The variable costs include fuel, labor, and maintenance. In general, fixed costs account for 10 to 30 percent and variable costs account for 70 to 90 percent.

The major issues for TL operation include utilization, consistent service, and backhauls. The major issues for LTL operation include the location of consolidation facilities, vehicle routing and scheduling, customer service levels, and vehicle utilization.

9.2.2 Railroad carrier

Prior to WWII, the railroad industry was the dominant domestic transportation mode. Railroads' main line mileage in the US has been gradually shrinking from its maximum length of 390,000 miles in the 1930s to approximately 152,000 miles today. However, railroads still play an important role in today's economy.

The ownership of the mileage is unequally divided between Class I and Class II railroads. Those with annual revenues of $87 million or more are classified as Class I railroads; these represent about 95 percent of the total railroad traffic in the US. A Class II classification is for short lines that connect shippers to the larger railroad lines. By 2012, there were nine major Class I railroads in the US.[3] This oligopolistic market structure gives large firms the opportunity to control pricing. The railroad has the ownership of right-of-way, which describes the equipment that the carrier uses to provide transportation service.

---

[3] Association of American Railroads, January 10, 2013.

The railroad industry is facing competition from the trucking industry. To increase the level of railroad service, railroad management developed the piggyback service (also called intermodal) that combines trailer-to-railroad or container-to-railroad transportation. Intermodal includes trailer-on-flatcar (TOFC) and container-on-flatcar (COFC) services. To compete effectively with a motor carrier, the railroad invests in terminal facilities for loading and unloading, as well as in changes to the railcars, trailers, and containers.

A railroad has high fixed cost and low variable costs. This situation exists because railroads and pipelines are the only transportation modes that own and maintain their own network and terminals. Thus, a large capital investment is initially required to invest in land, laying tracks, and building bridges and terminals. Annual equipment maintenance costs and labor costs account for a large portion of variable cost. Fuel and power costs are the next largest groups of variable costs. Shipment by railroad is a good choice for large, heavy, high density, and bulky commodities for a long haul at a low freight rate.

A major issue facing railroads is effective loading and freight scheduling to minimize both delays and early delivery, because customers do not want to pay for extra storage.

The role of high technology will continue to expand and increase the ability of the railroads to provide better customer services. For example, Advanced Train Control Systems, a joint venture between the US and Canada, has been developed to track the flow of the entire rail system. Additionally, new communication and signaling technologies provide timely communication among dispatchers, yard workers, field workers, and train crews.

9.2.3 Water carrier

The water carrier is the oldest economic mode of transportation and is still a viable part of the total transportation system. The water carrier system includes common, contract, exempt, and private service providers. The majority of water carrier traffic is exempt from regulation.

Competition among water carriers is limited as long as there are sufficient commodities for water carriers to transport. The water carrier competes with railroads and pipelines for the movement of low value and bulky commodities. For example, railroads and water carriers compete for contracts to move coal from West Virginia, Kentucky, and Pennsylvania to other parts of the US. Pipeline and water carriers compete to move petroleum and petroleum products.

The water carriers have high variable costs and low fixed costs. This is because water carriers pay for the use of right-of-way owned by the government. Additionally, water carriers usually use public-owned or shipper-owned terminals. Labor costs are not high for water carrier service because water carriers hire people at the terminals for special types of loading and unloading operations. Water transportation is a very low-cost service, but the transit time of water service is long and is subject to weather conditions.

9.2.4 Air carrier

In the early twentieth century, the airline industry began to grow. Both private and for-hire carriers operate as part of the airline transportation industry. The airline industry is dominated by its passenger services, but airfreight service has been growing recently, due to the increased volume of global sourcing. For example, Dell Inc. uses an airline carrier to ship chips from Taiwan to the US, and then uses motor carriers to ship computers to customers.

The deregulation of the US airlines in 1977 allows all cargo carriers to set rates, serve routes, and use any size airplane. This new legislative decision gave the opportunity to cargo carriers such FedEx and Air Borne to penetrate the airline market.

Airlines use a hub-spoke network system to effectively manage their services. The hub-spoke model gets its name from the analogy of a bicycle wheel, in which the spokes spread out from the central hub. To consolidate traffic flow, commuter airplanes transport customers on low-density routes to a central hub where customers are assigned to larger planes that fly the higher density routes. Sometimes, a customer might relay more than once, leading to a longer travel time.

Airlines have both a high variable cost and a low fixed cost structure. The relatively low fixed cost is due to the government investment in the operations of airports and airways. Airlines usually pay for the use of publicly provided airways and terminals; this, by nature, is a variable cost. Fuel and labor costs are important expenses of airline service.

Major issues facing airlines include the number of hubs and their locations, the locations of fleet bases and crew bases, flight scheduling optimization, fleet assignment, and crew scheduling. Additionally, airline safety issues have become especially important after the terrorist attack on September 11, 2001 in the US. Recently, escalating fuel costs have caused airline revenue problems, as well.

9.2.5 Pipeline

Pipeline transportation accounts for a large portion of the transportation industry, but is invisible to many people. Pipelines are a highly automated, efficient form of transportation and are very specialized in terms of the commodities that they can transport. Oil, natural gas, and chemical products move in large volumes at steady speeds through pipelines. Pipeline service is slow and has limited accessibility. However, it is very reliable with little damage.

The development of pipelines in the US began in the nineteenth century by the Pennsylvania Railroad. Oil companies gradually took ownership of pipelines. Today, pipelines are owned by both oil and non-oil companies. Because of large capital investment, joint ownership of several companies has become common.

A pipeline is a low-cost transportation mode. However, it has a high level of fixed cost because of the heavy capital investment for its pipeline infrastructure. Labor costs are very low due to highly automated operations.

9.2.6 Intermodal service

Intermodal transportation involves the joint efforts of two or more modes to complete the shipping movement. The most common forms of intermodal transportation include piggyback (rail-truck), water-rail (container-on- flatcar), and truck-air. The container improves the freight interchange efficiency between the modes and enhances the value of intermodal service.

In June 2006, Dr. Patrick Sherry, co-director of the National Center for Intermodal Transportation, addressed the US House of Representatives' Committee on Transportation & Infrastructure regarding the issue of major challenges facing the nation's transportation system.[4] Dr. Sherry told the panel that congestion, competition, capacity, conservation, and connectivity are the primary challenges facing the US logistics and transportation infrastructure today. Furthermore, he identified intermodal connectivity as the solution to the nation's transportation problems. A seamless intermodal transportation system can help to maximize interconnectedness while it improves the cost efficiencies of the various transportation modes.

Meanwhile, the globalization trend is giving rise to the development of new transportation services to meet the growing demand. In June 2006, Kansas City Southern (KCS) announced its strategic plan to provide a new daily service from Mexico to the southeastern US markets with its subsidiaries, Kansas City Southern de Mexico (KCSM) and The Kansas City Southern Railway Co (KCSR). This arrangement was made to develop an International Intermodal Corridor connecting Lazaro Cardenas to the southeast and central US for consistent and long-haul rail moves.

In 2006, Norfolk Southern and Kansas City Southern announced their joint venture to expand capacity for intermodal traffic between the southeast and southwest parts of the US. Kansas City Southern contributed a 320-mile line between Meridian, Mississippi and Shreveport, Louisiana to the joint venture, while Norfolk Southern invested $300 million cash for capital improvements to increase capacity and improve transit times over the line. This joint venture on a transcontinental rail corridor and intermodal service supports efficient and reliable traffic growth.

---

[4] http://www.eyefortransport.com.

9.2.7 Containerization

Since the introduction of containerization operations, international trade has grown more than twice as fast as the global economy. It is estimated that 90 percent of the world's trade today moves in containers. Each year, about 100 million container cargos in over 5,000 container ships crisscross the oceans. Containerization allows dramatic improvement in port and ship productivity and helps to lower the cost of imported goods. For example, in 1970, it took 50 days for a standard shipment to travel from Hong Kong to New York, but today, in containers, that same trip takes only 17 days.

The busiest container port ranking has changed since 1990. According to the container ports ranking published in 2013 by the American Association of Port Authority (AAPA), the top ten container ports are all in Asia.[5]

It is likely that world trade will double by 2020 and container traffic will grow seven percent a year or more. Consequently, the transportation infrastructure that would support this level of growth in port and container operations is not expected to be sufficient. As at the Port of Los Angeles, this influx of transportation will lead to two major infrastructure problems: 1) the limited available land left at a given site, and 2) the rate of capacity investment. To further support the increase in world transit using containers, major obstacles need to be overcome in infrastructure and in the capital investment that transportation requires. This is a global issue, not one that can be addressed singlehandedly by just one country.

9.3 The Network of Shipper and Carrier in e-distribution

The Internet has become part of our daily lives. Commercialization of the Internet has spawned online shopping, which in turn has established the need for e-distribution and sell-side and buy-side servers. Sell-side servers are electronic storefronts and catalogues that manage the

---

[5] www.worldshipping.org.

purchase process from the selection of items through payment. Buy-side servers provide the capabilities for purchase orders entered and fulfilled. Usually, there are well-established business rules that are incorporated into the e-commerce application. Since customers want to know the exact location of their shipments, marketplace applications enable electronic communities, both buyers and sellers, to track and trace orders.

9.3.1 Carrier side e-distribution

Today, transportation and logistics companies use the Internet to provide customer-side services. Transportation providers offer their customers the ability to log onto their Web sites to check their shipments. For example, the US Postal Service and FedEx allow their customers to log onto Web sites to track and trace their packages.

Many of these e-Business solutions have been developed due to the market requirements. When a customer opts to visit a Web site instead of calling the service center, the company usually benefits, as the option requires no paid employee. This option not only eliminates the risk of any unfavorable exchange between the customer and the service representative, it also reduces costs. Internet service becomes even more desirable when the supply chain serves a global market, one in which customers can call 24 hours a day. The range of these solutions has varied. Some companies have tried to create a competitive advantage with their Web pages by developing signature options unique to their brands. Others provide a customized portal for each customer, including offering the experience in languages other than English.

There are some obstacles in implementing carrier-side e-commerce. One is that if a shipper wishes to track an individual shipment using intermodal service, he must go to the Web page of each logistics provider. Multiple shipments, therefore, require constant movement between Web pages. Additionally, carriers have to know their shipment ID, which they may not have handy, in order to locate their shipments online. When intermodal transportation movement is involved, truckers usually are the last link in the intermodal chain. They must know when equipment is ready for movement. However, very often, they suffer from incomplete information.

Major port areas experience the same problem. Truckers have to log onto a number of Web sites for different steamship lines and marine terminals. Lacking timely information, truckers can find themselves unable to maximize their transportation capacity. For example, they may leave a terminal with an empty truckload, not realizing that a return move is available.

9.3.2 Shipper side e-distribution

The shipper-side of e-commerce determines the ultimate configuration of the market and the industry landscape. Although e-commerce is still in its early stage, some companies have already generated significant savings by moving their transportation purchasing to the Internet. In many cases, multiple vendors offer sales to multiple shippers, which give the shippers the opportunity to select the most suitable carrier.

9.3.3 Shipper and carrier in e-distribution

The transportation industry can be broken down into several groups. At the basic level, a carrier provides services directly to a customer. Thus, a one-to-one relationship is formed. Shippers have numerous bilateral contracts with carriers, and carriers have many one-to-one contracts with shippers.

Beyond this basic arrangement, there are two other marketplace arrangements. One arrangement is to post announcements on bulletin boards at truck stops or rest areas. Truckers post notes offering capacity and respond to requests for hauling capacity. This method is the simplest but requires actual presence at the truck stop or rest place. The other arrangement is to let truck brokerages perform a load matching task. Over time, truck brokerage has evolved into a third party logistic (3PL) provider.

The e-commerce bulletin board grows out of the traditional method. Here, the provider gathers and posts information online about available loads from carriers and desired loads by shippers. When shippers or carriers see an item online, they can contact the other party. This e-business model is simple. The bulletin board provider charges a monthly subscription fee and offers services.

Another type of e-commerce marketplace is the auction. Web sites serve as a freight rate auction marketplace. Shippers either place their desired bids on the website for carriers to view and offer bids, or just request the carriers' best rates. Carriers also take advantage of e-commerce. Some carriers advertise capacity and seek bids for it. This process is usually blind, taking place at a predetermined date and time; the winning bid will be announced.

Some carriers are afraid that e-commerce penetration may drive freight rates down. People with this concern may consider the following three arguments:

First, e-commerce penetration is determined by supply and demand in addition to market aggregation and intermediation. A market with a few major carriers (such as the railroad industry and the airlines) will be harder to penetrate than one with numerous carriers (such as interstate trucking).

Second, e-commerce solutions can be introduced more easily into markets that have well-established transportation intermediaries (the trucking industry) than to markets that do not traditionally rely on intermediaries.

Third, e-commerce business models will not cause rates to fall further than they should, but may drive shipping rates to fall a little faster.

Concerns on the shipper's side lie in the decision of when to purchase transportation services. If shippers suspect that demand is close to or exceeds supply, they will want contracts for their expected loads and transportation service. However, if they suspect that supply will exceed demand, they will tend to wait and purchase transportation service on the spot market.

Information is a critical component of the supply chain and will continue to drive change in the transportation and logistics markets. The number of transportation and logistics e-commerce products proliferates daily. While many B2B sites claim to eliminate the need for intermediaries, many are becoming intermediaries in their own right.

9.4 The Rise of Intermediaries in Transportation

9.4.1 The rise of intermediaries

During the middle and late 1990s, an increased awareness of core competencies became part of competitive culture. As more sophisticated financial tools, like activity-based costing and economic value-added activities, entered the corporate mainstream, management began to consider outsourcing non-core functions and began to concentrate on their core competencies and customers. Outsourcing non-core functions such as logistics and transportation allows a company to take advantage of greater operational flexibility. For example, Anheuser-Busch controls the majority of its supply chain functions including the agricultural supply, brewing, and distribution, but it outsources logistics functions, such as warehousing, to third-party providers.

Meanwhile, carriers may find pricing on the spot market unappealing because that pricing can leave them with a lack of an accurate demand forecast, effective information systems, or the personnel to handle such market dynamics. In order to avoid selling loading capacity at a steep discount, carriers seek contracts with 3PL providers for large cargo commitments. The rates for a large volume load may be lower than for a smaller volume load, but this option requires fewer employees, less time, and less information technology.

As such, intermediaries provide functions such as shipment consolidation, marketing, information collection, and the ability to match supply and demand between carriers and shippers. In general, intermediaries make purchased transportation decisions on two levels: buying and selling loading capacity and transportation services. Today, a transportation system is supported by a number of intermediary services, including shippers' associations, brokers, shipper's agents, owner-operators, and last-mile delivery companies. It has been estimated that more than 60% of the Fortune 500 manufacturers use some form of third-party logistics services. The following sections briefly discuss third-party logistics and fourth-party logistics (since we have discussed both topics in Chapter 4, *Supplier Relations and Strategic Sourcing*).

9.4.1.1 Freight forwarder

Freight forwarders specialize in arranging pick-ups, storage, and shipping of merchandise on behalf of their clients. They usually provide a full range of logistic solutions including preparing documents for shipping and exporting, negotiating competitive freight rates, booking cargo space, pooling small shipments, obtaining cargo insurance, filing insurance claims, warehousing, tracking inland transportation, completing customs clearance for importing goods, providing logistics service consultation, and more.

Freight forwarders usually ship under their own bills of lading. A **bill of lading** is a document issued on behalf of the carrier and is a contract of carriage by sea. The document has the following legal statements: (i) a receipt for goods, signed by a duly authorized person on behalf of the carriers; (ii) a document of title to the goods described therein; and (iii) evidence of the terms and conditions of carriage agreed upon between the two parties.

9.4.1.2 Transportation brokers

A **transportation broker** is legally authorized to act as an agent on behalf of shippers or carriers. A transportation broker is a licensed professional in a special area such as insurance, finance, or compliance who serves as a liaison between the shipper and carrier. Thus, the transportation broker plays an important role in moving cargo around and provides special services to connect the shippers and carriers who are willing to transport goods at a mutually acceptable rate. Freight brokers use their knowledge of the shipping industry and technological resources to help shippers and carriers accomplish their goals. The logistics services provided by transportation brokers help shippers to cut transportation costs, improve delivery efficiency and speed, and enhance customer service.

A freight forwarder and a freight broker perform some of the same tasks, including consolidating smaller shipments and arranging for the transportation of the consolidated shipments. The major difference between the two is that a freight forwarder takes possession of the items being transported while a freight broker never takes possession of the items being shipped.

9.4.1.3 Shippers association

Shippers Associations are usually non-profit, member-owned organizations that aim at providing their members with the lowest rates and best service for the movement of household goods throughout the world. For example, the **International Shippers Association** (ISA) is a non-profit association that moves members' cargo and consolidates small shipments to get a quantity discount. ISA members include international shippers and forwarders of commercial, military, and government household goods, unaccompanied baggage, and general commodities.

There are industry-based shipper associations as well. For example, the Food Shippers Association of North America (FSANA) was founded in 1996 around a core group of companies engaged in the export of frozen and chilled foodstuffs. The goal of FSANA is to help its members to maintain their competitiveness in the global marketplace. By pooling their resources and working together, FSANA members are able to obtain competitive ocean freight rates and other services. FSANA has signed contracts with most major carriers covering every major trade lane and it continues to grow larger and stronger.

9.4.1.4 Intermodal marketing company

Intermodal marketing companies, acting as intermediaries between intermodal rail carriers & shippers, combine the capabilities of railroads and ocean shipping with the accessibility of trucks to move containers, trailers, and other shipments. They also handle privately-owned containers and arrange for the vehicles needed to move goods. The major challenges facing the industry are coordination and channel leadership. Providing the right equipment is also a challenge because a variety of containers, trailers, and chassis sizes are all needed.

9.4.2 Third-party logistics in transportation services

Third-party logistics providers are firms that manage and execute certain value-added logistics and transportation functions on behalf of their customers, using their own assets and resources. Successful 3PLs provide services throughout the world using various modes such as highway, ocean, and air transportation.

Third-party transportation providers offer an array of logistics services, including carrier selection, route scheduling, shipment storage, partial assembly of parts, and transportation. Using 3PL services, businesses are able to reduce operating costs and capital expenses. Some customers believe that they can benefit from scope and scale economy that are unavailable from individual carriers. For example, Nortel Networks[6] is a global leader in telecommunications equipment and supplies industry customers in 150 countries. Its customers require Nortel to deliver products just-in-time to their production sites. At the beginning of 2002, Nortel outsourced its entire $200 million in logistics operations to Kuehne & Nagel.[7] Kuehne & Nagel created a separate company, KN Lead Logistics (KNLL), to handle Nortel's more than 80 primary and 200 secondary logistics service providers. After using 3PL service, Nortel only needs to contact KNLL for a range of logistics and transportation operations such as warehouse storage, shipment delivery, distribution network design, and global systems connectivity. Thus, Nortel was able to strengthen its core competencies and provide differentiated value to the customer. Both Nortel and KNLL were able to share the financial benefits of supply-chain performance improvement.

A survey of industry executives and managers confirms that third-party logistics providers not only provide strategic and operational value, but also develop new and innovative ways to improve logistics effectiveness. In general, shippers spent 42% of their total logistics

---

[6] Nortel Networks Corporation was a multinational telecommunications and data networking equipment manufacturer headquartered in Mississauga, Ontario, Canada.

[7] Kuehne & Nagel is a global transportation and logistics company based in Schindellegi, Switzerland.

expenditures (which is 12% of their sales revenue) on 3PL services. In this sense, 3PLs are key contributors to shippers' overall business success.[8]

9.4.2.1 Last-mile delivery

Online shopping is becoming an increasing trend for consumer goods shoppers and is even more popular among holiday shoppers. However, the product a consumer has ordered online through cyberspace has to be delivered to the customer's space or residence. The phrase, "last-mile delivery" means the delivery of the product ordered online to the customer's home. E-commerce has created many users of last-mile delivery services because of the relatively small volume of products being shipped. Many companies turn to 3PL providers to make sure that their packages get to their final customers. UPS and FedEx, to name just two, are major last-mile delivery service providers. These companies offer a range of services such as home delivery, business-to-business delivery, and customized logistics services. Usually, these 3PL providers can provide a better value to businesses than having the businesses incur the cost of maintaining their own vehicle fleets or expanding their delivery teams. 3PLs usually concentrate on logistics service. Therefore, 3PLs are more efficient and cost-effective at getting things delivered in the right condition, at the right time, and to the right place.

9.4.2.2 A last-mile delivery case: The collaboration of Talbots, DHL, and US Postal Service

Talbots, a leading US national specialty retailer, e-retailer, and catalogue sales provider of women's apparel, shoes, and accessories, outsourced its business-to-consumer (B2C) delivery service to DHL, a leading logistics company. Talbots operates over 500 stores throughout the US and Canada; their catalogs and an e-commerce site reach a vast audience of customers around the world.[9]

---

[8] John Langley, Jr. (2012). "2012 Third-Party Logistics Study," Capgemini.
[9] Available August 2013 www.Talbots.com.

Focusing on its core competencies in apparel and in maintaining an unbeatable customer service level, Talbots identified a collaboration opportunity with DHL that would reduce the home delivery time of ground shipments from the company's distribution center in Lakeville, Massachusetts to the West Coast from six days to four days.

DHL, on the other hand, created a 3PL solution called DHL@home in 1999 to provide business-to-residential delivery service. How does DHL deliver the shipments to the end users? Through the @home service, DHL picks up parcels at the Talbots warehouse in Lakeville., sorts parcels according to customers' zip codes, and delivers the parcels via its logistics network to the US postal facility that is closest to the consumer.[10] Collaborating with DHL, the US Postal Service (USPS) then performs the last-mile delivery with its daily mail delivery routes. Fig. 9.2 illustrates the delivery process.

Since Talbots requires' over 10,000 shipments a day, DHL has developed a customized logistic solution for Talbots that includes flexible delivery options of 2-4 days or 2-7 days, Saturday delivery, and delivery to US postal facilities. Additionally, a proactive account was set up to ensure that customer orders will be fulfilled on time.

This example of 3PL operation represents modern thinking. DHL is taking advantage of the existing US postal mail delivery network to reduce the number of delivery routes, since the number of post offices (many, many fewer than the number of individual householders) is fixed. By collaborating with US postal service, DHL is able to reduce the complexity of route scheduling, which leads to cost reduction.

---

[10] DHL To Serve as Talbots' Preferred Residential Delivery Provider for Catalog and Online Customers, December 2, 2004, www.businesswire.com.

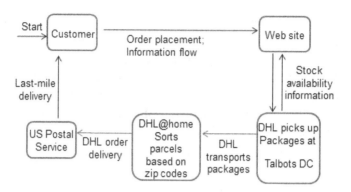

Fig. 9.2 Last-mile delivery.

9.4.2.3 Managing less-than-truckload (LTL) shipments

Less-than-truckload (LTL) shipments are also called small shipments. When transportation is a peripheral function of a company, using a for-hire carrier or 3PL for delivery is a common practice. The strategy for managing small shipments is: 1) to consolidate small shipments through door-to-door pickup, 2) to use 3PL or for-hire carriers to transport shipments to a transportation facility such as a terminal or warehouse, and 3) to share the services offered by the carrier or 3PL. Managing small shipments effectively can help a company reduce costs and maintain a high level of customer service.

9.4.3 Fourth-party logistics in transportation service

A fourth-party logistics (4PL) provider is the "head logistics provider" of a supply chain which manages the 3PLs in the supply chain. As shown in Fig. 9.3, 4PL integrates various supply chain activities to create a virtual business environment; its role includes, but is not limited to:

- Helping clients develop strategic objects
- Integrating the operations of 3PL providers, IT providers, manufacturers, distributors and retailers involved along the supply chain

- Directing the planning, steering, and controlling of all of the logistics procedures of its clients
- Managing supply chain operations
- Supervising the activities of 3PL
- Creating and utilizing business information and knowledge

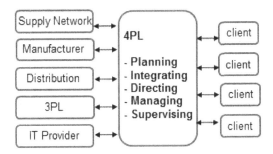

Fig. 9.3 The role of 4PL in the supply chain.

In general, people agree that fourth-party logistics providers have emerged to cover information technology's needs in transportation. However, the true evolution of the 4PL is due to the growth of the global marketplace. Companies which operate in the global marketplace have become aware of the fact that logistics is not a commodity or a simple client/service relationship; it is a critical means to steer them toward boosting their cost savings, enhancing their cash flow, and improving their service levels in getting their products to market. In this sense, a 4PL provider is a supply chain integrator that synthesizes and manages the resources, capabilities, and technologies of its own organization with those of complementary service providers to deliver an e-commerce supply chain solution to its customers. A 4PL company provides strategy: consulting, reviewing, and redesigning its customers' business processes, integrating various technologies, and leveraging human resources. When a 4PL company provides 3PL services, it becomes known as an *infomediary*. Thus, a 4PL provider is a strategic partner instead of a tactical transportation service provider such as the 3PL.

9.5 Trade-Off of Transportation and Inventory Costs

When making transportation decisions, a number of factors need to be considered. These factors include inventory-holding costs, facility costs, order processing costs, transportation costs, and other relevant costs. Supply chain managers often consider the following trade-offs:

* the trade-off between inventory and transportation costs
* the trade-off between the transportation mode and the customer service target.

The following is an example problem regarding trade-offs between transportation choices and inventory costs.

Example problem 9.1: Trade-off of transportation and inventory costs

Located near Norfolk, Virginia, the Flow Pump Corporation offers a wide range of pump types, from pre-engineering process pumps to highly specialized pumps and systems. It purchases all of the motors for its pumps from Quik Motors, Inc. Flow Pump has an average demand of 30,000 motors annually. Each motor averages about 40 pounds in weight. Quik Motors charges Flow Pump $600 per motor. Usually, it takes one day for Quik Motors to process the orders from Flow Pump, which means, for example, that if Quik Motors receives the order from Flow Pump on Monday, it will ship the order on Tuesday.

Flow Pump has an order processing cost of $50 per order. Its inventory holding cost is 25% of the item-purchasing price. At its assembly plant, Flow Pump carries a safety inventory equal to five percent of the average demand during the carrier's delivery lead time. Flow Pump operates 300 days a year.

The plant manager at Flow Pump wants to balance inventory costs and transportation costs before he selects a transportation option. Available transportation options are given in the table below:

Carrier	Volume shipped (in pound)	Shipping cost ($/lb.)	Lead time
Southern Railroad	20,000 & more	0.10	6 days
Eastern Trucking TL	10,000	0.15	3 days
Flex Trucking LTL	no weight limit	0.20	4 days

The less-than-truck-load (LTL) option consolidates small shipments for intercity movement and then disaggregates the truckload at the destination. Thus, the LTL option has a longer lead time than the Truckload (TL) option. The manager would like you to figure out the following:

a. What is the lot size for each option?
b. What is the number of orders for the year?
c. What is the cycle inventory?
d. What is the safety inventory?
e. What is the ordering cost?
f. What is the transportation cost?
g. What is the cycle inventory holding cost?
h. What is the safety stock holding cost?
i. What are the total costs (including cycle inventory cost, safety stock cost, order cost, and transportation cost) for each option?
j. Which option would you recommend to the plant manager based on the cost analysis? What other relevant factors would you suggest to the manager?

Solution to example problem 9.1

Below, we show the detailed computational procedures for the choice of Southern Railroad, along with answers to all three choices that are presented in Table 9.1.

a. The railroad's shipping quantity is 20,000 pounds and each motor averages about 40 pounds in weight.

$$\text{Lot size} = \frac{20{,}000 \text{ lb}}{40 \text{ lb}} = 500 \text{ units}$$

b. The number of orders for a year is determined by annual demand divided by order lot size.

Number of orders for a year = $\dfrac{30,000}{500}$ = 60 orders

c. The cycle inventory is the order size divided by 2.

Cycle inventory = $\dfrac{Q}{2}$ = $\dfrac{500}{2}$ = 250 units

d. The safety inventory is five percent of the average demand during the carrier's delivery lead time as stated in the problem. The company operates 300 days a year.

Safety inventory = $0.05 * 6 * \dfrac{30,000}{300}$ = 30 units

e. The order cost per order should be multiplied by the number of orders.

Ordering cost = $50 * 60 = $3,000

f. First, multiply number of units by unit weight, and then multiply by the shipping rate.

Transportation cost = 0.10 * (30,000*40) = $120,000

g. The inventory holding cost is 25% of the item-purchasing price for each unit for a year. The cycle inventory cost is computed as cycle inventory multiplied by inventory unit holding cost.

Cycle inventory cost = ($600 * 0.25) * 250 = $37,500

h. The safety inventory cost is computed as safety inventory multiplied by the inventory unit holding cost.

Safety inventory cost = ($600 * 0.25) * 30 = $4,500

i. Total cost = order cost + transportation cost + total inventory cost

= $3,000 + $120,000 + ($37,500 + $4,500) = $165,000

j. Based on the cost analysis shown in Table 9.1, the plant manager decides to purchase transportation service from Southern Railroad. Other factors that can be considered include on time delivery, flexibility, customer service level, cash flow, etc.

Calculate the lot size for Flex Trucking (LTL):

$$\text{Lot size} = \sqrt{\frac{2DS}{H}} = \sqrt{\frac{2(30000)50}{600(0.25)}} = 141 \text{ units}$$

Please note, if you use a spreadsheet, the numbers may be a little different due to rounding. For example, the lot size for Flex Trucking LTL can be 141.42. Additionally, the cycle inventory of Flex Trucking LTL is a fraction. We keep the fraction to demonstrate the idea. In practice, this number can be rounded to integer.

Table 9.1 Solution to example problem 9.1.

	A	B	C	D	E	F	G	H	I	J
1	Carriers	Lot Size	# of Orders	Cycle Inv	Safety Inv	Order Cost	Transport Cost	Cycle Inv Cost	Safety Inv Cost	Total Cost
2	Southern Railroad	500	60	250	30	3,000	120,000	37,500	4,500	165,000
3	Eastern Trucking TL	250	120	125	15	6,000	180,000	18,750	2,250	207,000
4	Flex Trucking LTL	141	213	70.5	20	10,650	240,000	10,575	3,000	264,225

9.6 Vehicle Routing and Scheduling

A good selection of transportation mode can provide a company with competitive cost advantages because transportation costs usually range from one-third to two-thirds of total logistics costs. It is vital in transportation to find the best travel route, one that minimizes the distance or the time for a vehicle. Vehicle routing and scheduling are important aspects of last-mile delivery.

There are a number of factors need to be considered when developing a vehicle route and schedule. These factors include loading and unloading at each stop, the use of multiple vehicles with similar or different capacities in volume and weight, the maximum driving period limitation (e.g. an eight-hour shift), and a time window for pickup and delivery to avoid traffic time or to meet a business's most demanding hours of the day, such as delivering beer to a restaurant before dinnertime.

One of the most important decisions in vehicle transportation management is the selection of routes and the scheduling of deliveries. A route is a sequence of pickup and/or delivery points which the vehicle must follow in order. A schedule is a set of arrival and departure times for the pickup and/or delivery points specified in the route.

When arrival times are specified at facilities on an existing road, we refer to the problem as a scheduling problem. When arrival times are unspecified, the problem is a straightforward routing problem. When time windows and precedence relationships exist, both routing and scheduling functions are performed.

9.6.1 Characteristics describing vehicle routing

The objectives of motor services are to minimize routing costs incurred, to minimize the sum of fixed and variable costs, and to provide the best service possible. There are a number of factors that a motor carrier needs to consider when offering motor services:

- *Demand.* The nature of demand can be stable or sporadic, and delivery time can be specified in advance or unspecified.
- *Facility and equipment.* There are various kinds of facilities and equipment. For example, there can be one terminal or several terminals; the type of vehicles can be one size or different sizes; vehicle capacity constraints can be imposed either consistently or at certain time windows; and routes can be direct, indirect, or even mixed.
- *Costs.* There are a number of costs for providing service: for example, purchasing a vehicle or leasing a vehicle, fixed operating costs such as the terminals fee and the airport gates ticket, trip-related costs such as labor costs and fuel expenses, and quantity related costs such as loading /unloading costs and overhead costs.
- *Type of service.* The type of service offered can be pickup only, drop off only, like UPS service. Alternatively, a mix of pickup and drop off service (such as by a post office mail carrier who picks up the outgoing mail we leave in the mailbox and drops the in-coming mail in the mailbox).

There are a number of factors that affect a shipper's decision. Various costs related to transportation must be considered, including mode related transportation costs, load-related inventory costs, facility costs, order-processing costs, and service level costs.

9.6.2 Solution procedure for vehicle routing and scheduling

Vehicle routing and scheduling problems have become more complicated as more constraints have been added. A number of solution procedures have been developed over the years. Among them, the Saving Method suggested by Clarke and Wright is one that is able to handle a range of constraints. The following steps are taken to create routes and to make travel schedules based on the model suggested by Clarke and Wright. The first three steps are used to assign customers to routes, and the fourth step creates a schedule for each vehicle to minimize the distance traveled, as well as the transportation costs.

1. Compute the distance matrix. The distance between the warehouse and the customer (or a pair of customers) is determined using the following formula.

$$\text{Distance (between store and customer)} = \sqrt{(\text{store}_x - \text{cust}_{ix})^2 + (\text{store}_y - \text{cust}_{iy})^2}$$
$$(9.1)$$

where:
  Store_x = x coordinate of the store location
  Store_y = y coordinate of the store location
  Cust_{ix} = x coordinate of the location of customer i
  Cust_{iy} = y coordinate of the location of customer i

2. Compute the savings matrix. The savings in distance between two customers i and j is determined by

$$\text{Saving (Cust}_i, \text{Cust}_j) = \text{distance (store, Cust}_i)$$
$$+ \text{distance (store, Cust}_j) - \text{distance (Cust}_i, \text{Cust}_j) \qquad (9.2)$$

Where:

$Cust_i$ = customer i

$Cust_j$ = customer j

3. Create routes. Assign customers to routes. Initially, we assume that there are as many routes as there are customers. Search the Savings Matrix created in Step 2 for the intersection of $customer_i$ and $customer_j$ that has the largest savings. Consider combining route x with route y, if adding additional customers to the route will not exceed the vehicle capacity, and if neither route x nor route y has been combined with some other route. If a single customer's load exceeds the capacity of a truck, split the load into two vehicles.

4. Develop a delivery schedule. First, sequence customers within the route to make a schedule. The nearest insertion method is applied. Based on the distance matrix computed in Step 1, the customer closest to the current trip should be inserted first.

The nearest insertion method. This procedure is called the nearest insertion method because it adds the customer that is closest to the route. The procedure is as follows:

- With a given route, determine the minimum increase in distance and insert the closest customer to the route.
- Continue this process until all of the customers assigned to the vehicle are inserted to the route.

Example problem 9.2: Vehicle routing and sequence

Farm Fresh, a grocery store, delivers customer orders that have been placed online. One morning, the manager at Farm Fresh has orders from nine different customers that are to be delivered. Table 9.2 shows the locations of the store and the customers, as well as the customer order size. There are four minivans available; each is capable of carrying up to 260 kilograms.

a. Using the Savings Method to determine the number of routes (minivans) needed to deliver orders that morning:

- Create a distance matrix
- Create a savings matrix
- Assign customers to route (vehicle)

b. Make a schedule for each route (vehicle) using the Nearest Insertion Method.

Table 9.2 Vehicle routing and sequence.

	X coordinate	Y coordinate	Order Size (kilogram)
Store	0	0	
Customer 1	5	13	38
Customer 2	2	9	91
Customer 3	8	16	57
Customer 4	9	11	47
Customer 5	13	2	30
Customer 6	18	1	56
Customer 7	15	-6	92
Customer 8	10	-9	43
Customer 9	4	-11	36

Solution to problem 9.2 Vehicle routing and sequence

Step 1: Create distance matrix

Use equation (9.1) to compute the distance matrix. The results of the distances between the store and all of the customers, and among the customers are reported in Table 9.3. For example, compute the distance from the store to customer 1:

$$\text{Distance (store, Cust1)} = \sqrt{(\text{store}_x - \text{cust}_{ix})^2 + (\text{store}_y - \text{cust}_{iy})^2}$$

$$= \sqrt{(0-5)^2 + (0-13)^2} = 13.93$$

Now, compute the distance from customer 3 to customer 4:

$$\text{Distance (Cust3, Cust4)} = \sqrt{(8-9)^2 + (16-11)^2} = 5.10$$

The distance between all pairs of store to customers, and customer to customer are presented in Table 9.3.

Table 9.3 Distance matrix.

	Store	Cust1	Cust2	Cust3	Cust4	Cust5	Cust6	Cust7	Cust8	Cust9
Cust1	13.93	0.00								
Cust2	9.22	5.00	0.00							
Cust3	17.89	4.24	9.22	0.00						
Cust4	14.21	4.47	7.28	5.10	0.00					
Cust5	13.15	13.60	13.04	14.87	9.85	0.00				
Cust6	18.03	17.69	17.89	18.03	13.45	5.10	0.00			
Cust7	16.16	21.47	19.85	23.09	18.03	8.25	7.62	0.00		
Cust8	13.45	22.56	19.70	25.08	20.02	11.40	12.81	5.83	0.00	
Cust9	11.70	24.02	20.10	27.29	22.56	15.81	18.44	12.08	6.32	0.00

Step 2: Create savings matrix

Use equation (9.2) to compute the savings matrix. The results of savings between a pair of customers are reported in Table 9.4.

Table 9.4 Savings matrix.

	Cust1	Cust2	Cust3	Cust4	Cust5	Cust6	Cust7	Cust8	Cust9
Cust1	0.00								
Cust2	18.15	0.00							
Cust3	27.58	17.89	0.00						
Cust4	23.67	16.15	27.00	0.00					
Cust5	13.48	9.33	16.17	17.51	0.00				
Cust6	14.27	9.36	17.89	18.79	26.08	0.00			
Cust7	8.62	5.53	10.96	12.34	21.06	26.57	0.00		
Cust8	4.82	2.97	6.26	7.64	15.20	18.67	23.78	0.00	
Cust9	1.61	0.82	2.30	3.35	9.04	11.29	15.78	18.83	0.00

Note: the savings matrix is computed based on the distance matrix. The answers could be a little different due to rounding.[11]

---

[11] The savings between customer 1 and customer 2 can also be computed as follows: Distance (store ↔ customer 1, store ↔ customer 2)=13.93+13.93+9.22+9.22=46.30. If the van travels from the store to customer 1, and then from customer 1 to customer 2, and travels back from customer 2 to the store, the total distance (using Table 9.3 the distance matrix) will be:
Distance (store → customer 1 → customer 2 → store) = 13.93+5+9.22 = 28.15
Savings between customers 1 and 2 is: 46.30 – 28.15 = 18.15.

Let's use customer 1 and customer 2 as an example using values from Table 9.3 Distance Matrix. Table 9.4 Savings Matrix presents the savings of all pairs.

Saving = distance(store, $Cust_1$)+distance(store, $Cust_2$)–distance($Cust_1$, $Cust_2$)
= 13.93 + 9.22 – 5 = 18.15

Step 3: Build routes

The solving procedure used to build routes is as follows:

1) Assume that each delivery to a customer is a route or a trip. There are nine routes to start with.
2) Find the largest savings between a pair of two locations from the Savings Matrix.
3) Check load constraint before combining customers that have the largest saving between them.
4) Continue the search until all customers are assigned to a route.

First, make each customer an independent route. There are nine routes to start with. Then, search for the largest savings between two customers from Table 9.4 Savings Matrix. The saving between customers 1 and 3 is the largest: 27.58. Check order sizes and van capacity: 38 + 57 < 260. Customers 1 and 3 can be combined to form a new route. We call this route 1.

The next largest saving is 27, which is between customers 3 and 4. Check order sizes and van capacity: 38 + 57 + 47 < 260. Customer 4 can be combined into Route 1. Now, Route 1 has three customers: 1, 3, and 4.

The next largest saving is 26.57, which is between customers 6 and 7. Customers 6 and 7 do not intersect with customers 1, 3, and 4 in Route 1. But also, if both customers 6 and 7 are added to Route 1, its total load of 5 customers will exceed its van's capacity. Therefore, let's create a new route for customers 6 and 7. This route is named Route 2.

Continuing the search, Route 1 ends up with 4 customers (1, 3, 4, and 2) and a total load of 233 (38+57+47+91 = 233). Route 2 has five customers (6, 7, 5, 8, and 9) and a total load of 257 (56 + 92 + 30 + 43 + 36 = 257).

Step 4: Sequence customers within the route

Next, we use the Distance Matrix in Table 9.3 to make a delivery sequence.

1) For each route, find the shortest distance from the store to customer (since we start at the store).
2) Find the shortest distance from the chosen customer to the next customer; add the customer to the route.
3) Repeat step (2) until all of the customers within the route are scheduled.
4) Compute the total distance traveled for each route.

Fig. 9.4 shows the two routes.

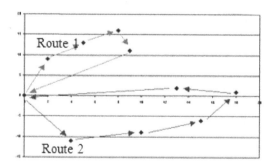

Fig. 9.4 Routes.

Route 1: The shortest distance from the store to customers 1, 2, 3, and 4 is between the store and customer 2. Therefore, the route starts from the store and goes to Customer 2. The next shortest distance between customer 2 and customers 1, 3, and 4 is between customer 2 and customer 1. The route is extended to store – Cust2 – Cust1. Continue this procedure until the sequence is complete. Route 1 now has the following sequence:

Store → Cust2 → Cust1 → Cust3 → Cust4 → store.
The total distance is: 9.22 + 5 + 4.24 + 5.10 + 14.21 = 37.77

Route 2 has the following sequence:

Store → Cust9 → Cust8 → Cust7 → Cust6 → Cust5 → store.
The total distance is: 11.70+6.32+5.83+7.62+5.10+13.15 = 49.72

9.6.3 e-Business tools for creating routes

Some Internet search engines offer a convenient way to build delivery routes. For example, using Google maps and Mapquest, readers can enter the addresses they want to visit and create a route. But these tools do not provide ways to handle delivery time-window constraints or the weight capacity of vehicles. Consequently, human intelligence is needed to create delivery routes that take such constraints into consideration.

9.7 Railway Freight Car Scheduling

With the globalization of the world economy and the birth of free-trade zones, railway freight services have played an important role in the development of modern transportation networks in Asia, Europe, the United States, and many other countries. The offshore sourcing of goods in the Pacific Rim countries has led to the increased use of water-rail-truck intermodal service. Thus, railroad transportation has gained renewed attention for its capacity to transfer bulk commodities over long distances at a lower freight rate.

In practice, it is difficult to allocate the freight cars and to determine how to load a variety of goods into them using a large-scale railway network. Railway freight service requires sophisticated algorithms as well as flexibility. Both practitioners and researchers have indicated that a knowledge-based system can be useful for making decisions in railway freight services. Geng and Li have suggested a model for freight car loading and routing, and a knowledge-based system for railway freight service that is integrated into an existing railway information system.[12] The combination of loading rules, routing algorithms, logic programming and database technology provides railway managers with a practical way to manage railway freight service.

9.7.1 Railway system

A railway system is a network of track sections connected to one another by stations and terminals. The advantage of using railway service is that it delivers large-volume/low-value items over long distances at low cost. With the advancements in supply chain management, the railroads have expanded their operations to include intermodal services that lead to increased growth in loadings.

The carload is the basic unit of measurement of freight handled by the railroad. Therefore, loading and routing are two major operational issues to be considered in order to ensure reliable service for shippers. The overall objective is to maximize freight car utilization and minimize distance traveled.

In railway service, there is usually a start station which dispatches a freight train, a stop station where the freight train completes its trip, and transfer stations that serve as depots and cover a number of stations within a network of vertices. Commodities of smaller quantity from ordinary stations or other transfer stations are transported to the transfer station for consolidation, loading, and unloading.

---

[12] Geng, G. & Li, L. (2001). "Scheduling railway freight cars" *Knowledge-based Systems,* 14, pp. 289-297.

9.7.2 Characteristics describing railway freight scheduling

Freight car loading usually uses some sort of priority rules. Loading priority is a function of commodity attributes, delivery due date, delivery time window, delivery date priority, core shipment status, and commodity weight.

Possible commodity attributes include fresh and live goods; coal, chemical, and allied products; farm products; motor vehicles; equipment; military goods; food and kindred products; and non-metallic minerals, among others. A great number of chemicals and allied products are classified as hazardous.

Core shipment is a shipment of heavy weight. Railway authorities determine the weight; for example, if a shipment exceeds 5000 kilograms, it is a core shipment. The purpose of determining the core shipment is to realize more loading in a freight car with fewer stops. A core shipment may include only one commodity. Several small shipments can be arranged into a core. The commodities of a core shipment are transported to the same stop station or transfer station. Using the core shipment priority method, the railway storage utilization is improved, and so is transportation efficiency.

In general, shipments with a heavy weight but a small volume are not to be placed in the same freight car, nor are the goods with large-volume light weight to be placed in the same freight car. A mix of heavy weight, small-volume commodities and light-weight, large-volume goods better utilizes freight car space.

When a train arrives at a transfer station, some goods are unloaded and additional goods are loaded onto the freight car. In this case, additional goods loaded into the rail car at the current stop should not disturb the unloading operation at the next station. What must be determined is which item should be loaded into the railcar first and which should be loaded next. Transference range must be considered when loading additional goods.

Loading hazardous goods is a tough job. Any carelessness can result in an accident. Therefore, considerable attention is paid to loading hazardous goods.

The railway network is pre-existing. The length of the legs between consecutive stations is fixed. The speed on the leg between any two stations is assumed to be constant. The selection of the best routes for each freight train determines the workloads and the general consolidation strategies for each station of the railway system.

The input information for arranging freight car loading and scheduling includes commodity attributes, commodity weight, commodity volume, hazardous/perishable goods, number of days the commodity will be in the rail yard, loading priority rating, neighborhood distances, transfer range (the distance from a transfer station to every station within the transfer range), and transfer path (the shortest path between two transfer stations). The output of freight car scheduling includes the loading sequence of the commodity by freight car, primary route, the 2nd and 3rd possible routes, freight car capacity utilization by each freight car, and day of week.

9.8 Enhance Value through Transportation

The transportation industry is a significant factor in world trade and economic growth. Over the past ten years, U.S. international trade in goods has doubled, and this rate is not likely to slow in the next decade. The low transportation rates enhance the competitiveness of US products in world markets and enable importers to bring a variety of industry and consumer goods to the US as well. For example, transportation adds a dollar to the cost of bringing a VCR from Hong Kong to the US market; ocean shipping services from Asia add about 40 cents to the price of the sneakers.[13] As the supply chain is further extended, transportation service truly adds value to supply chain management.

---

[13] The World Shipping Council.

The US Federal Highway Administration anticipates freight volume to grow by 70% by 2020. More investment is needed to support this expected doubling of freight volume by 2020. In order to support the US trade flow and to add value to the world economy, a seamless and efficient multi-modal transportation system is needed. The intermodal operation should be able to link large-size cargo vessels, complex cargo handling, effective storage operations, reliable rail service, and extensive trucking coverage.

Tight collaboration among supply chain companies will be more popular in the years to come. Mark Colombo, vice president for strategic marketing at FedEx, talked about a survey of lean supply chain manufacturing in the electronics industry.[14] In that survey, 87 percent of respondents said they expected their level of imports to increase beyond where it is now. These companies are already implementing global supply chains and may add another sub-production facility in Asia, South America, or even in Europe. In this case, they will transport their products from the production center to the customer-centered markets. The loads can start out as ground-into-air or ground-into-ocean. The issue is how integrated their logistics and transportation networks are going to be, in order to support their supply chain needs. In the same survey, 68 percent of the respondents said that they expected collaboration and tight integration with their transportation providers, because their customers are expecting short lead times and high responsiveness.

---

[14] http://www.worldtrademag.com/CDA/Archives/.

9.9 Summary

In this chapter, we have offered an overview of various transportation modes and their roles in supply chain management. The rise of intermediary, third party logistics, and fourth party logistics has rapidly changed the landscape of the transportation industry in the US and throughout the world. E-distribution has become the new way of doing business in a global market. Transportation is no longer a minor function of a company; it has strategic importance to the success of a supply chain.

Questions for Pondering

1. Compare and contrast the cost structure, market structure, customer service policy, business infrastructure, and operations management of the truckload and LTL segments of the motor carrier industry in the US.
2. The railroad industry contributed significantly to the development and growth of cities and economic centers prior to WWII. The trucking industry contributed to the development and growth of cities and economic centers in the second half of the twentieth century. The airline industry has grown very quickly since 1978 and is currently facing financial difficulties. Discuss the political, economic, social, technological, and industry-competitive factors that contribute to the growth and decline of various transportation modes. In your opinion, what will be the next dominant transportation mode? Why?
3. Discuss the advantages and disadvantages of the rise of intermediary, third-, and fourth-party logistics. Provide industry evidence with your discussions.

Problems

1. Suzuki, Inc. supplies window fans to Best Appliances Distributor. Best Appliances Distributor is responsible for transportation arrangements and costs. Best Appliances Distributor purchases 100,000 units annually at an average of $10.00 per fan. Inventory cost is 25% of the unit purchasing cost. Order processing cost is $30 per order. Best Appliances operates 350 days a year and carries 5% of the average demand during the carrier's delivery lead time.

   The director of transportation at Best Appliances has collected the following information and has hired you to complete the analysis. You need to present a solution that will minimize transportation and inventory costs. Consider order costs, the costs of cycle inventory and safety stocks, and transportation costs.

Transportation Mode	Transit Time	Rate Per Unit	Lot Size / Shipment Size
Railway	30 days	$1.00	1,000
Piggyback	12 days	$1.20	500
Truck	4 days	$1.30	200

2. FreshBread delivers customer orders daily to 10 grocery stores. One morning, the manager at FreshBread had the orders as shown in the following table. There are two vans available; each is capable of carrying up to 500 loaves of bread.

	X coordinate	Y coordinate	Order Size
FreshBread warehouse	0	0	
Store 1	6	12	128
Store 2	3	2	95
Store 3	9	15	157
Store 4	10	10	140
Store 5	11	1	130
Store 6	8	0	150
Store 7	5	-7	102

   a. Use the Savings Method to determine the number of routes (vans) needed to deliver orders that morning.
   b. Make a schedule for each route (van) using the Nearest Insertion Method.

3. A warehouse that distributes kitchen appliances is considering proposals from two trucking companies. Demand and inventory costs are given below.

Forecast demand	5000 units /year
Order cost	$117 / order
Product price	$ 75 / unit
Inventory holding cost	25% of unit price

The warehouse operates 365 days a year and uses EOQ as its order quantity. The safety stock is 20% of the average demand during the carrier's delivery lead-time. The information about the two trucking companies is given below.

Trucking Company	Lead-time	Transportation Rate Per Unit	Variability in Delivery Lead time (std. dev.)
Swift Trucking	3 days	$15	1day
On Time Trucking	4 days	$13.5	2days

   a. What is safety inventory without variability in delivery time?
   b. What is safety inventory with variability in delivery time?
      Consider one standard deviation case only.
   c. What is the total cost?
   d. Which trucking company should the warehouse select?
   e. What other factors should be considered other than the cost?

References

Ballou, R.H. (2004). Business Logistics Management, 5th edition (Prentice Hall, New Jersey).

Bodin, L. and Golden, B. (1981). "Classification in Vehicle Routing and Scheduling," *Networks*, 11, pp. 97-108.

Chopra, S. and Meindl, P. (2013). Supply Chain Management, 5th ed. (Prentice Hall, New Jersey).

Clarke, G. and Wright, J.W. (1963). "Scheduling of vehicles form a central depot to a number of delivery points." *Operations Research*, 11, pp. 568-581.

Coyle, John J., Novack, Robert A., Gibson, Brian J., and Bardi, Edward J. (2011). Transportation, 7th edition, (South-western: Cincinnati, OH).

Prince, Theodore (2000). E-Commerce: It's Impact on Transportation, Logistics, and Supply Chain Management, April 15, *ASCET*, Vol. 2.

Simchi-Levi, D., Kaminsky, P., and Simchi-Levi, E. (2003). Designing and Managing the Supply Chain, 2nd edition, (McGraw-Hill Irwin, New York).

Appendix 1: World Busiest Container Ports: Top 25 2012

Rank	Port, Country	2012 (Million TEUs)	Website
1	Shanghai, China	32.53	www.portshanghai.com.cn
2	Singapore, Singapore	31.65	www.singaporepsa.com
3	Hong Kong, China	23.10	www.mardep.gov.hk
4	Shenzhen, China	22.94	www.szport.net
5	Busan, South Korea	17.04	www.busanpa.com
6	Ningbo-Zhoushan, China	16.83	www.zhoushan.cn/english
7	Guangzhou Harbor, China	14.74	www.gzport.com
8	Qingdao, China	14.50	www.qdport.com
9	Jebel Ali, Dubai, United Arab Emirates	13.30	www.dpworld.ae
10	Tianjin, China	12.30	www.ptacn.com
11	Rotterdam, Netherlands	11.87	www.portofrotterdam.com
12	Port Kelang, Malaysia	10.00	www.pka.gov.my
13	Kaohsiung, Taiwan, China	9.78	www.khb.gov.tw
14	Hamburg, Germany	8.86	www.hafen-hamburg.de
15	Antwerp, Belgium	8.64	www.portofantwerp.com
16	Los Angeles, U.S.A.	8.08	www.portoflosangeles.org
17	Dalian, China	8.06	www.dlport.cn
18	Keihin ports*, Japan	7.85	www.city.yokohama.lg.jp/en
19	Tanjung Pelepas, Malaysia	7.70	www.ptp.com.my
20	Xiamen, China	7.20	www.portxiamen.gov.cn
21	Bremen/Bremerhaven, Germany	6.12	www.bremen-ports.de
22	Tanjung Priok, Jakarta, Indonesia	6.10	www.priokport.co.id
23	Long Beach, U.S.A.	6.05	www.polb.com
24	Laem Chabang, Thailand	5.93	www.laemchabangport.com
25	New York-New Jersey, U.S.A.	5.53	www.panynj.gov

Source: *The Journal of Commerce*, August 20, 2012 and August 19, 2013.

Appendix 2: World's Busiest Airports by Cargo Traffic: Top 25 2012

Rank	Airport	Location	Cargo Metric Ton
1.	Hong Kong International Airport	Chek Lap Kok, Hong Kong	4,062,261
2.	Memphis International Airport	Memphis, Tennessee, United States	3,916,535
3.	Shanghai Pudong International Airport	Pudong, Shanghai, China	2,939,157
4.	Incheon International Airport	Incheon, Seoul National Capital Area, South Korea	2,456,724
5.	Ted Stevens Anchorage International Airport	Anchorage, Alaska, United States	2,449,551
6.	Dubai International Airport	Dubai, United Arab Emirates	2,267,365
7.	Louisville International Airport	Louisville, Kentucky, United States	2,187,766
8.	Paris-Charles de Gaulle Airport	Seine-et-Marne/Seine-Saint-Denis/Val-d'Oise, Île-de-France, France	2,150,950
9.	Frankfurt Airport	Flughafen (Frankfurt am Main), Frankfurt, Hesse, Germany	2,066,432
10.	Narita International Airport	Narita, Chiba, Kantō, Honshū, Japan	2,006,173
11.	Miami International Airport	Miami, Florida, United States	1,929,889
12.	Singapore Changi Airport	Changi, East Region, Singapore	1,898,850
13.	Beijing Capital International Airport	Chaoyang, Beijing, China	1,787,027
14.	Los Angeles International Airport	Los Angeles, California, United States	1,688,351
15.	Taiwan Taoyuan International Airport	Dayuan, Taoyuan, Taiwan	1,577,728
16.	London Heathrow Airport	Hayes, Hillingdon, Greater London, United Kingdom	1,556,203
17.	O'Hare International Airport	Chicago, Illinois, United States	1,512,186
18.	Amsterdam Airport Schiphol	Haarlemmermeer, North Holland, Netherlands	1,511,824
19.	Suvarnabhumi Airport	Racha Thewa, Bang Phli, Samut Prakan, Greater Bangkok, Central, Thailand	1,345,487
20.	John F. Kennedy International Airport	New York City, New York, United States	1,283,663
21.	Guangzhou Baiyun International Airport	Baiyun, Guangzhou, Guangdong, China	1,246,467
22.	Indianapolis International Airport	Indianapolis, Indiana, United States	932,105
23.	Tokyo International Airport	Ōta, Tokyo, Kantō, Honshū, Japan	909,684
24.	Shenzhen Bao'an International Airport	Bao'an District, Shenzhen, Guangdong, China	854,901
25.	Leipzig/Halle Airport	Leipzig, Germany	846,092

Source: Airports Council International. "Cargo Traffic 2012 Preliminary from Airports Council International". 2013-07-11; 2012 preliminary statistics.

Part 5

Emerging Issues in Supply Chain

Chapter 10
Emerging Issues in Supply Chain Management

Chapter 11
Information Flow and Big Data Science in Supply Chain Management

Chapter 10

Emerging Issues in Supply Chain Management

10.1 Green Supply Chain

In order to sustain the competitive advantage of the global supply chain for the 21st century, companies must be aware of the importance of the green supply chain and enhance green initiatives. The phenomenon of global warming and the concept of green supply chain are impelled by the increasing level of air and water pollution, overuse of natural recourses, overflow of waste, and faster deterioration of the environment.

Greenness in a supply chain requires collaboration among supply chain partners to ensure environmental, social, and ethical compliance from upstream to downstream in the supply chain. It has been very well reported that green collaboration requires a substantial commitment of both resources and organizational capabilities. The goal of green supply chain management is to ensure that the current level of supply chain consumption will not overuse resources and pollute the environment, so that the needs of future generations will not be compromised. Green supply chain management promotes environmental responsibility, minimizes waste, enhances efficiency, and should achieve cost saving through supply chain collaboration. Fig. 10.1 presents a list of the logical steps in the implementation of a green supply chain initiative.

Fig. 10.1 Steps to implement a green supply chain (GSC) initiatives.

Step one in Fig. 10.1 notes the importance of top management involvement in leading a green supply chain management (GSCM) initiative. Green supply chain projects usually require the internal cooperation of different functional areas and external collaboration among the supply chain partners. Therefore, with top management serving as the helmsman, both employees and suppliers should actively engage in green supply chain management.

Step two is to assess the firm's current green supply chain commitment. The current level of commitment to natural resource utilization, waste emissions, involvement in reuse, recycling, refurbishment projects, and health and safety programs should be analyzed and assessed.

Step three is to identify and set up objectives for a list of Rs (reduce, reuse, rework, refurbish, recycle, remanufacture, reverse logistics, etc.). During this process, A SWOT (strengths, weaknesses, opportunities, and threats) analysis can be conducted to better understand the internal elements as well as the external requirements.

Step four is to implement green supply chain initiatives. In order to implement green supply chain tasks, it will be necessary to involve the suppliers from various echelons of the supply chain. At this step, an effective strategy of partnership collaboration should be formulated in accordance with the regulatory requirements, consumer pressures, and the supply chain's objectives.

Step five is to evaluate the outcome of the green supply chain initiatives after the GSC has been implemented. This is a feedback control loop that measures the result of each element, compared with the objectives defined in Step Three.

The International Organization for Standardization (ISO) has published standardized methodologies that reduce hazardous impacts on the environment and maximize the benefits of physical products from material procurement to product manufacturing, product use, and end-of-life. The ISO 14000 certification requires firms to identify all of the environmental impacts of their operations, including the procedures that safely handle waste and dispose of hazardous materials, and the firm's level of compliance with relevant environmental regulations.

10.1.1 Green sourcing and procurement

Green sourcing and procurement is the process of the selection and acquisition of raw material, parts, components, and products that minimize the negative impact over the lifecycle of manufacturing, distribution, recycling, and reverse logistics. Green sourcing and procurement consists of a set of sustainability criteria, supplier certifications, and supplier codes of conduct for supporting sustainable purchasing practices, in order to minimize environmental impact. If the supplier's commitment to a green supply chain is neglected, serious problems can occur. In 2007, Mattel, a producer of Barbie dolls, Matchbox Toys, and many other games, recalled about one million toys due to their use of lead paint. This incident damaged the brand and forced the company to conduct an extensive investigation of its supply chain. The problem stemmed from a third-tier supplier who had sold leaded yellow pigment to a paint company with a fake certification indicating that the paint did not contain lead. Then, the paint company sold the paint to one of Mattel's longtime contract manufacturers. This lesson teaches us how to treat supply chain sustainability as an integral part of the entire process – from the raw material producer to the end user. Green sourcing and procurement should consider multiple facets of specific issues: inventory, cycle time, quality, the costs of materials, production, and logistics.

As one of the top supply chain companies, Walmart formulated a Carrot Strategy to motivate suppliers to reduce their energy consumption during production. When the initiative began, many small and medium suppliers in China were hesitant to participate in the program because they worried about increased production costs and uncertain revenue income. Walmart helped to mitigate the revenue risks of its suppliers through purchasing guaranteed quantities from those suppliers who would participate in the energy saving program. As a result, an audit in year 2009 of more than 100 Chinese factories serving Walmart found that they had become 5% more energy efficient in the program's first year.[1]

10.1.2 Green product design

Green design includes certain environmental considerations during the product design phase. These considerations, made during new product and process development, are associated with waste reduction and carbon emission reduction over the full life cycle of the product. The scope of green design encompasses many disciplines, including environmental risk management, product safety, pollution prevention, resource conservation, and waste management. For example, Procter & Gamble (P&G) publicly stated its green goals as "the product is concentrated so that packaging materials are reduced, and by not requiring hot water, it minimizes the consumption of energy during its use, thereby reducing carbon emissions."[2]   As a major laundry product producer, P&G discovered that the worst impacts of its Tide laundry product on the environment was neither during the extraction of raw materials during manufacturing nor in the use of the resources required to deliver the product to retail stores. Rather, it was found as consumers used heated water when washing their clothing. This increased energy consumption and caused heat emission problems. Based on this finding, P&G redesigned its product and developed Tide Coldwater Liquid Detergent, a product that no longer requires the consumer to use hot water for laundry. This product design improvement helps green the environment.

10.1.3 Green manufacturing

Green Manufacturing is the latest addition in the green objectives of supply chains. The goal of green manufacturing is for companies to reduce the ecological burden on the globe by using appropriate material

---

[1] Source: Lee, H. (2010). "Don't Tweak Your Supply Chain – Rethink It End to End." *Harvard Business Review*, Oct., pp. 63-69.

[2] Melanie Warner (2008). "P&G's Sustainability Initiatives - Not So Sustainable." Date of access: July 1. www.fastcompany.com/.

and manufacturing technologies in the production of their products. Green manufacturing and remanufacturing are a very important area within green operations. The techniques used for green manufacturing include reducing the use of energy and raw materials, improving production efficiency, reducing environmental and occupational safety expenses, and improving the corporate image.

The mounting pressure from the government, stakeholders, and consumers to conduct business in a sustainable fashion has made many companies rethink their manufacturing production processes from end to end. For example, Esquel, an apparel producer in Hong Kong, put great effort into balancing the trade-offs among environmental sustainability, social responsibility, and business performance. Noticing the overuse of water during cotton farming production, Esquel assisted its independent farms to implement green production techniques and encouraged farmers to adopt drip irrigation so as to reduce water consumption during the process of producing organic cotton. Additionally, Esquel advised its cotton producers to implement natural pest-control and disease-control programs, such as breeding disease-resistant strains of cotton, to reduce reliance on pesticides.[3] After analyzing its own manufacturing process, Esquel implemented a greener manufacturing process for washing, ginning, and spinning organic cotton fiber. Additionally, it developed new dyes that consist of greener chemicals than those previously used to color conventional cotton fiber. In this way, it reduced the use of other chemicals in fabric manufacturing.

Remanufacturing is part of green manufacturing. Paired with reverse logistics, remanufacturing combines recover, re-use, recycle, repair, and refurbish, and adds even more Rs to the manufacturing process.

10.1.4 Green packaging and distribution

The development and management of green packaging and distribution puts even more stress on the ability to create green distribution of goods and services. Delivering goods, either done by the companies

---

[3] Lee, H. (2010). "Don't Tweak Your Supply Chain – Rethink It End to End." *Harvard Business Review*, Oct., pp. 63-69.

themselves or by a 3rd party logistics provider, generates emissions, increases pollution, and damages the environment. Green distribution consists of the reduction of packaging size and layers, the use of environmental responsible packaging material, and the implementation of green logistics.

Green packaging paired with green loading techniques can reduce material usage, and can increase space utilization in the warehouse, in the ocean vessel, and in the trailer to reduce the amount of handling required. During the past few decades, many green innovations have been developed in the packaging and distribution areas. The delivery of flat furniture is one of many examples to reduce packaging size and material so as to reduce transportation cost and waste. The container box, which "made the world smaller and the world economy bigger[4]" has standardized packaging dimensions, eased loading operations, reduced hazardous emission, and saved total logistics costs. Cross-docking, a loading method initiated at Walmart, takes finished goods from the manufacturing plant and delivers them directly to the customer with little or no handling in between.

10.2 Reverse Logistics

Reverse logistics refers to the physical flow of the discarded materials that have lost their original value for consumption. Reverse logistics includes the maintenance, return, repairing, recycle, reprocessing, remanufacturing, recovering, reuse, and waste disposal of used materials. Its main purpose is to recapture the useful value of products or to properly dispose of the discarded products.[5] The Supply Chain Operations Reference (SCOR) model, which was introduced by the Supply Chain Council (SCC), benchmarks operational measurement to a

---

[4] http://www.amazon.com/The-Box-Shipping-Container-Smaller/dp/0691136408.

[5] Shi, X., Li, L., Yang, L., Li, Z., Choi, J.Y. (2012). Information flow in reverse logistics: an industrial information integration study, *Information Technology and Management*, 13(4), pp. 217-232.

Wang, D. and Gao, S. (2003). "Recycling of used batteries and environmental protection." *Recycling Research*. 6 pp. 20–24.

prioritized improvement portfolio tied directly to a company's balance sheet. In the SCOR model, return, which indicates reverse logistics, is considered to be both an important intra-organizational function and a critical inter-organizational process. Narrowly speaking, reverse logistics is a process which collects and processes used products through a distribution network. In a broad sense, reverse logistics includes reusing materials, saving resources, and protecting the environment.

The supply chain that supports reverse logistics is significantly more complex than the forward supply chain. The reverse logistics supply chain involves more participants, covers a wider region, and has higher randomness than a traditional supply chain. Therefore, when managing a reverse logistics system, information sharing, transaction coordination, decision support, and the allocation of resources become inseparable from the support of the information systems or e-logistics systems. As such, many companies now outsource their reverse logistics components to a third-party logistics provider. After examining its reverse logistics program regarding warranty parts, General Motors, one of the world largest automakers, collaborated with UPS Supply Chain Solutions for its parts under warranty programs. UPS invested in the advanced information technology needed to streamline and control the GM material recovery supply chain to support GM's goal of a green supply chain.[6] The program ranges from door-to-door package delivery to inventory management. GM dealers no longer need to package warranty parts, write mailing labels, take the packages to the local post office, and pay postage costs in order to ship the warranty parts to GM's remanufacturing center. Through its collaboration with UPS, GM is able to focus on its core competency, to reduce the complexity of its reverse logistics program, to enhance its energy saving commitment, and to improve its customer services.

In August 2013, Apple, the smart phone producer, announced its "reuse and recycling" program, which allowed customers to trade in a functioning smartphone and receive a credit to use toward the purchase

---

[6] UPS Supply Chain Solutions, "GM Accelerates Warranty Parts Recovery with Specialized Logistics." 2004.

of a new iPhone.[7] This green supply chain program showed a win-win strategy. Apple was able to establish its image as a strong environmental supporter through emphasizing its commitment to recycling after iPhones have been used. Customers were able to upgrade their iPhones by receiving a credit for their returned phone.

10.3 Disaster Relief Supply Chain

In recent years, the world has experienced many disasters, either caused by nature (such as the 2004 Tsunami in Asia or the 2012 Kamaishi earthquake in Japan), or by terrorist attacks (such as the bombing of the World Trade Center on September 11, 2001 or Kenya's Westgate shopping mall attack in 2013).

The disaster relief supply chain can be defined as "a process of planning, managing and controlling the efficient flows of relief, information, and services from the points of origin to the points of destination to meet the urgent needs of the affected people under emergency conditions."[8] A disaster relief supply chain faces three pressing issues after the disaster attack: (i) repairing the basic infrastructure, such as the roads, utility power lines, and telephone lines; (ii) transporting humanitarian personnel, such as doctors and firefighters, to the site; and (iii) delivering life support materials, such as drinking water, food, medicine, and clothes, to the disaster area. The objective is to get the right aid to the right people, at the right place, and at the right time.

Emergency relief planning is an important component of such a supply chain. A relief plan should focus on the emergency response to a short-duration event, but should also consider any long-duration effects. Some critical drugs, for example, are produced at only one production site. If the manufacturing facility were destroyed, it would take a couple of years to resume production. Therefore, an effective contingency plan

---

[7] Sherr, I. (2013). "Apple to Pay up to $280 for Used iPhones," Wall Street Journal, August 30.

[8] Sheu, J. (2007). "Challenges of emergency logistics management." *Transportation Research Part E*, 43, pp. 655–659.

should consider issues such as alternative manufacturing facilities, safety stocks, alternative delivery routes, and offsite backup warehouse capacity. Contingency planning before a disaster helps firms deal with unexpected disruptions. One information technology executive manager talked about the aftermath of the New York City's 2001 World Trade Center disaster. He was relieved that the company's data bank was safe and that the company was operational the next day. Fortunately, the company had an IT disaster recovery plan in place, and was able to convert a warehouse in New Jersey into a temporary IT operation room.

To develop and maintain an effective disaster relief supply chain is a challenge. It presupposes the availability of resources needed to execute tightly coordinated tasks, such as regularly checking food and medicine inventory for expiration, procuring relief items, fund raising, maintaining vehicles, etc. Such a supply chain must be created "on the go" in order to execute emergency aid tasks.

10.4 Managing Disaster Relief Material Flow and Inventory

Natural disasters and political disruptions happen often and strike nearly anywhere. After a disaster attack, the immediate challenge is to deliver humanitarian aid and life support materials to the stricken community. This may require unprecedented forms of communication, cooperation, and coordination among various organizations and relief teams.

The fundamental issues related to relief supply inventory management are how much to acquire, where to store the goods, and how to deliver those goods to the community. An effective disaster relief supply chain synchronizes and orchestrates relief material acquisition, storage, and delivery. Some of the characteristic of disaster relief inventory management are found in Table 10.1.

A just-in-time inventory acquisition approach can be applied to respond to a rapid surge of goods. Unlike the inventory management of companies that operate during calm periods, disaster relief organizations usually do not have ongoing relationships with suppliers. Furthermore, demand quantity, time, and place are highly uncertain. In this case, planning on demand volume, acquisition, and storage becomes important information for decision support. About ten years ago, the United Nations formed an office to centralize its disaster relief resource information and included data on inventories available for emergencies. The UN Office for the Coordination of Humanitarian Affairs (United Nations, 2004) oversees the program.

Table 10.1 Material flow and inventory management for disaster relief.

	Regular Time Material Flow & Inventory Management	Disaster Relief Material Flow & Inventory Management
Acquisition	• Ongoing relationship with suppliers • Orders are placed with estimated lead time and safety stock	• No regular relationship with suppliers • Demand quantity, time, and place are highly uncertain
Storage	• Location of storage is a business decision • Security is mostly an internal issue • Information is available to manage product expiration and storage life	• Location of storage is a political decision • Security involves government regulation • Information on inventory is not integrated • Product expiration and storage life require special attention
Distribution	• Commercial transportation is commonly used • Deliveries are pre-scheduled	• Transportation may require special carriers • "Last mile" delivery is a big challenge

Source: Adapted from D.C. Whybark (2007). "Issues in managing disaster relief inventories." *International Journal of Production Economics*, 108, pp. 228-235.

Acquisition of relief inventory can be categorized to two ways. One is to acquire and store disaster relief items before the disaster occurs, as anticipation inventory. The other is to acquire items for humanitarian aid during a disaster relief operation. Both approaches require demand forecast, planning, and execution.

The decision about the location of relief inventory must take into consideration the accessibility for inventory monitoring when auditing is conducted and the ability for shipping when the need arises. Additionally, security and safety considerations should be incorporated. Many relief items, such as medicine, water, and food have expiration dates that must be honored.

Effective transportation of food, goods, and crucial equipment such as vehicles is extremely important, in order to deliver goods to the people who are in need of aid. The task of distributing goods to the disaster location is often referred to as "last mile delivery." After the 2008 Wen Chuan earthquake in China, for example, locations near the disaster were flooded with food and medicine. The pressing problem was how to transport the goods downstream, from the depots and harbors to the people who were in urgent need of the aid. There were many factors that made it difficult to deliver the humanitarian aid to the hands of those who needed it most. Heavy rain was pouring, roads were either damaged or congested with traffic, and the rescue teams may not have known precisely the location of the disaster epicenters. The Wen Chuan Government immediately set up a relief center in a stadium off the intersection of a highway. Every county and city set up a flag with its name on it, so that the residents of the county were able to find relatives or get information at the site. Additionally, the old, the children, and the sick were placed in the middle of the covered stadium. Using this organized program, the last mile delivery problem was eased.

10.5 Summary

Resilient supply chain management is a relatively new area of research. In recent years, the world has become increasingly uncertain and vulnerable. We have experienced or witnessed many types of unpredictable disasters, such as earthquakes, tsunamis, bird flu, SARS, terrorist attacks, wars, computer virus penetration, economic crises, etc. To address these issues, we need to develop protocols and measures to secure our supply chains. It becomes important to assess the benefits and costs associated with the creation of resilient supply chain.

In order to sustain the competitive advantage of global supply chains, companies need to be aware of the importance of the green supply chain and enhance their commitment to building a green supply chain. Greenness in a supply chain requires collaboration among supply chain partners to ensure environmental, social, and ethical compliance from upstream to downstream. It has been well reported that green collaboration requires a substantial commitment of resources and organizational capabilities. The goal of green supply chain management is to ensure that the current level of supply chain consumption will not overuse resources and pollute the environment.

Questions for Pondering

1. Why have so many firms recognized the detrimental effects of supply chain disruptions, yet have committed so few resources to mitigating supply chain risks?
2. What kind of data would you need to prepare a disaster relief plan?
3. Compare and discuss various disaster relief approaches in different countries. What can we learn from each other's experiences?
4. What is the impact of green sourcing on social responsibility and supply chain performance?
5. Map Mattel's supply chain. How important is sourcing to Mattel's reputation of social responsibility and supply chain performance? (hint: you may use information from the Internet).
6. What is Wal-Mart's carrot strategy in supplier development? How does it work? What is the result?

References

Angeles, R. (2011). "Roadmap to charting a green supply chain." *Proceedings of Northeast Decision Sciences Institute*, pp. 1455-1471.

Boin, A., Kelle, P. and Whybark, DC (2010). "Resilient supply chains for extreme situations: Outlining a new field of study." *International Journal of Production Economics*, 126, pp. 1-6.

Cervera, C.M. and Flores, J.L.M. (2012). "A conceptual model for a green supply chain strategy." *Proceedings of Global Conference on Business and Finance*, pp. 269-273.

Christensen, J., et al. (2008). A practical guide to green sourcing. *Supply Chain Management Review*, 12(8), pp. 14-21.

Dhanda K. and Peters A. (2005). "Reverse Logistics in the Computer Industry," *International Journal of Computers, Systems and Signals*, 6(2), pp. 57-67.

Fleischmann M, Bloemhof-Ruwaard J, Dekker R et al. (1997). "Quantitative model for reverse logistics: a review." European *Journal of Operational Research*. 103(1), pp. 1-17.

Goldsby, T.J. and Closs, D.J. (2000). "Using activity-based costing to reengineer the reverse logistics channel." *International Journal of Physical Distribution & Logistics Management*, 30(6), pp. 500-514.

Goleman, D. (2009). Ecological Intelligence: How Knowing The Hidden Impacts of What We Buy Can Change Everything. (Broadway Books, New York, NY).

Hervani, A.A., Helms, M.M., and Sarkis, J. (2005). "Performance measurement for green supply chain management." *Benchmarking: An International Journal*, 12(4), pp. 330-353.

Ho, J., et al. (2009). "Opportunities in green supply chain management." *The Coastal Business Journal*, 8(1), pp. 18-31.

Hoek, R. (1999). "From reversed logistics to green supply chains." *Supply Chain Management: An International Journal*, 4(3), pp. 129-135.

Oloruntoba, R., Gray, R. (2006). "Humanitarian aid: an agile supply chain?" *Supply Chain Management: An International Journal*, 11 (2), pp. 115-120.

Ostlin, J., Sundin, E., and Bjorkman, M. (2008). "Importance of closed-loop supply chain relationships for product remanufacturing." *International Journal of Production Economics*, 115(2), pp. 336-348.

Sherr, Ian (2013). "Apple to Pay up to $280 for Used iPhones." Wall Street Journal, August 30.

Shi, X., Li, L., Yang, L., Li, Z., Choi, J.Y. (2012). "Information flow in reverse logistics: an industrial information integration study." *Information Technology and Management*, 13(4), pp. 217-232.

Srivastava, S.K. (2007). "Green supply-chain management: A state-of-the-art literature review." *International Journal of Management Reviews*, 9(1), pp. 53-80.

United Nations. Office for the Coordination of Humanitarian Affairs (OCHA) (2004). Central Register of Disaster Management Capacities. Date of access: June 2007. http://www.reliefweb.int/cr/.

Whybark, D.C. (2007). "Issues in managing disaster relief inventories." *International J. of Production Economics*, 108, pp. 228-235.

Chapter 11

Information Flow and Big Data Science in Supply Chain Management

11.1 Data Science in Supply Chain Management

In the Information Age, productivity is based on not only labor and material, but also on information and knowledge. More data was collected and stored during the two-year period from 2011 to 2012 than in all of previous human history.[1] Some new phrases such as "Big Data" and "Data Science" have emerged to attempt to describe the huge volume of data collected through various integrated information systems, social media, and the Internet. The term "Data Science" can be defined as "the application of quantitative and qualitative methods to solve relevant problems and predict outcomes."[2] Combining data resources, data analysis methods, and business applications, Data Science and Big Data are providing supply chain managers the opportunity to design better supply chain management models at the strategic, tactical, and operational levels. The rapid progress of data warehouse technologies and data mining tools have helped the supply chain to be able to respond to customer demands more quickly. Data Science is quietly revolutionizing supply chain dynamics.

---

[1] IBM, www-01.ibm.com/software/data/bigdata, available March 27, 2013.

[2] Waller, M.A. and Fawcett, S.E. (2013). Data Science, Predictive Analytics, and Big Data: A Revolution That Will Transform Supply Chain Design and Management. *Journal of Business Logistics*, 34(2), pp. 77-84.

11.1.1 Data collection and organization

Data is a representation of facts in a formalized manner suitable for interpretation or processing. Firms are often buried in a sea of data collected by various business units. In a supply chain, information including customer names, product prices, production lead time, inventory levels, inventory data with numerous descriptive fields (such as the size of the product, the color of the product, the expiration date, the warranty information, and the return and exchange rules) are useful data for business planning. Data can be stored in some sort of technology system which is called a database. Managers may not always have the data they need to make effective business decisions. In this case, data may be obtained from existing data storage.

The backbone that enables the making of effective business decisions is twofold: data and information. Companies may have obtained data from different sources, but that data is often not available in a ready-to-use format. It is fairly common for a data analyst to spend 70% of data analysis time on preparing data. Data comes in many categories. The most common types include *categorical* and *continuous*:

- Categorical data or nominal data: e.g. customer gender and race
- Binary data: e.g. female and male
- Ordinal data: such as ranks in a survey, strongly agree or disagree
- Continuous data: e.g. customer income level, purchasing amount

A data warehouse is an extension of database system. Data warehouses make full use of historic data to provide valuable information on products, suppliers, and customers. The process of data organizing and data mining includes the following phases:

- Data - collect data on demand: supply, inventory, lead time, cost, and many other supply chain aspects
- Database - create client database: define attributes, process transactional data
- Data warehouse - extract and transform transactional data

- Select data mining technique - summarize, classify, cluster, perform regressions, etc.

11.1.2 Information extraction and analytic models

In supply chain management, managers often suffer from an overabundance of data. What they really want to know is what makes a customer more likely to purchase the product produced by their companies. To meet this objective, unstructured or fragmented data needs to be filtered and condensed, and then transformed into relevant information.

Extracting and organizing data alone does not generate value. Advanced analytic models are needed to transform data into information. Information is different from data. Information is data processed for a certain purpose. Information has meaning. The relationship between information and data can be classified as follows:

- Contextualization: the purpose of data gathered is known. For example, customer purchasing data is gathered.
- Categorization: the units of analysis or the key components of the data are known. (For example, customers' incomes have been categorized.)
- Calculation: the data has been analyzed mathematically or statistically. For example, the correlation of customer incomes and their purchasing behavior has been studied. This correlation then offers useful information to the marketing department to develop an effective promotion strategy.
- Correction: errors in the data have been removed. (For example, the number "668" was keyed in as "688" and this error has been corrected.)
- Condensation: the data has been summarized in a more concise form. (For example, the mean and standard deviation of demand for low fat ice cream have been summarized.) The mean and standard deviation of demand for a product have now become information for production planning.

Fig. 11.1 illustrates the forward and backward flow of data and information in a supply chain. Information is extracted from data, whereas knowledge is derived from information. However, if there is too much information, it can be reduced. One of the important issues in applying information for decision-making is to know how your competitors are applying the same information that you are using. Armed with this business intelligence, your company is able to identify business applications that will lead to top performance and may have applicability elsewhere.

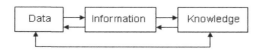

Fig. 11.1 Three components of a knowledge system in supply chain.[3]

11.1.3 Knowledge management

Knowledge is the fact or condition of knowing something with familiarity gained through experience or association.[4] According to Davenport and Prusak, "knowledge is a fluid mix of framed experience, values, contextual information, and expert insight that provides a framework for evaluating and incorporating new experiences and information. It originates and is applied in the minds of knowers."[5] In a supply chain, knowledge becomes embedded not only in demand and inventory documents but also in the routines, processes, practices, and norms of the supply chain. Knowledge can be derived from information, just as information can be derived from data. Interestingly, a substantial amount of knowledge may be required to infer an essential set of data. These relationships are illustrated in Fig. 11.1.

---

[3] Source: adapted from Li, L. and Xu, L. (2001). "Knowledge-based problem solving," Encyclopedia of Microcomputers, 28(7), pp. 149-167.

[4] Merriam Webster's Collegiate Dictionary (1996).

[5] Davenport, T., and Prusak, L. (1998). Working Knowledge: How Organizations Manage What They Know. (Harvard Business School Press, Boston, Mass).

It has been recognized that supply chain management knowledge generation and application are at the core of many organizations. It is obvious that the growing importance of knowledge regarding customer demand, inventory levels, supplier relations, and production scheduling helps strategic decision making.

Currently, information technology helps in the generation of business data, information, and knowledge. In the total enterprise integration (TEI) environment, usage of knowledge is moving from traditional knowledge-based problem solving to integrated knowledge-based problem solving. Substantial efforts have been made in this direction, including the exploration and development of multi-dimensional knowledge structures.

11.1.4 Data warehousing

The **data warehouse** is a significant component of supply chain business analytics. A supply chain data warehouse is subject-oriented; data in a data warehouse is integrated; the data collected is kept in the data warehouse; and data is associated with specific time periods. A data warehouse integrates various types of data. For example, it integrates multiple and heterogeneous data sources, such as relational databases, on-line transaction records, flat files, etc. Focusing on the modeling and analysis of data for decision makers, the data warehouse provides a concise view of particular subject issues. For example, if a supply chain manager would like to know specific customer demographic information, he can extract useful information and can exclude data that is not useful in the decision support process. By handling numerous enterprise records for integration, aggregation, cleansing, and query tasks, the data warehouse supports the physical propagation of data and is used to support managerial decision making process.

A data warehouse is time-variant. The time horizon for the data warehouse is significantly longer than that of the operational database that keeps transactional information. A data warehouse provides information from a historical perspective. For example, its 65-week point-of-sale information provides Walmart with historical information about its sales.

A **data mart** is a collection of subject areas organized for decision support that are based on the needs of a given topic. For example, a logistics department has its own data mart, which barely resembles marketing's data mart. A logistics department has its own interpretation of what a data mart should look like. Similar to data warehouses, data marts contain operational data that helps logistics experts to strategize, based on analyses of past data and future trends. There can be multiple data marts inside a supply chain data warehouse.

Business intelligence relies on data warehousing technology. The main objective of business intelligence is: 1) to integrate and consolidate the supply chain's data from disparate sources to a single location and in a flexible format so as to provide a basis for companies to categorize and aggregate the data meaningfully for their supply chain; and 2) to provide decision support information. Data warehousing is an action that processes, constructs, and uses the data collected. The state-of-the-art technology in data warehousing has created a technical foundation for applying Collaborative Planning, Forecasting, and Replenishment (CPFR) in a supply chain. As early as 1966, Sam Walton, the founder of Walmart, started to automate the Walmart retail distribution system. Today, Walmart possesses one of the largest commercial databases in the world, which includes data such as inventory, forecasts, demographics, sale promotions, exchanges and returns, and market baskets (the products in a shopping cart that a shopper buys in a single trip). Walmart's data warehouse is stocked with 65 weeks of data categorized by item, store, and day. Using data mining techniques, Walmart develops accurate forecasts about customer demand. Its sixty-five week point-of-sale data enables Walmart to conduct full comparisons between the current year and the past year for the same quarter. The completeness of its data warehouse has enabled Walmart to gain competitive advantages through its data mining solutions.

11.1.5 Data mining

Data mining is a process of discovering knowledge in a data warehouse or a database. Some people refer to this process as "knowledge discovery in databases" (KDD). In supply chain management, data mining extracts previously unknown knowledge or patterns of demand, lead time, production, sales, etc. Data mining is an especially useful tool to use in profiling customers and demand to a level not possible before. Some people refer to this as "one-to-one" marketing. Very soon, data mining will be a requirement of supply chain management, rather than a competitive advantage as we see in today's market.

Data mining is a process of model building and analytics. Various models, such as clustering, decision trees, genetic algorithms, neural networks, statistics, hybrid models, etc., can be used to discover useful trends, patterns, and correlations, as well to make predictions based on historical data. In general, data mining extracts a portion of a data warehouse which is large enough to contain the significant information, yet small enough to manipulate quickly. It explores the data by searching for unknown or unanticipated trends to gain an understanding of market dynamics and generate new ideas. Data mining modifies the data by creating, selecting, and transforming the variables to focus on decision formulation. It searches the database automatically to predict a desired outcome and assesses the data by evaluating the usefulness of the findings. For example, the number of inventory turns in a year, or the number of weeks of supplies using existing inventory at the distribution center can be used to evaluate a company's supply chain performance and retune its inventory management strategy.

11.2 Big Data-based Supply Chain Management Decisions

Data Science tools decoupled with enterprise information systems can produce strikingly rich information. However, these outputs are valuable only if supply chain managers understand them and are able to translate them into tangible business actions, such as a clear interface for scheduling employees, cross-selling suggestions for call-center agents, or a way for marketing managers to make real-time decisions about discounts. Many companies fail to complete this step in their thinking and planning, so that they are not able to be benefitted from the new models and insightful information.

The major components of a business intelligence system include data warehouse, data mining, and OLAP (online analytical processing system). The capabilities of business intelligence include statistical analysis, forecasting, and decision support.

The front end of the business intelligence solution must incorporate a user interface that aims at making raw data meaningful. Key performance indicators must be multi-dimensional and must include, for example, history, trends, and predictors — without becoming too obscure or overwhelming. Supply chain managers must be empowered to view data from their relative perspectives as the supply chain trend evolves and their needs for analysis change.

The key driver in the creation of a successful intelligent supply chain is to consolidate data from many different enterprise operational systems into an enterprise data warehouse. This data warehouse allows intra-enterprise and inter-enterprise data to be extracted, integrated, and analyzed. Companies which are capable of harnessing the copious amounts of data and converting that data effectively into intelligent information will have the inside track in the global supply chain arena. Managing the supply chain using business intelligence will enable firms to gain a better understanding of customer needs, to identify demand trends earlier, and to capitalize on business opportunities faster than their competitors.

Table 11.1 provides three examples of ways to apply intelligent supply chain decisions to cope with demand with various time frames such as time-of-day, day-of-week, and month-of-year.

7-Eleven Japan is the largest convenience store chain in Japan and is the country's most profitable retailer. The company has invested in an advanced information system which provides it with timely and comprehensive indications about market demands, and it has built a strong network of suppliers and logistics providers. For instance, the company observed demand for milk at various times of day. Smaller size milk cartons were preferred in the early morning hours by commuters on their way to work and by school children on their way to school; medium-size milk cartons sold fast at lunch hour to business people; and larger size milk was bought by home-makers in the late afternoon. The sizes of milk bought by customers were different at certain **times of the day**. After converting the raw data to meaningful demand patterns, 7-Eleven Japan developed an intelligent milk replenishment strategy to make sure that customers were provided with what they wanted at the various times of day.

Table 11.1 Big data-based supply chain decisions.

	Demand Management	Time frame	Supply Chain Decision
7-Eleven Japan	• Integrated and timely information systems • supply partnerships • agile logistics	Time-of-day	• Perform statistical analyses of correlations among trends of product demands, timing differences, customer characteristics; develop intelligent replenishment plans & product offerings
The Kroger Co.	• Timely demand information, • targeted promotion • agile logistics	Day-of-week	• Study the flow of customers on different days of week and demand pattern analysis; make intelligent decision about store product offerings
Perdue Farms	• Collaboration & sharing of critical information about forecasting • promotion activities • inventory replenish plans	Month-of-year	Perform seasonal demand analysis, analysis of point-of-sales info., demand patter projection; make intelligent collaborative decisions on supply chain, anticipating inventory management for holiday season

The Kroger Company, headquartered in Cincinnati, Ohio, is one of the nation's largest grocery retailers as measured by total annual sales. In the fiscal year 2011, Kroger's sales revenue was $90.4 billion.[6] The Kroger Co. spans many states with store formats that include grocery and

---

[6] Fortune 500 (2012). http://money.cnn.com/magazines/fortune/fortune500/2012.

multi-department stores, convenience stores, and mall jewelry stores. The company takes positive steps to build strong local ties and loyalty from its customers. After analyzing the customer flow on different days of the week, the company designated Tuesday as senior citizen day to attract business on a slow day of a week. Senior citizens who shop on Tuesday get 5% off on everything they purchase at the Kroger store. After applying business intelligence to analyze demand data, the Kroger Co. is able to balance the customer flow based on different **days-of-week** and can replenish store shelves to target that customer segment.

PERDUE is one of America's best-known brand names in the food industry. Ranked third in sales in the poultry industry, the company is a leading international food and agriculture business. It has 14 food-processing facilities in the U.S. and produces about 2.7 billion pounds of chicken and turkey annually. Since the late 1990's, Perdue Farms has radically reshaped the company's supply chain infrastructure to implement CPFR and to provide high quality products and the highest level of service to their customers. Their $20 million investment in the cutting edge supply chain information system Manugistics, a CPFR software solution, has enabled Perdue to collaborate and share critical information on forecasting, point-of-sale data, promotion activities, inventory, and replenish plans with its partners. Manugistics forecasting software and supply chain planning tools generate timely and comprehensive signals about market demands. As such, PERDUE is able to intelligently deliver the right number of poultry products to the right customers at the right time. Usually, the third week of November is Perdue's busiest **time of year**. However, the company's output does not change drastically. The big difference is the form the turkeys take. Most of the year, turkey is prepared for food parts and deli meats, while in mid-to-late November, PERDUE prepares whole birds for sale. Getting turkeys from farm to table is a race against time, so PERDUE has turned to CPFR technology solutions to make sure that its products arrive fresh and safe. Each of its delivery trucks is equipped with a global positioning system that allows dispatchers to keep tabs on the turkeys en route from each of the company's four distribution centers to their destinations. In case of a flat tire, a truck breakdown, or another emergency, intelligent logistic control is applied. A replacement will be sent to rescue the pallets of poultry to ensure that the customers receive fresh poultry products.

The potential of the intelligent supply chain is not only for cost savings, but for profit and for sales enhancements which can eventually lead to higher market values for the firm. Business intelligence allows companies to best utilize the information from point-of-sales, demand forecasts, inventory, capacity, shipment plans, and to take advantage of many other kinds of supply chain data.

11.3 Business Intelligence

War intelligence can be traced back to Sun Tzu's *The Art of War*, written during the 6th century BC. Sun Tzu asserts that to succeed in war, one should have complete knowledge of one's own strengths and weaknesses as well as complete knowledge of one's enemy's strengths and weaknesses, which means "know yourselves and know your enemy, one hundred battles one hundred victories." An analogy can be drawn between the war intelligence and the business intelligence in a supply chain. Business intelligence should detect patterns of market, estimate changes in those patterns, use data to derive insights, develop intelligent business decisions, and gain a competitive advantage.

Business intelligence is an umbrella term used to describe the application of data collection and organization, information extraction and analysis, and decision support insights about markets, customers, suppliers, and products. Additionally, competitive business intelligence applications provide supply chain managers with tools for performance data analysis that help to uncover potential problems and to predict business trends. As technology advances at an exponential rate and market competition is getting fiercer each day, business intelligence has moved to the center of supply chain management. Most organizations have some sort of in-house business intelligence function: some are a part of the IT department, some are a part of marketing research, and others are an independent department.

The tools used to realize business intelligence in a supply chain include data warehousing, data mining, online analytical processing, reporting and query tools, and data visualization tools. The application of these tools can transform data into valuable information, can transform information into competitive decisions, can transform decisions into forward-looking actions, and can transform actions into sustainable high performance.

11.3.1 Intelligent value chain

To meet supply chain challenges, timely information about the market, customers, and competitors are crucial. An intelligent value chain is an interrelated process of suppliers, manufacturers, distributors, and customers that uses data, information, and knowledge to pilot a company toward competitive success.

Business intelligence (BI) is grounded in various supply chain activities and processes that serve as the sources of BI data and information. Enhanced intelligence analysis and awareness of the latest developments in data collection and information analysis, as well as networking, are vital components of value chain management. While some supply chain managers may attempt to cruise blindly through the local, national, or even the global marketplaces, it becomes more and more clear that being able to make informed decisions about alternative courses may help businesses avoid potential risks and lead to their enhanced bottom-line success.

There are several levels of business intelligence application in a supply chain, as indicated in Table 11.2. They are strategic, tactical, operational, and R&D and data analysis.

Strategic decisions are made at the top management level. Chief executives usually require long-term historical data, along with integrated information about environmental changes and industry trends, combined with business performance, to drive decisions. Insightful business decisions can create unprecedented success by adjusting supply chain directions. For example, eBay bought Billpoint in May 1999 in hopes of beating the rival PayPal. Nevertheless, despite heavy promotion, Billpoint was not able to win an appropriate electronic payment market share from PayPal. Comprehensive analysis of market data indicated that it was easier to acquire PayPal than to beat it because

PayPal had some 20 million registered account holders and about $1.5 billion in payments sent to its customers, just in the second quarter of 2002.

Merrill Lynch analyst Justin Baldauf commented on the market power of PayPal and eBay: "PayPal is the gorilla in the online payment market and eBay is the gorilla in the online auction market." In July 2002, eBay purchased PayPal, based on the result of business data analysis. Today, the implication of this strategic decision is obvious: eBay and PayPal together make online trading more compelling; together, they have built a vibrant virtual market on the Internet.

Table 11.2 Intelligent value chain.

BI Decision Level	Data Needed	Information	Knowledge	Decision	Intelligent Supply Chain Action
Strategic	Long term, historic	Integrated cross business & industry	Environment, supply chain wide, customers & competitors	**e-Bay**: Purchase an online payment company	Acquire PayPal
Tactic	Periodic, historic	Aggregated across business units	supply chain wide, company level, customers & competitors	**Anheuser-Busch**: determine inventory level based on demand	Create appropriate demand profiles, replenish responsively through updating demand forecast
Operational	Daily & real-time	Aggregated across departments	customers & competitors	**Walmart**: Collect real-time customer purchasing data at retail stores	Invested a software "RetailLink" to connect all of its stores to corporate headquarters
R&D and data analysis	Long-term, periodic, daily, & real-time	Supply chain information	Environment, supply chain wide, customers & competitors	**Pharmaceutical company**: Determine the effectiveness of a new medicine	Use historical data from clinical trials to assimilate the new drug

At the tactical level, aggregate information is needed to provide visibility across multiple processes within a supply chain in order to facilitate actionable changes. Management Information systems (MIS) or intra-organization enterprise systems are commonly used by managers at this level. Aggregated data across business units assists managers in making informed decisions, analyzing business trends, and delivering promised services or products with a consistent quality. For example, the vice president in charge of forecasting at Anheuser-Busch needs to determine the correct amounts of beer needed to arrive from the breweries to support the distribution centers in order to maintain satisfactory inventory levels. Given a maximum life of 110 days from brewery to consumption (to ensure freshness), forecasts must be fairly accurate. Collecting data from various business units, the vice president aggregates information from the trend of past seasons, the cyclical patterns of beer consumption, and external factors, such as special promotions offered by grocery stores, the weather, holidays, and special local events. Based on intelligence information, the vice president formulates forecasts six weeks in advance to help him or her decide on a trend pattern, as well as to cover last minute orders from clients. The forecasts are then sent to the host brewery via Anheuser-Busch's computer information system "BudNet."

Operational level decisions require daily and real-time data in order to satisfy customer demand on time. The product line manager is responsible for the day-to-day business of certain business processes. Line managers may use real-time monitoring tools to access data and to make timely decisions. For example, Walmart installed an information system called RetailLink, which connects all of its stores to corporate headquarters and to each other. Store managers frequently hold videoconferences to exchange information on what is happening in the field, such as which products are selling and which are not, which promotions work and which do not. Feasible decisions are then made right on the retail store floor.

At the R&D and data analysis level, professional staff members may not be directly involved in daily decision making, but they collect and organize data, analyze data through modeling and simulation to extract supply chain information, and uncover knowledge about customers and competitors that is embedded in the supply chain process. For example, a research scientist of a pharmaceutical company may use historical data from clinical trials to assimilate the effectiveness of a new medicine.

11.3.2 The value of business intelligence

Prior to the information age of the late 20th century, businesses usually collected data from non-automated sources and made decisions primarily based on intuition or on expert experience. As computer power has increased exponentially in recent years, more and more data about supply chain activities has become available through the employment of integrated information systems such as Enterprise Resource Planning (ERP) and Customer Relationship Management (CRM). However, ERP and CRM collect so much data that it can be difficult for the supply chain manager to focus on specific decision support insights. Business intelligence provides a hope for managers to extract information embedded in ERP and CRM; it analyzes the information in order to bring out the most important aspects of the data. A recent report on the benefits of BI and information management indicates that the type of benefits that BI can generate include faster and accurate reporting, improved decision making, improved customer service, increased revenue, savings on non-IT costs, and IT savings.[7]

11.3.3 Applying business intelligence to reduce bullwhip effects

The bullwhip effect is essentially the artificial distortion of consumer demand volumes as they are transmitted back to the suppliers from the retailer. Many suppliers and retailers have observed the phenomenon of demand fluctuation in the upstream of the supply chain.

To understand the impact of increasing variability on the supply chain, consider the demand management of a wholesaler of window blinds. The wholesaler receives the order from the retailer and places the order to the manufacturer. To determine the order size for window blinds, the wholesaler must predict the demand from the retailers and must place orders to the manufacturer. If the wholesaler does not have the information about the demand from the retailer, it must estimate the demand and then place orders to the manufacturer. In this case, the

---

[7] Olin Thompson (2012). "Business intelligence success, lesson learned," retrieved from www.technologyevaluation.com.

wholesaler has to carry more safety stock in order to protect itself from stock-out.

The following are some strategies that can be considered, in order to reduce bullwhip effects through applying business intelligence:

• Forge strategic partnerships within the supply chain to share demand, inventory, and production information to reduce inventory. This decision takes place at the strategic level and uses long-term historical data, integrated information on environmental changes, and industry trend.

• Reduce demand uncertainty through data-mining customer purchasing patterns. This decision takes place at the tactical level. Aggregated data across business units is needed in order to make informed decisions on demand patterns.

• Reduce demand variability through reducing the variability inherent in the customer demand process. Possible approaches include Everyday Low Price (EDLP), which can lead to stable customer demand patterns; and vendor-managed inventory (VMI), which can reduce order variability to the upstream of the supply chain. This practice takes place at the tactical level.

• Shorten lead time through data analysis and information sharing all along the supply chain. This decision takes place at the operational level. Application of real-time monitoring tools is needed to make timely decisions.

11.3.4 Effects of information flow on material flow

The customer eventually gets physical products from a supply chain. Therefore, managing material flow is an important task facing a supply chain manager. The new paradigm in supply chain management is to reduce inventory using information by cutting non-value-added activities.

In the past, inventory was often the result of a misinformed decision to produce large batches of an item in order to take advantage of economies of scale. The good side of inventory is that it allows organizations to satisfy customer demand immediately from stock. The down side of inventory is that it represents a large investment. In a supply chain, inventory can be found in many places. Raw materials, parts, and components are held at various stages of a supply chain, as are finished goods inventories that can be found at suppliers, manufacturers, distributors, and retailers. Obviously, large investment in inventory makes the supply chain less competitive.

With the assistance of the Internet, information sharing among members of the supply chain has increased dramatically. Consequently, material management decisions can be better made if accurate demand information is available. The ubiquity of new telecommunications and the Internet has made real-time, online communications throughout the supply chain a reality. Effective information enables supply chains to reduce paperwork, to improve communication, and to reduce lead time. Ultimately, a better information flow reduces inventory held due to distorted demand projections and accelerates the delivery of physical goods to the customer.

11.4 Using Social Media Text Mining to Improve Customer Service in a Supply Chain

More and more supply chains are using social media tools such as Facebook and Twitter to provide various services and to interact with suppliers and customers. As a result, a large amount of user-generated content is freely available on social media sites. To effectively assess the competitive environment of businesses, supply chain managers need to monitor and analyze the customer-generated content on their own social media sites, even as they monitor and analyze the textual information on their competitors' social media sites.

Traditionally, pizza restaurants promote sales to customers through various marketing channels such as direct mail, newspapers, magazines, and TV advertising. As social media applications are getting more popular among customers, pizza stores are promoting their products via Facebook, Twitter, and YouTube. Through social media, customers can engage in activities such as customizing pizzas, discussing pizza quality and tastes, interacting with peer customers, giving praises and complaints, and providing feedback. On the other hand, pizza restaurants are using social media as a customer service tool to understand customers' needs and concerns.

Comparing textual data from Pizza Hut, Domino's Pizza and Papa John's, using a query search, researchers found that context data can be applied to speed up the ordering and delivering process, to improve product quality, and to analyze customers' purchasing decisions.[8] The following (Table 11.3) is an example of clustering textual data about a pizza store's service.

Table 11.3 Textual data clustering.

Topic	Examples
Customer sharing positive experiences with online ordering and delivery	Having the iPhone app to order pizza is the greatest thing ever! It's almost as awesome as delivery! You guys totally rock.
Customer sharing negative experiences with online ordering and delivery	Order did not have discount applied. I had to cancel the order for pizzas. Delivery so slow. Late almost 1 hour & 10 min.
Responses from customer service representatives of the pizza store	Thanks for the great feedback! We're so glad you like our iPhone app! Can you pls give details and city where this happened? We take this seriously & I'd like to look into it. Thanks! We are very sorry for the experience you had! Can you pls DM your # so we can help make things right!

In order to help their companies understand how to perform a social media competitive analysis and transform social media data into

---

[8] This section is based on W. He, S. Zha & L. Li (2013). "Social media competitive analysis and text mining: A case study in the pizza industry." *International Journal of Information Management*, 33(3), pp. 464-472.

knowledge for decision making, supply chain professionals need to analyze unstructured text content on Facebook and Twitter sites, categorize the data, and analyze patterns. Text mining is an effective technique to extract business value from the vast amount of available social media data.

11.5 Technology Designed to Combat Fakes in the Global Supply Chain

With the increase of globalization in trading and online shopping, the amount of counterfeit goods and fake products has skyrocketed. In 2011, U.S. Customs officers confiscated over a billion dollars-worth of phony handbags, sportswear, electronics items, etc. As markets have become more global, business competition has evolved from a firm-versus-firm race to a supply-chain-against-supply-chain battle, and a wrestling match between lawful manufacturers and counterfeiters.[9]

There are a range of anti-counterfeiting technologies that are available to authenticate products or packaging, and to trace and track products in the supply chain. All of these technologies aim at detecting fake products or deterring counterfeiting. Some anti-counterfeiting technologies are low cost and user friendly, while others are highly sophisticated, yet expensive. Table 11.4 categorizes currently available anti-counterfeiting technologies into two areas:

(i) Technologies for product authentication; and
(ii) Technologies for tracing and tracking products as they move along the supply chain. Technology for product authentication deal with the process of determining whether the product is in fact what it declares to be, whereas technologies for tracing and tracking products use technologies such as the Electronic Product Code (EPC) and radio frequency identification (RFID) to follow products as they move along the supply chain.

---

[9] Source: this section is based on the article by Li, L. (2013). "Technology designed to combat fakes in the global supply chain." *Business Horizons*, 56 (2), pp. 167-177.

Table 11.4 Category of anti-counterfeit technology.

Categories	Product Authentication Verification		Product Tracking and Tracing
Technology	<u>Overt</u> • Holograms • Optically variable devices • Color-shifting films / inks • Security thread • Fluorescent inks • Intaglio printing • Security paper • Watermarks • Sequential product numbers	<u>Covert</u> • Security inks / coatings • Hidden printed messages • Digital watermarks • Taggants (biological, chemical, or microscopic) • Cryptoglyph • Others	<u>Machine Readable Technology</u> • Radio Frequency Identification (RFID) • Electronic product code (EPC) • Bar code • Laser marking • Optically stored marks
Advantages	• User verification • Improved & more secure • Serve as deterrent to counterfeiters	• Low implementation cost • No need of regulatory approval • Easy upgrading • Flexible implementation	• No manual data collection & entry • Convenient tag reading • Digital networking capability • Encoding and security features from a single source
Disadvantages	• User training • Subject to imitation & reuse • High level security requirement • Commitment on the supply side • Appropriate disposal procedure	• Easily imitated • Costly, if more security options are required • Risk, if the device is solely administered by suppliers	• No one-stop platform technology available • Remote access security requirement • Overhead cost

Source: Adapted from Li. L. (2013). Technology designed to combat fakes in the global supply chain. *Business Horizons*, 56 (2), pp. 167-177.

Under the product or packaging authentication area, *overt* and *covert* are two major technologies (Table 11.4). Overt technology is visible. It is easy for users to authenticate products. The major advantages of overt technology include product verification by users and improved security. For example, a manufacturer's product barcode labels display important information about the brand owner, the product, its production dates, series numbers, tracking details, etc. The current product authentication technology, to a great degree, remains at the packaging level, rather than being built into the product. The possible downsides of overt technology include user training, possibilities for imitation and reuse, and possible false assurance. Moreover, overt devices require a high-level security commitment on the device-supplier side and an appropriate disposal procedure on the user side to avoid unauthorized use or reuse. As such, overt technology can increase the cost of production.

Covert technology, on the other hand, is hidden and invisible. Covert devices enable the producer or the brand owner to identify counterfeit products. Covert technology is controlled and only those who have administrative responsibility have access to the details. Customers are neither able to detect the technology's presence nor have they a means to verify covert devices. The advantages of covert technology include low implementation cost, no need for regulatory approval, easy upgrading or addition, and flexible implementation either by the device supplier or the manufacturer. The potential downsides of covert technology include easy imitation (if widely applied), increased cost (if more security options are required), and risk of compromise (if the device is solely administered by the component's suppliers).

Many industries have incorporated advanced anti-counterfeiting solutions in order to enhance their brand reputation and to ensure product safety. This initiative is most evident in the pharmaceutical supply chain. By applying anti-counterfeiting labels on medicine cases, users can conveniently recognize product information and be in compliance with regulations.

The global internet pharmacy supply chain faces increasing risk from fraudulent drugs which not only put patients' health at risk but also cost pharmaceutical companies billions of dollars. Phony drugs are a huge safety issue faced by the entire pharmaceutical supply chain from pharmaceutical companies through to wholesalers, hospitals, drug stores, and down to patients and end users. In 2012, Roche's Genentech unit warned doctors and patients about fake Avastin (which treats cancer) that was sold in the U.S. If consumers paid close attention to the drug's packaging, they would notice that the fake packaging was different from the authentic packaging in terms of barcode for batch numbers and dates.

In Avastin's case, anti-counterfeiting solutions, such as labels and barcodes on a medicine package, provided consumers with a means to detect fraudulent drugs.

Other than the pharmaceutical industry, beverage, wine, and food producers are constantly looking for anti-counterfeiting solutions in order to ensure the authenticity of their products, to protect public safety and to ensure their branded product. For food, wine, and beverage products, shrink-wrapped cases embossed with a 3D motif anti-counterfeiting solution give each case a unique pattern. The manufacturers claim that heat-shrink labels with integrated holograms help the wine and beverage industry in the fight against counterfeiting and forgery. Anti-counterfeiting technology provides a true service to food and beverage supply chains through offering high quality security solutions to protect both the interests of producers and the legitimate rights and safety of consumers, so that people can eat and drink with peace of mind.

11.6 Enhancing Value through Managing Information Flow and Big Data in the Supply Chain

Distilling knowledge out of a supply chain data warehouse will be a major focus of managing any supply chain successfully, both today and for years to come. The global network of supply and demand will depend increasingly on knowledge generation. This trend requires us to understand how to manage data and information flow, how to transform data into relevant information, and how to generate knowledge out of data and information. An ideal business intelligence system should permeate the entire supply chain, should span all functions and members, and should coordinate information flows.

Nevertheless, good information and a thorough knowledge of the market will not automatically lead to competitive decisions. Managers need to absorb and digest information in order to use it to assist in their decision-making. Better decisions may require different organizational governance, processes, and rules, such as collaboratively shared data, information, and knowledge about business with all of the players in the same supply chain. Ultimately, the managers are the ones who should evaluate and control the business intelligence system (rather than be controlled by it).

As part of its business intelligence strategy, a company needs to align its business intelligence environment with its business objectives and develop a phased plan that is best suited to the current and evolving needs of its business. When a company decides to implement a business intelligence system, it should assess its staff's business intelligence awareness, the cultural fit of the BI system, and the support offered by top management. Upon completion of the assessment, the company will have a better understanding of its information requirements and how the right BI system can help generate integrated, high quality information.

11.7 Summary

In this chapter, we have discussed the relationships among data, information, and knowledge in a business context. We have also discussed the latest developments in social media, textual data, data warehousing, and data mining. As the next natural phase of data mining, business intelligence provides the supply chain with the technological foundation for building a complete knowledge system. The system allows the supply chain to rapidly develop and deploy data warehouses with an integrated array of query, reporting, analysis, alerting, data integration and business intelligence application development capabilities.

Questions for Pondering

1. Discuss the possible benefits and risks of business intelligence as it faces supply chain players.
2. Supply chains control extensive customer private information through customer purchasing history using data mining technology. What are the legal implications of this practice?

3. Will data mining and knowledge management improve the forecasting accuracy of customer demand patterns and overall supply chain performance?

References

Davenport, T., and Prusak, L. (1998). Working Knowledge: How Organizations Manage What They Know. (Harvard Business School Press, Boston, Mass).

Fernandez, G. (2002). Data Mining Using SAS Application. (Chapman & Hall/CRC, New York, NY).

Groth, R. (1998). Data Mining. (Prentice Hall PTR, Upper Saddle River, NJ).

Li, L. and Xu, L. (2001). "Knowledge-based problem solving," Encyclopedia of Microcomputers. 28, Supplement 7, pp. 149-167.

Li, L. (2013). Perdue Farms: A vertically integrated supply chain, in The Supply Chain Management Casebook, Chuck Munson ed. (Pearson Education, Inc. One Lake Street, Upper Saddle River, NJ).

Manglik, A. (2006). "Increasing BI adoption: An enterprise approach." *Business Intelligence Journal.* 11(2), pp. 44-52.

Manugistics Forum Keynote Speakers. Date of access: Aug. 30, 2005. http://www.manugistics.com/envision2005/speakers.html

Sahay, B.S. and Ranjan, J. (2008). Real time business intelligence in supply chain analytics. *Information Management & Computer Security*, 16(1), pp. 28-48.

http://www.webopedia.com. Date of access: Aug. 2006.

Part 6

Supply Chain Performance and Evaluation

Chapter 12
Performance Measures: From Order Winning to Order Fulfillment

Chapter 12

Performance Measures: From Order Winning to Order Fulfillment

12.1 Introduction

Performance measures are gauges that are typically applied to a supply chain, as businesses look for ways to sustain competitive positions in the market place. The front-runners, Dell Inc., Walmart, and many others use best practices to capture and retain the right customers. Consequently, performance measures become crucial yardsticks for businesses to improve their market images and revenue. There is a well-known saying: "You can't improve what you can't measure." Having taken this to heart, businesses are making use of a few supply chain measurement models that have been introduced recently. Among them, order winning, order fulfillment, financial measurement, the Supply Chain Operations Reference Model (SCOR), and the balanced scorecard are particularly well accepted.

12.2 Order Winning in the Supply Chain

12.2.1 Identify and capture the right customers

A good supply chain model wins orders in the market place. As such, the supply chain model begins with the careful selection of customers and a look at the company's identity in the market place. Scholastic, the world's leading publisher and distributor of children's books, serves as a good example of capturing the right customers. By applying a unique marketing strategy to attract the customers it wants, Scholastic has won orders by combining a diverse portfolio of titles, such as *Clifford the Big Red Dog*, *the Babysitters*, and *Harry Potter*. This approach has led the direct-sale-to-classroom book club model in the United States. Scholastic treats each teacher as an individual customer and promotes its new titles to the teachers. Meanwhile, Scholastic's direct-sale-to-classroom book clubs provide students with a defined set of books and other media from which they can choose. Scholastic offers what it has in stock within a fixed period of time, responds to predictable order patterns, and manages prices relative to a given offer. Moreover, Scholastic works to enhance school-channel loyalty by providing credits for free books, classroom technology support, and syllabus-support materials. The direct-sale-to-classroom model has effectively created a barrier against Scholastic's competitors entering the same market because the teachers are the point-of-order contact with students. Due to its effort to identify and capture the right customers, Scholastic has been able to double its revenue in recent years.

12.2.2 Create a customer-responsive supply chain

Linking supply chain operational processes directly to the customer order process serves to increase sensitivity to ever-changing customer demands. Technology greatly enables supply chain responsiveness. For example, Dell Computer has completely automated its process to take hundreds and thousands of orders, translate them into millions of component requirements, and work directly with its suppliers to build and deliver products in order to meet individual customer requirements. Today, even if a company's operating model differs from that of Dell's, its response to customer demands can be more efficiently achieved through connecting to online devices.

Operating within the customer's operations is a more recent quick response strategy. This strategy has been the key to Dell's effort to dominate the corporate PC market. By creating custom-tailored account pages for each corporate customer, Dell provides "in-customer" services, which include customer-specific asset tagging, a kind of software image support that integrates Dell with its corporate customer operations.

Similarly, Hewlett-Packard has designed electronic appliances specifically for Walmart, in order to meet the customer profile of Walmart.

Creating a customer-responsive supply chain through integrating the supplier's process with customer's order process has dramatically enhanced both Dell Inc.'s and Walmart's responsiveness. This level of response has provided both companies with a cutting-edge competitiveness that has been difficult for their competitors to replicate within a short period of time.

12.3 Order Fulfilling in the Supply Chain

12.3.1 Creating a collaborative, flexible, and cost-efficient order fulfillment process

Order fulfillment comes close to an order winning business model. Leading companies employ a variety of strategies to reduce the cost of operations and to maintain agility during order fulfillment process.

The Collaborative Planning, Forecasting, and Replenishment (CPFR) model that we discussed in chapters 1, 5, and 6 enables supply chain members to work together to design products that offer the greatest potential return across the supply chain and, indeed, across the complete product lifecycle. Collaboration brings tremendous gains to companies seeking to reduce development costs and time-to-market cycles.

Since it acquired McDonnell Douglas Corporation's and Rockwell International Corporation's A&D businesses, Boeing has collaborated with Dassault Systems. Dassault's Catia computer-aided-design environment enables Boeing engineers worldwide to share design ideas among themselves and with suppliers, which increases the flow of innovative ideas. This design collaboration process contributes significantly to supply chain performance in terms of faster time-to-market, increased revenue, reduction in the cost of goods sold, reduction in service and support expenses, and cuts in research and development costs.

Flexible and cost-efficient supply chains keep a strong focus on supply network consolidation. Dell consolidated its supply base, invested in make-to-order manufacturing capability, and implemented a demand-fulfillment system. All of these moves have made Dell extremely agile and able to schedule assembly production with real-time order data and to fulfill customer orders in a JIT fashion. In a similar manner, Walmart consolidated its supply base and invested heavily in demand management analysis. The result is that it now has better estimates regarding market demand and has been able to reduce its order fulfillment cycle time.

To become more cost efficient and flexible, supply chain managers combine regional order fulfillment functions with centralized manufacturing and sourcing. It is becoming increasingly common to centralize product design and development, and to decentralize order fulfillment tasks to local markets. Sport Obermeyer is a high-end fashion ski-wear designer and merchandise company headquartered in Aspen, Colorado. Although the company has a global supply network, it keeps its critical skiwear design center at its headquarters and outsources production to its joint venture partner, Obersport Ltd., a Hong Kong-based company. With this order fulfillment process, Sport Obermeyer is able to introduce high-quality design products while maintaining a low manufacturing cost. Sport Obermeyer's experience depicts the importance that partnership selection strategy plays in order fulfillment, as discussed in Chapter 3.

12.3.2 Choosing the right technology to support supply chain operations

Technology is a core component in the order winning and order fulfillment process. E-auctions, event management software, ERP, and private exchange networks, are just a handful of the technology innovations that are changing the way that supply chains do business today. The Internet brings immediacy to the supply chain by enabling business partners to capture real-time customer demands and to maximize visibility into the inventory positions, the locations of in-transit inventory, and the suppliers' production schedules. Walmart's

RetailLink system has been considered to be one of the best practices in technology management. This system provides vendors with up-to-date access to point-of-sale prices and inventory positions, as well as estimated demands. Furthermore, the system helps the vendors to position the right inventories and to talk with Walmart about the movement and promotion of their products.

However, simple investment in technology is not the whole story. By investing in a combination of technology and supply chain capabilities, companies like Dell and Walmart have successfully leveraged their business models and created market differentiation. When it is integrated properly with supply chain infrastructure, technology can support a supply chain's market competitiveness, can improve collaboration, can increase production flexibility, and can help to achieve cost-efficient results.

12.3.3 Fulfilling customer orders in the supply chain

A successful order fulfillment process connects the back-office information to the front office operations. The fulfillment-focused processes focus on tight, synergistic relationships in areas such as warehousing, transportation, customer service, and the transaction flow. Working together, these innovations are helping companies reduce order-entry-cycle times, respond to order-fulfillment needs more effectively, and manage customers' expectations more reliably.

Amazon.com, Gap, and Toys "R" Us are a few good examples of "e-tailers." These retailers show online customers precisely what is available in their warehouses. Integrating order winning in the front-end office and order fulfillment in the back-end office makes it possible for these companies to formulate better and more timely decisions about transportation, distribution, manufacturing, and marketing. A more sophisticated function lies in being able to integrate event management and supply chain visibility systems. This innovation validates customer-requested shipping dates, and notifies a customer when an out-of-stock item replenishes.

12.4 Using Financial Data to Measure Supply Chain Performance

A supply chain involves managing the flow of material, information, and funds. In fact, financial measures are the most commonly used yardstick to evaluate performance. Good performance in the realms of cost, revenue, and profit gives a company a solid market presence and attracts investors to make investment decisions.

12.4.1 Metrics for material flow

Inventory represents the material flow in a supply chain and is considered an investment because it is an asset created for future use. Additionally, inventory ties up funds that might be used for operations that are more profitable.

Usually, companies want to have just enough inventory to cover demand, since excess inventory is a cost. Typical material flow and inventory performance measures include average annual aggregate inventory value, weeks of supply, and inventory turns.

Average aggregate inventory value is the total value of all inventory including raw material, work-in-process inventory, and finished goods inventory. Average aggregate inventory is expressed in dollar values. The methods used to estimate aggregate inventory values, weeks of supply, and inventory turns are discussed in section 7.2.6.

Inventory turnover ratio (INVT). Inventory turnover ratio measures the speed at which inventory can be sold in a year (as discussed in section 7.2.6). Inventory represents material flow in a supply chain. A higher inventory turnover ratio usually generates higher profits and is more desirable. The formula used to compute inventory turnover (INVT) is as follows:

$$INVT^1 = \frac{\text{Annual cost of sales}}{\text{Average aggregate inventory value}}$$

Weeks of Inventory Supply (WKS). Weeks of Inventory Supply means the number of weeks' supply that a company holds as on-hand

---

[1] Formula 7.2 in section 7.2.6.

inventory and that can be used to fulfill orders. From an inventory cost perspective, the fewer the weeks of supply, the less the inventory cost. Weeks of inventory supply (WKS) is determined as follows:

$$WKS^2 = \frac{\text{Average aggregate inventory value}}{\text{weekly sales at cost}}$$

Inventory expenses relate to inventory control policies, supply networks, and demand prediction. Better demand estimation and more reliable suppliers can reduce the level of safety stock.

12.4.2 Metrics for fund flow

The outcomes of business models and supply chain activities profoundly affect a company's financial performance. Some well-accepted financial measures that use data from income statement include those for accounts receivable, accounts payable, working capital, return-on-equity, and cash-to-cash cycle time. An income statement shows the company's financial performance, estimates its cash flow, and assesses its future growth. Table 12.1 shows the correlation between income statement items, supply chain activities, and performance metrics.

Net sales. Net sales are related to demand management and to customer relations management, which is a key indicator of a firm's order winning and order fulfilling capability, as well as its revenue performance.

Cost of goods sold. Cost of goods sold is determined through the firm's financial arrangements with suppliers, production costs, and other overhead costs. Quality problems in the supply chain can also increase the cost of goods produced, and consequently, the cost of goods sold. On the other hand, increasing the percent of on-time delivery from suppliers enables a firm to reduce its amount of safety inventory, which leads to reduced inventory cost and cost of goods sold.

Selling and administrative expenses. Selling and administrative expenses represent expenses needed to sell products or to deliver services. These expenses include salaries, commissions, advertising,

---

[2] Formula 7.3 in section 7.2.6.

freight, shipping, warehouse management, and the depreciation of sales equipment. The effect on selling and administrative activities is found in order fulfillment rate and speed, logistics, transportation, and overhead costs.

Return-on-assets (ROA). Return-on-assets is an important financial measure which indicates how effectively a supply chain capitalizes its resources. ROA is achieved through dividing the net income by total assets and shows the level of profitability of a firm's assets in generating revenue. Inventory, cash, and accounts receivables are components of a firm's short-term assets. Since reducing the aggregate inventory investment reduces a company's total assets, reduction in inventory will increase return-on-assets if the amount of net sales remains the same. The appropriate asset management strategy is not to have the least amount of inventory, but to have the proper amount of the right products in stock.

$$\text{ROA} = \frac{\text{Net Income}}{\text{Total Assets}}$$

Accounts receivable turnover (ART). Accounts receivable turnover measures the efficiency with which a firm uses its assets and inventory. The role of accounts receivable is to indirectly extend interest-free loans to customers. Accounts receivable turnover ratio is computed as "sales revenue divided by accounts receivable value." A high ratio implies either that a company operates on a cash basis or that its credit collection of accounts receivable is efficient.

$$\text{ART} = \frac{\text{Sales revenue}}{\text{Accounts receivable value}}$$

A firm's accounts receivable may be large due to its sales promotions (such as "no pay for 6 months) or due to its customers with bad credit history. Any cash tied up in the accounts receivable costs the company other profitable investment opportunities.

Accounts payable turnover. Accounts payable turnover is a key metric that measures a supply chain's financial leverage. The accounts payable turnover ratio is calculated by taking the total cost for purchased goods and dividing it by the average accounts payable amount during the same period. The accounts payable turnover ratio formula is shown below:

$$APT = \frac{Cost \ of \ goods \ sold}{Accounts \ payable}$$

Table 12.1 Financial data and performance measures.

Financial Data	Supply Chain Management Variables	Performance Measures
Net sales	Demand management; Customer relationship management (CRM); Order winning	Number of orders; Revenue
Cost of goods sold	Purchasing; Supply network; Production planning & control	Cost; Profit
Selling & administrative expenses	Order processing; Transportation; Packaging & warehousing; Promotion; Other support activities	Order fulfillment costs; Transportation & logistics costs; Overhead costs
Income before taxes	Orders; Revenue	Profit contribution
Return on assets	Inventory control; Cash flow	Profit contribution
Accounts receivable turnover	Payment to a company by its customers for goods provided on credit.	Cash flow; Liquidity
Inventory turnover ratio	The number of times inventory is sold in a year	ROA; Profit contribution
Accounts payable turnover	Amount owed by a company to suppliers from whom it has purchased goods on credit	Liquidity; Supply chain interactive money flow
Cash-to-cash cycle time	The supply chain's money flows	Cash flow; Liquidity

A larger accounts payable turnover ratio indicates that a firm's short-term liquidity level is good. This ratio is used to quantify the rate at which a company pays off its suppliers; it measures supply chain interactive money flow.

Working capital. Working capital is money used to finance ongoing operations. It is a surrogate indicator for inventory turns and for weeks of supply. An increase in inventory investment requires increased payments to suppliers. As such, decreasing the number of weeks of inventory supply or increasing the number of inventory turns can help to reduce pressure on working capital and can improve cost performance.

12.4.3 Metrics for supply chain interactive activities using cash-to-cash cycle time

Cash-to-cash cycle time (C2C). Cash-to-cash cycle time measures a supply chain's money flow from its suppliers (in the form of accounts payable) to its customers (in the form of accounts receivable). C2C is computed as the number of days it takes for a firm to be paid by its customers plus the number of days it takes to sell its inventory, subtracting the number of days it takes for the firm to pay its suppliers. It represents the duration between the time that cash is invested in goods to the time that that investment produces cash for the business. The formula is as follows:[3]

C2C= days receivable outstanding + avg. days to sell inventory –
        days payable outstanding

$$= (365 \text{ days } / ART) + (365 \text{ days } / INVT) - (365 \text{ days } / APT)$$

When a firm purchases materials on credit, it creates accounts payable; when it sells the inventory to its customers on credit, it generates accounts receivable. The shorter its cash-to-cash cycle, the better a supply chain's money flow. A long cash-to-cash cycle may indicate that the company is holding a large volume of outstanding

---

[3] Penman, H. S. (2010). Financial Statement Analysis in security valuation, 4th Ed. (The McGraw-Hill Companies, New York).
Chopra, S. and Meindl, P. (2001). Supply Chain Management: Strategy, Planning, and Operations, 5th ed. (Prentice Hall, Upper Saddle River, NJ).

receivables or has low inventory turnover ratio. The longer the cash-to-cash cycle time, the more current assets (such as cash) will be needed to fund supply chain inventory because it takes more days to convert inventories and receivables into cash.

12.4.4 Performance analysis — Kroger and Whole Foods

In this section, we apply the financial data of a firm to measure its supply chain material flow and fund flow performance. Generally speaking, comparisons are best made within the same industry. Therefore, we choose Kroger and Whole Foods, both of which are grocery supermarkets in the US. Table 12.2 reports selected financial data from the financial statements and balance sheets of Kroger and Whole Foods.

(1) Return on assets: $\text{ROA} = \dfrac{\text{Net Income}}{\text{Total Assets}}$

Kroger's ROA = $\dfrac{\$602}{\$23,476} \approx 2.56\%$

Whole Foods' ROA = $\dfrac{\$466}{\$5,294} \approx 8.8\%$

(2) Inventory turnover: $\text{INVT} = \dfrac{\text{Annual cost of sales}}{\text{Average aggregate inventory value}}$

Kroger's INVT = $\dfrac{\$71,494}{\$5,114} \approx 13.98$ turns

Whole Foods' INVT = $\dfrac{\$7,543}{\$374} \approx 20.17$ turns

(3) Weeks of supply: $\text{WKS} = \dfrac{\text{Average aggregate inventory value}}{\text{weekly sales at cost}}$

Kroger's WKS $= \dfrac{\$5,114}{\$71,494/52} \approx 3.72$ weeks

Whole Foods' WKS = $\dfrac{\$374}{\$7,543/52} \approx 2.58$ weeks

Kroger's ROA is lower than that of Whole Foods (Kroger: 2.56 vs. Whole Foods: 8.8). One explanation can be that Kroger holds more inventory than Whole Foods. Regarding Weeks of Supply (WKS), Kroger holds 3.73 weeks of inventory while Whole Foods holds 2.58 weeks of inventory. Additionally, Whole Foods turns its inventory much faster than does Kroger (Whole Foods: 20.17 turns vs. Kroger: 13.98 turns). Whole Foods has made less investment in inventory than has Kroger. Therefore, whole Foods' ROA is higher than Kroger's.

(4) Accounts receivable turns: $\text{ART} = \dfrac{\text{Sales revenue}}{\text{Accounts receivable}}$

Kroger's ART = $\dfrac{90{,}374}{949} \approx 95.23$

Whole Foods' ART = $\dfrac{11{,}699}{197} \approx 59.39$

Kroger had 95 accounts receivable turns in 2012 and Whole Foods had 59 turns. We may conclude from this that Kroger gets paid by its customers sooner than does Whole Foods. The explanation might be that customers use cash more often at Kroger than they do at Whole Foods.

(5) Accounts payable turns: $\text{APT} = \dfrac{\text{Cost of goods sold}}{\text{Accounts payable}}$

Kroger's APT = $\dfrac{\$71{,}494}{\$4{,}329} \approx 16.52$

Whole Foods' APT = $\dfrac{\$7{,}543}{\$247} \approx 30.54$

Kroger made $71,494 million in purchases from suppliers in 2012 and held an average accounts payable of $4,329 million. Its accounts payable turnover ratio for the period was 16.52. Whole Foods' accounts payable turnover ratio, on the other hand, was higher than Kroger. This means that Whole Foods paid its suppliers faster than did Kroger. Whole Foods was able to pay its suppliers more quickly because it turns its inventory more quickly. Every inventory turn could generate some profit for Whole Foods.

Table 12.2 Selected financial data for Kroger and Whole Foods.

Row	Company	Kroger	Whole Foods
	Period	FY 2012	FY 2012
		in million $	in million $
1	Revenue	90,374	11,699
2	Cost of Revenue	71,494	7,543
3	Gross Profit	18,880	4,156
4	Operating Expenses	17,602	3,355
5	Operating Income	1,278	800
6	Interest Expense	435	0
7	Net Non-Operating Losses (Gains)	0	48
8	Pretax Income	843	752
9	Income Tax Expense	247	286
10	Income Before XO Items	596	466
11	Minority Interests	-6	0
12	Net Income	602.00	465.57
13	**Assets**		
14	Cash & Near Cash Items	188	89
15	Short-Term Investments	0	1,131
16	Accounts & Notes Receivable	949	197
17	Inventories	5,114	374
18	Other Current Assets	1,074	312
19	Total Current Assets	7,325	2,103
20	Total Long-Term Assets	16,151	3,192
21	Total Assets	23,476.00	5,294.22
22	**Liabilities & Shareholders' Equity**		
23	Accounts Payable	4,329	247
24	Short-Term Borrowings	1,315	1
25	Other Short-Term Liabilities	3,461	729
26	Total Current Liabilities	9,105	977
27	Total Long-Term Liabilities	10,405	515
28	Total Liabilities	19,510	1,492
29	Total Equity	3,966	3,802
30	Total Liabilities & Equity	23,476	5,294

Source: Bloomberg data, retrieved July 2013.

(6) Cash-to-cash cycle time

C2C= days receivable outstanding + avg. days to sell inventory –
days payable outstanding

$$= (365 \text{ days} / ART) + (365 \text{ days} / INVT) - (365 \text{ days} / APT)$$

Kroger C2C cycle time $\quad = \dfrac{365}{95.23} + \dfrac{365}{13.98} - \dfrac{365}{16.52}$

$$= 3.83 + 26.11 - 22.09 = 7.85 \text{ days}$$

Whole Foods C2C cycle time $= \dfrac{365}{59.39} + \dfrac{365}{20.17} - \dfrac{365}{30.54}$

$$= 6.15 + 18.09 - 11.95 = 12.3 \text{ days}$$

Returning to the current time, cash-to-cash cycle time measures the number of days between the time when Kroger and Whole Foods pay their suppliers and the time when they receive payments from their customers. Kroger keeps its inventory for an average of 26 days, gets paid by its customer (on average) within 4 days, and pays its suppliers (on average) in 22 days. Therefore, its cash-to-cash cycle is about 8 days.

Whole Foods keeps its inventory for an average of 18 days, gets paid by its customer (on average) in a little over 6 days, and pays its suppliers (on average) within 12 days. Therefore, its cash-to-cash cycle is between 12 to 13 days.

Kroger has a short cash-to-cash cycle because it receives cash from its customers at the time of sale, and it controls its inventory well. Whole Foods' cash-to-cash cycle is longer than Kroger's.

The C2C represents the duration between the time when cash is invested in goods to the time when that investment produces cash. When a firm purchases materials on credit, it creates accounts payable; when it sells the inventory to its customers on credit, it generates accounts receivable. The shorter its cash-to-cash cycle, the better a supply chain's money flow. A long cash-to-cash cycle may indicate that the company has a large volume of outstanding receivables or a low inventory turnover ratio. The longer the cash-to-cash cycle time, the more current assets, such as cash, will be needed to fund supply chain inventory because it takes more days to convert inventories and receivables into cash.

12.4.5 The shortcomings of financial measurements

Financial measures are very important indicators of supply chain performance, but they sometimes cannot reflect a firm's true performance. For example, when gas prices go up, trucking companies experience higher fuel costs which result in lower profits. Therefore, in recent years, more comprehensive performance measurement models have been introduced to measure supply chain performance. The Supply Chain Operations Reference (SCOR) Model and the balanced scorecard model are two commonly applied supply chain measurement approaches. We are going to introduce these two models in the following sections.

12.5 The Supply Chain Operations Reference (SCOR) Model

The Supply Chain Operations Reference (SCOR) Model is introduced by the Supply-Chain Council (SCC), an independent, not-for-profit, global corporation with membership open to all companies and organizations interested in applying and advancing state-of-the-art methods in supply-chain management systems and practices. The SCC was organized in 1996 by Pittiglio, Rabin, Todd, and McGrath (PRTM) and AMR Research, and initially included 69 voluntary member companies. Now, the Council has established international chapters in Europe, Japan, Korea, Latin America, Australia, New Zealand, and Southeast Asia.

According to the SCC, the SCOR-model integrates the concept of business process re-engineering, benchmarking, and process measurement into a cross-functional framework.[4] The model spans all customer interactions, from order entry to paid invoicing; spans all product transactions, from the supplier's supplier to the customer's customer; and spans all market interactions, from the understanding of aggregate demand to the fulfillment of each order. The SCOR-model

---

[4] Supply Chain Council's SCOR model, Date of access: June 2013. www.supply-chain.org.

comprises five components: Plan, Source, Make, Deliver, and Return. Each of these components is considered both an important intra-organizational function and a critical inter-organization process. This framework can be viewed as a strategic tool for describing, communicating, implementing, controlling, and measuring complex supply chain processes, in order to help a firm achieve good performance.[5]

The SCOR-model contains four levels of process details. Level 1 defines the scope and content of a supply chain and contains the five basic processes: Plan, Source, Make, Deliver, and Return. For example, the 'Plan' process comprises those processes that balance aggregate demand and supply for generating best-fit decisions to meet sourcing, production, delivery, and return requirements.

Level 2 specifies the configuration of processes in line with operations strategies. For example, the 'Make' component can be positioned as make-to-stock, make-to-order, or engineer-to-order.

Level 3 details each process category into elements, to be further decomposed into activities in practical implementations. For example, a make-to-order company embraces schedule production activities, issues a sourced-in-process product, produces and tests products, etc.

Level 4 is an implementation stage. This level, though is recognized in the model, lies outside of its current scope. The rationale for its exclusion is that the SCOR-model has been created as a process tool that describes, measures, and evaluates any supply-chain configuration. Companies need to define their unique set of competitive priorities, operations strategies, and business conditions in order to achieve the desired level of performance.

The SCOR-model specifies the five performance metrics in two categories: customer-facing metrics, which include reliability, responsiveness, and flexibility; and internal-facing metrics, which include cost and assets.

---

[5] Li, L., Su, Q. and Chen, X. (2011). Ensuring supply chain quality performance through applying SCOR model. *International Journal of Production Research*, 49(1), p. 33-57.

At the request of the Supply Chain Council, all companies that use the SCOR-model should share their implementation experiences with the Supply-Chain Council members. Consequently, the widespread use of the SCOR model results in better customer-supplier relationships, better system integration, and better knowledge dissemination of best supply chain practices.

12.6 The Balanced Scorecard

Using the balanced scorecard to measure business performance was initiated by Kaplan and Norton in 1992. The balanced scorecard aligns an organization's performance measures with its strategic plan and goals. By 1998, 60 percent of the Fortune 1000 companies had experimented with the balanced scorecard.[6] Companies such as Mobil Oil, Tenneco, AT&T, Intel, and Ernst & Young have reported noticeable success using the balanced scorecard approach.

The balanced scorecard considers both financial and non-financial indices when measuring short-term and long-term performance. The balanced scorecard approach includes four areas: customer, financial, learning and growth, and internal business processes.[7] Fig. 12.1 provides a framework of using the balanced scorecard in supply chain management.

The *customer perspective* focuses on customer requirements and satisfaction including customer satisfaction ratings, customer retention, new customer acquisition, customer valued attributes, and market share.

The *financial perspective* addresses revenue growth, product mix, cost reduction, productivity, asset utilization, and investment strategy.

Learning and growth focuses on the organization's people, systems, and procedures, including intellectual assets, re-training employees,

---

[6] Silk, S. (1998). "Automating the balanced scorecard," *Management Accounting*, May, pp. 38-44.

[7] Kaplan, R.S. and Norton, D.P. (1996). Linking the balanced scorecard to strategy. *California Management Review*, 39(1), pp. 53-79.

enhancing information technology and systems, and employee satisfaction.

The *internal business process* addresses critical business process issues, such as quality, flexibility, innovation, and time-based measures.

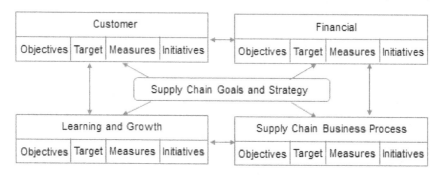

Fig. 12.1 Balanced scorecard: Supply chain management application.

These four measurement areas reflect the strategic goals of an organization or a supply chain, and are linked together to measure both the company's long-term and short-term performance. The process of developing a balanced scorecard begins with defining the company's strategy, then translates the company's strategy into operational activities, and finally translates the scorecard into a system of performance measures.

12.7 The Future of Supply Chain Management

The supply chain is facing a paradigm change in the e-Biz environment, as we indicated in Chapter 1. The four noticeable paradigm changes are summarized as follows:

(i) Supply chain operations are moving from cost management to revenue management, thus emphasizing customer relationship management and order winning;

(ii) Supply chain operations are moving from a functional focus to an order fulfillment process focus, thus emphasizing integrated goods and the service delivery flow;

(iii) Supply chain operations are moving from inventory management to information management, thus emphasizing quick response systems and knowledge management; and

(iv) Supply chain operations are moving from arm's length transactional relationships to strategic alliances, thus emphasizing a win-win strategic collaborative relationship.

The term "collaboration" has become today's hottest buzzword. To be competitive, a supply chain must be cost-efficient, responsive, flexible, and agile. If so, it will be able to provide the right product, in the right quantity, at the right place and time, at the right price, and with the right quality.

Today, many companies view the global expansion of markets and the use of international suppliers as strategies for enhanced profitability and competitiveness. Apple, Dell, and many other market leaders are profiting greatly from their use of global supply chain. Global expansion of the supply chain has also increased the need for third party and fourth-party supply chain service providers. UPS has acquired over twenty-five transportation and logistics companies in recent years and has created a global logistics footprint network. At the same time, UPS has been building up a technology infrastructure to help customers control the global supply chain by enhancing e-commerce capabilities.

The future of supply chain management lies in globalization, collaboration, technology application, and process re-engineering.

Questions for Pondering

1. In building supply chain competencies, what are the trade-offs that must be considered?
2. Explain why cost-based performance measures are important to a company.
3. What is a realistic way to measure a supply chain that includes many companies?
4. What makes a performance measurement system "world class"?

Problems

1. The following table reports selected financial data from the financial statements and balance sheets of JB Hunter Transport Services Inc. and Swift Transportation Co.

   (1) Compute the following financial performance measures using the data from the table.
      (a) Return on assets;
      (b) Inventory turnover;
      (c) Weeks of supply;
      (d) Accounts receivable turns;
      (e) Accounts payable turns;
      (f) Cash-to-cash cycle time
   (2) Learn the business background of both companies from the Internet or news and discuss their supply chain and/or logistics strategies and practices.
   (3) How do different supply chain and/or logistics strategies and practices affect their financial performance?

Selected financial data of JB Hunt Transport Services Inc. and Swift Transportaion Corporation is provided below.

	A	B	C
		Services Inc.	Swift Transportation Co.
1	Company	Services Inc.	Swift Transportation Co.
2	Period	FY 2011 (million $)	FY 2011 (million $)
3	Revenue	4526.842	3333.908
4	Cost of Revenue	3962.729	2753.251
5	Gross Profit	564.113	580.657
6	Operating Expenses	119.88	283.118
7	Operating Income	444.233	297.539
8	Interest Expense	28.508	145.973
9	Net Non-Operating Losses (Gains)	-0.008	2.734
10	Pretax Income	415.733	148.832
11	Income Tax Expense	158.727	58.282
12	Income Before XO Items	257.006	90.55
13	Minority Interests	0	0
14	Net Income	257.006	90.55
15	**Assets**		
16	Cash & Near Cash Items	5.45	82.084
17	Short-Term Investments	0	0
18	Accounts & Notes Receivable	411.479	330.49
19	Inventories	20.932	17.441
20	Other Current Assets	75.681	236.12
21	Total Current Assets	513.542	666.135
22	Total Long-Term Assets	1753.79	1972.53
23	Total Assets	2267.332	2638.665
24	**Liabilities & Shareholders' Equity**		
25	Accounts Payable	251.625	81.688
26	Short-Term Borrowings	50	59.339
27	Other Short-Term Liabilities	136.89	175.788
28	Total Current Liabilities	438.515	316.815
29	Total Long-Term Liabilities	1261.274	2235.661
30	Total Liabilities	1699.789	2552.476
31	Total Equity	567.543	86.189
32	Total Liabilities & Equity	2267.332	2638.665

2. Cycle time management is an important performance measure. Suggest three kinds of cycle time in a supply chain and discuss how they affect a firm's financial performance and customer service level.

References

Christopher, M. (1998). Logistics and Supply Chain Management, 2nd edition, (Prentice Hall, Great Britain).

Gable, R. (1997). "The history of consumer goods: How supply-chain management is driving the next consumer goods revolution." *Manufacturing Systems*, 15(10), pp. 70-84.

Kaplan, R.S. and Norton, D.P. (1992). "The balanced scorecard – Measures that drive performance." *Harvard Business Review* 70(1), pp. 71-79.

Li, L, Su, Q., and Chen, X. (2011). "Ensuring supply chain quality performance through applying SCOR model." *International Journal of Production Research*, 49(1), pp. 33-57.

Silk, S. (1998). "Automating the balanced scorecard." *Management Accounting*, May, pp. 38-44.

Index

Company Index

Printed in the United States
By Bookmasters